Sports: Why People Love Them!

Tim Delaney and
Tim Madigan

UNIVERSITY PRESS OF AMERICA,® INC.
Lanham • Boulder • New York • Toronto • Plymouth, UK

Library of Congress Control Number: 2009922989
ISBN: 978-0-7618-4496-9 (clothbound : alk. paper)
ISBN: 978-0-7618-4489-1 (paperback : alk. paper)
eISBN: 978-0-7618-4490-7

Back cover photo: Tim Delaney and Tim Madigan outside of Dodger Stadium.
Courtesy of William "Bear" Konopka.

Dedicated to the memory of Martin (Uncle "Marty") Delaney, who had the greatest childhood impact on Tim Delaney and his love of sports, especially for the Dodgers; and to the memory of Peter Hare, who demonstrated to Tim Madigan what true sportsmanship is all about.

Contents

Preface

In August of 2008, while this book was being completed, much of the world was riveted by the incredible record-breaking phenomenon of Michael Phelps at the Summer Olympics in Beijing. The sheer joy of watching him, time and again, go for the gold in various swimming contests, brought millions of people together, giving thrills of excitement to countless individuals and bonding together total strangers, most of whom had never even heard of Phelps before the Olympic Games began. There's something about the breaking of athletic records that excites even the most tepid follower of sports.

But why exactly is it that so many people all across the globe, and throughout recorded time, have devoted so many of their waking hours to participating in and/or avidly following various sporting contests? In *Sports: Why People Love Them!* we will attempt to answer these questions through an examination of sport in all its facets, from sorting out various types of sporting activities to giving an overview of the history of sport from the earliest days to the present-time, with a constant focus upon the social conditions through which sport arises and by which it continues to thrive.

It is not an exaggeration to say that billions of people around the world *love* sports. While we all are aware of troubling aspects related to sports—such as violence, cheating, and overemphasis on winning—we also realize that such problems occur with all social institutions. They should not be underestimated, but nor should they dominate the discussion of why it is that sports enthrall us. Our popular media is dedicated more and more to the heated rivalries of sports teams; our academic institutions are thoroughly connected with various sporting activities; our newspapers and websites report continuously on the various athletic competitions occurring on a daily basis; most of us take part in some sort of team sport or athletic contest ourselves; and our very language is filled with sports-related metaphors. Just what *is* sport and why does it so fascinate us? In the following pages, we'll do our best to find out. And we hope you'll find it an exciting endeavor. Let's begin!

Acknowledgments

The authors would like to thank the folks at the University Press of America, especially Brian DeRocco and Patti Belcher for their assistance in putting together this text. Tim Delaney would like to offer special thanks to Christina.

Chapter One

What is Sport?

When people hear the word "sport" a number of images come to mind. Ask someone for illustrations of sports and they are likely to respond with traditional examples such as football, baseball, basketball, and hockey. But asking someone to define "sport"—especially to provide a definition that clearly distinguishes activities that may otherwise be labeled as forms of recreation and leisure—is more challenging than one might think. For example, recently one of the authors was asked, "Is playing video games a sport?" The immediate response was, "No, of course not." However, upon further reflection, this gut reaction response may actually require further thought. At the very least, it requires a working definition of the word "sport."

THE VAST ARRAY OF SPORTS: FROM "A" (ANVIL SHOOTS) TO "Z" (ZEBRA HUNTING)

If you ask someone to name three sports, most likely he or she will be able to comply with ease. After all, nearly everyone has an idea about what types of activities constitute as sports and which do not. Like Supreme Court Justice Potter Stewart's famous remark about pornography—"I know it when I see it"—most of us think we know what sports are. However, as we shall soon see, the line drawn between examples of sports, leisure, and play is not always clear. In fact, devising a definition that establishes clear and clean parameters around what types of activities should be included and excluded is relatively difficult to do. For example, many people once played badminton in their backyards but this activity was hardly considered a sport. Since 1992, however, badminton has been an Olympic sport! Badminton, an Olympic sport? Say it ain't so! Before purists get too upset over the notion of badminton as a sport, let alone one deserving of inclusion in the Olympics, consider some of these early Modern Olympic sports: tug-of-war, rope climbing, club swinging, tumbling, one-hand weightlifting, dueling pistol (where shooters, thankfully, fired at mannequins rather than at each other) and a game similar to hopscotch—the standing hop, step, and jump (Marshall, 2008). (Note: The Olympics will be discussed in further detail in chapter 2.)

According to the International Olympic Committee (IOC), badminton is a sport. For now, we will agree with the IOC. Trying to determine whether or not badminton is a sport leads us to ponder about other sporting activities. This lets us to play a little game—"Sport or not a sport?"—with you. In the following pages, we will review a few other non-traditional sporting activities. This will allow us an opportunity to determine, is it a sport, or not?

Anvil Shoots

In certain rural areas of the South anvil shoots have become a relatively popular "sporting" activity. According to the World Anvil Shooting Society, anvil shooting dates back to the Civil War when the Union army marched through the South and destroyed their metal-working capabilities (Taylor, 2008). The Union Army put powder underneath the anvils and tried to blow them up; instead, they shot straight up in the air. Before the Civil War it had been common for the Southern States to incorporate cannon fire into their July 4th celebrations. This tradition has been revitalized with anvil shoots.

The roots of modern anvil shooting date back to the early 1990s when a small group of explosion enthusiasts from Mississippi and other Southern states began to compete with one another for bragging rights over who could shoot an anvil the highest distance. According to a spokesperson for the National Anvil Shooters Association, anvil shooting is primarily "a guy thing" (Hoffman, 1996). What is anvil shooting? "Anvil shooting involves placing one large blacksmith anvil upside down on the ground and filling its cavity with a fine grade of black powder. A second anvil weighing up to 150 pounds is then placed upright on top of the bottom one. The powder is ignited and the top anvil is thrust as high as 125 feet into the air. The earth literally shakes; and the deafening boom, it is said, can be heard from as far away as 15 miles" (Source: Museum of Appalachia, 2005).

According to the Museum of Appalachia, anvil shoots have a long history in the United States with "accounts that the shooting of the anvil was employed to celebrate the nation's independence, Christmas, and even Davy Crockett's election to the United States Congress." Today, anvil shoots are becoming increasingly common at July 4th celebrations throughout the South, especially at local fairs. "Odd as the sport sounds—and lethal as it could be among bumblers—it is growing in popularity among those fond of antique tools, rending noises and gravity-defying acts. The usual venues are old engine shows and blacksmith get-togethers along rural highways in the South" (Hoffman, 1996:A-18).

Cup Stacking

An activity that is far more popular that anvil shooting is cup stacking. Cup stacking (also known as "sport stacking" and "speed stacking") has become increasingly popular over the past decade at many elementary schools, and, to a lesser extent, at high schools and colleges. The goal of cup stacking is to stack and unstack a number of plastic cups (usually either 9 or 12) as fast as possible. Cup stacking can be both an individual and team activity. Participants place cups in multiple stacks and sequences (such as "three-six-three" or "three-three-three") and compete against the clock or each other.

For years, cup stacking has been relegated to summer camps, church youth groups, and special-education classes. Recently, however, promoters of cup stacking claim that stacking is much more than a simple fun game. Research has shown that it helps a person's development to be able to use both sides of the brain at the same time (Sunkin, 2007). Therapists utilize cup stacking with stroke victims "to help them regain strength and coordination" (Sefton, 2004:A-16). Exercise and sports scientists report findings that indicate cup stacking significantly improves eye-hand coordination and reaction time among participants. Proponents of cup stacking also point out size and strength are not variables to successful stacking; therefore, anyone can excel at this activity. Furthermore, because stackers need to use both hands, cup stacking also augments ambidexterity. It can be particularly helpful for stroke victims and others who have suffered similar afflictions in regaining physical control (see Chapter 9 for further discussions on how sports can be beneficial to people with physical disabilities).

Cup stacking has an official governing body, the World Sport Stacking Association (WSSA). According to its online "Homepage," the WSSA "promotes the standardization and advancement of sport stacking worldwide. This association serves as the governing body for sport stacking rules and regulations and provides a uniform framework for stacking events, and sanctions sport stacking competitions and records" (World Sport Stacking Association, 2008). By mid-July 2008, the WSSA recognized four new records: Individual 3-3-3 stack (1.86 seconds); Individual Cycle Stack (6.21 seconds); doubles stack (7.65 seconds); and Timed 3-6-3 Relay (13.19 seconds) (WSSA, 2008). In 2007, cup stackers around the world participated in the "WSSA Stack Up!"

competition and set a Guinness record with 143,530 stackers from 846 schools and organizations from countries around the world (WSSA, 2008).

Dodgeball

There was a time when school-aged kids played dodgeball in physical education classes. A number of "concerned" people (e.g., parents and administrators) feared potential injuries and impending lawsuits due to this game and eliminated it from the curriculum. However, there has been a rebirth of interest in dodgeball, especially with the 2004 film release of *Dodgeball: A True Underdog Story*. As demonstrated in the film, the game of dodgeball is usually played indoors at a gym. However, it is also an outdoor activity. There exists a governing body for one variation of the outdoor version of dodgeball. Furthermore, as with cup stacking, outdoor dodgeball has a governing body, the National Amateur Dodgeball Association (NADA). According to its homepage, NADA "was created as a recreational pursuit for nontraditional sport enthusiasts. It is an alternative sport requiring minimal equipment, set up and playing experience. Teamwork and strategy are more valuable factors in dodgeball than athletic skill and individual competitiveness. Anyone can play! Experience is countered by enthusiasm. Dodgeball promotes maximum social enjoyment" (National Amateur Dodgeball Association, 2008).

There is also another form of outdoor dodgeball—beach dodgeball. While on vacation in Redondo Beach, California, one of the authors witnessed a few variations of beach dodgeball. First, there was the traditional version of the indoor game with teams consisting of an equal number of participants who stay on their half of the divided playing area and throw balls at each other in an attempt to "knock" an opponent out of the game. Of course, a player can also be knocked out of the game if his or her opponent catches a thrown ball. In this scenario, teams were picked before the competition begins. However, a second type of beach dodgeball involved an unusual set-up wherein two players were located at the extreme end (one on each side) of the playing surface and took turns throwing balls at the remaining players (who were divided equally) standing in the middle. In this set-up, any player hit with the ball joined the team of the player who threw the ball. Eventually, there would be only one player left in the middle and he or she "won" that part of the game. However, the game continued based on preliminary round team formation and then followed the traditional playing of dodgeball, albeit with potentially uneven teams.

Kickball

Possessing a governing body seems characteristic of most "real" sports. Then again, cup stacking and dodgeball have a governing body, and the jury is still out as to whether or not they are sports. Kickball is a sporting activity that also possesses a governing body—World Adult Kickball Association (WAKA)—and is generally not considered a "true" sport. According to their website WAKA (2008) is a social-athletic organization created to advance the joy of kickball around the world. WAKA's mission statement says it all—"To provide a unique club with an inclusive co-ed social culture and establish the WAKA Kickball experience as the new American Pastime." As the mission statement implies, organized adult kickball is a co-ed sporting endeavor.

Despite the many other options that present themselves to amateur sports enthusiasts in the summer, Summer Kickball Leagues are growing in popularity. One of the authors, Tim Delaney, belonged to a local kickball league sponsored by his brother's restaurant—The Blarney Stone. He was forced into early retirement, however, due to an unrelated knee injury. (The fact that most kickball participants are in their 20s or 30s should have tipped off the author not to be out on the pitch in the first place!) Although the primary purpose of kickball leagues is to foster friendship, competitiveness and good times, a number of teams take this game very seriously. To that end, teams from across the world may qualify for the WAKA's annual "Founders Cup" championship.

Co-ed adult kickball leagues are growing in popularity throughout the U.S. (Courtesy Tim Delaney)

Zebra Hunting

Rounding out our brief "A to Z" look at sport-or-not-a-sport is zebra hunting. Zebra hunting is usually conducted while on safari and is generally located on conservation sites. Zebra hunters are generally assisted by trained guides. As with most forms of hunting, the debate over whether or not zebra hunting is a sport is reflected in the greater debate over whether *any* form of hunting is a sport. There are those who argue strongly that an activity involving the deliberate killing of an animal can never be classified as a sport, while others argue just as forcefully that the skills and knowledge involved in hunting are fully consistent with the aims and goals of sportsmanship. Perhaps the emotional attachment many people (especially professional referees!) have toward the zebra species makes this category particularly controversial.

So, what do you think? Are anvil shoots, cup stacking, dodgeball, kickball, and zebra hunts examples of sports (and do you foresee a day when these activities will be added to the Olympic Games)? Will kickball some day gain professional sport status? Only time will answer the latter question; but answering the former question is a matter of one's definition of sport.

Defining Sport

Nearly all definitions of sport include the notion that it involves some sort of competitive physical activity beyond the realm of play. Harry Edwards (1973), the person who coined the term "sport sociology" argues, "One of the most salient features of sports is that they always involve physical exertion. This physical exertion is an imperative characteristic that cannot be overstressed. Without it there simply is no sport activity" (p.55). Thus, playing cards (e.g., poker) is not a sport because it does not involve physical activity. Notions of sport also include the assumption that such an activity is *institutionalized*; that is, rules are clearly established and enforced by some governing body. As Edwards explains, in order for a physical activity to qualify as a sport, it must involve "activities having formally recorded histories and traditions, stressing physical exertion through competition within limits set in explicit and formal rules governing role and position relationships, and carried out by actors who represent or who are part of formally organized associations having the goal of achieving valued tangibles or intangibles through defeating opposing groups" (pp. 57–58). It is often argued that certain playful and leisure activities may also qualify as sport so long as the use of relatively complex physical skills is involved. It is this aspect that allows golf, for example, to be classified as a sport.

With the above ideas in mind, we define "sport" as an institutionalized, structured competitive activity beyond the realm of play that involves physical exertion and/or the use of relatively complex athletic skills. We maintain the consistent perspective that sport must imply physical activity and/or the ability to use relatively multifaceted skill to gain an advantage over an opponent and we want to make it clear that there is a distinction between leisure and play and sports.

Based on this definition of sport, which of the previously described activities of anvil shoots, cup stacking, dodgeball, kickball, and zebra hunting, if any, would you label as "sport?"

DISTINCTIONS BETWEEN LEISURE, PLAY, AND SPORT

Nearly anyone can play basketball, but a group of friends playing hoops on a paved driveway with a hoop stand does not qualify as playing sport. Instead, it is a leisure or playful activity. When the game is played in an organized structured manner such as on a high school, college, or professional level, basketball becomes a sport. Let's examine the differences between leisure, play, and sport more closely.

Leisure

"Leisure" refers to "unobligated" time wherein we are free from work or maintenance responsibilities. Thus, a teacher who brings home his or her students' assignments to grade at home is not engaged in a leisure activity. Also, mowing the lawn and shopping for groceries are not leisure pursuits because they are necessary maintenance tasks. On the other hand, attending a ball game, window shopping at the mall, going to the movies, and feeding the ducks at a pond *are* leisure activities because we are not obligated to do these things. In fact, there are countless examples of leisure activities that people engage in.

Although it may be argued that leisure time is time that one could spend to "get ahead" (in work obligations or maintenance responsibilities) there are many mental health professionals who argue that leisure provides a number of benefits to participants, including personal and creative growth, self-actualization, and necessary rest in order to perform more efficiently at work. For obvious reasons, most of us look forward to our leisure time and we feel that we deserve time off to recharge our "battery." The idea that we "deserve" leisure time is a relatively new notion because historically most people had little time to pursue leisure. In fact, leisure was generally reserved for the upper class; but all this would change with the rise of industrialization and the corresponding middle class. Members of the middle class generally have enough time and money to pursue any number of leisure pursuits. Consider, for example, that Americans, 100 years ago, worked an average of 57.7 hours per week (earning an average of $3.75/hr.) and had a life expectancy of 48.7 years (American Sociological Association, 2005). In 2005, the average work week for Americans was down to 33.8 hours per week (earning an average of $15.86/hr.) and life expectancy rose to 77.6 years. Clearly, we have far more leisure time and money to spend than our great-grandparents. Members of the working and middle classes may not be financial capable of living a "life of leisure," but we are afforded down time from work. After all, simply watching television represents a leisure activity.

Play

Play has been a constant characteristic of human and other animal societies throughout history. It seems only "natural" that younger members of any species enjoy such playful activities as playing tag, wrestling with one another, jumping, and throwing various objects. As with leisure, play represents an absence of obligated time. In fact, play is engaged in voluntarily during one's leisure time. Generally, as people age, they have less time and/or energy for play and more interest in pursuing leisure interests. Lucky members of society are able to play games for a living. For most of us, however, play is something we do with others for the mere enjoyment of the activity.

Play may be spontaneous or relatively organized. *Spontaneous play* is self-initiated in accordance with personal goals or expressive impulses; is voluntary; open to innovation and tolerates a wide range of flexibility; it is temporal; and possesses no substantial outcome. A group of young girls playing with their dolls or young boys building a fort and playing "army" represents spontaneous play. *Recreation* is a type of spontaneous play. Derived from the Latin word "recreatio," recreation carries with it the connotation of restoration or recovery from something (Arnold, 1980). Recreation, whether a pastime, diversion, or exercise, affords participants a sense of relaxation and enjoyment.

Certain types of play are a little more serious and may be classified as *organized play*, or as *games*. Thus, hop-scotch is not random jumping (spontaneous play), but organized jumping that allows for the determining of success or failure. Games may also be divided into two sub-categories: noncompetitive games (e.g., hacky sack) and competitive games (e.g., poker). Hacky sack is a co-operative form of play (with origins dating to ancient China,

Narrative 1.1.   An interview with Scott G. Eberle, Ph.D., Vice President for Historical Interpretation and Director of Play Studies, Strong—National Museum of Play®

1. How do you define "play"?

   That's the $64k question. Most scholars say they can't define it. Some, including the dean of the study of play, Brian Sutton-Smith, say one shouldn't try. Most mention 5 features of play. Play is:

   - special – set off and demarcated from ordinary life in a way that removes play activities from ordinary consequences
   - voluntary – not required or compulsory
   - fun or pleasurable
   - rule-bound (even if the rules are spontaneously generated or loose and labile)
   - and I'd add "harmless"

   You can get an argument on all of these grounds, especially the last one. I prefer to think of play as a psycho-biological process that's socially constructed, and historically contextualized. It's all over the place, and, as a result, what it is always depends upon when and where. (Actually the pronoun "it" is misleading. Play isn't a thing, it's a process.)

2. What connections do you see between play and sports?

   Sports fit into the first four categories above. I'd make a big tent for play – even including dangerous, grueling, or morally dubious play such as boxing, mountain climbing, car and bicycle racing, and gambling. Though I'd modify the fifth feature. I'd say in these instances play is "mostly harmless." There are surely times within these play activities where all the play drains out. But most other sports I can think of fit the criterion.

3. Why do you think there was a need for a National Museum of Play?

   These days, thanks to the explosion of children's museums and hands-on science centers and the dedicated work of researchers and scholars like those who form the Association for the Study of Play, play is increasingly an object of attention and sophisticated examination. We now know that when we play, we grow physically, intellectually and socially. We gain strength, balance and coordination. We imagine, experiment, create and discover. And we learn to communicate, share and cooperate. Children at play practice adult roles and learn to solve problems and make decisions. They socialize, discover appropriate ways of self-expression and gain confidence. When we don't play, we are less creative and productive. We are more sedentary, more easily fatigued, more susceptible to obesity and more likely to encounter social and emotional stress and issues.

   Despite our growing knowledge of play, however, free play for children is under attack from various forces. TV and electronic games are competing for

(continued)

Narrative 1.1. (*continued*)

children's attention. Issues of urbanization and government are restricting the development of new playgrounds. Risk aversion, high-stakes testing and the mistaken belief that physical education classes are an appropriate substitute for free play are reducing recess in schools. And organized youth sports don't make up for it. At the same time, despite all the communications gadgets we have and all the sophisticated management techniques we employ—or perhaps because of them—adults, too, have less time for uninterrupted play.

4. How is the Museum involved with play scholarship?

In the summer of 2008 we launched the *American Journal of Play*. We edit the *Journal* in-house, and the University of Illinois Press handles printing and distribution. They tell us that they have never seen subscriber numbers climb like they have in a new periodical. The first issues feature cultural historians, neuroscientists, anthropologists, folklorists, physicians, sociologists, mathematicians, and a psychiatrist. It is an eclectic mix, fittingly for the subject that spans the disciplines. We've entered into a cooperative relationship with The Association for the Study of Play, too. Many TASP members serve on the board of our *American Journal of Play*. We hosted TASP's national conference in 2007 and we will host TASP's web page. We are housing archival material from play scholars. The Middle Atlantic American Studies Association and the Great Lakes American Studies Association held their joint conference at the museum in 2008. The American Association of State and Local History will also bring nearly a thousand to their gathering at Strong National Museum of Play in 2008. I'll have two books coming out in the next couple of years—one about toys, and the other about play theory that is informed by cultural history, neuroscience, and evolutionary biology. From this vantage we are looking at an encouraging trend in play studies as more scholars are recognizing the gravitas and import of the subject.

5. What benefits does play have for a child's development?

This is a big question. It seems like most every philosopher, educational psychologist, historian of education, ego psychologist, sports sociologist, coach, pediatrician, and evolutionary biologist who could pick up a pen has written about this. Here's a useful way to begin to look at it. Play is development itself. Language acquisition, literacy and numeracy, practicing and refining motor skills, building muscles, "socialization," and exercising a capacity for fantasy are all realized in large part through play.

Thailand, and Native America) that involves participants kicking a bean bag around to each other without allowing it to fall to the ground (Bellis, 2008). Hacky sack is a noncompetitive game in that, once the ball drops to the ground, all participants "lose" and must start over. Thus, the goal of the hacky sack is to cooperate with one another in order to extent the game.

As games become more competitive they tend to involve more rules with designated time limits and/or boundaries and the determination of a clear-cut winner (and loser) becomes paramount. Competitive games are further divided into two categories: intellectual contests (e.g., poker) and physical contests (competitive eating). Poker does not involve physicality, and although success is as much about luck as it is about skill, it does involve a relative amount of intelligence. In other words, each participant in a game of poker is subject to the random draw of cards; however, the manner in which each player utilizes strategy enhances the probability of winning. Thus, a player who utilizes deception (knowing when to bluff), is capable of reading the "tells" (most people give off clues as to whether they have a "good" hand or a "bad" hand) of opponents, and engaging in strategic betting will succeed more often in poker than relying merely on chance. In short, competitive poker represents a competitive game, but despite what ESPN would have us believe, it is certainly not a sport.

An interesting example of a competitive physical contest is the ever-growing popular activity of competitive eating. "Competitive eating," as the term implies, involves a field of gurgitators (eaters) competing against one another in an effort to consume the most food during a designated period of time. As with cup stacking, kickball, and other sporting activities already discussed, competitive eating is governed by an international body, the International Federation of Competitive Eating (IFOCE). The IFOCE requires that all of its competitive eaters must be at least 18 years old. Any contestant who throws up during competition is disqualified. According to its website, the IFOCE (2008) "helps to ensure that the sport remains safe, while also seeking to achieve objectives consistent with the public interest—namely, creating an environment in which fans may enjoy the display of competitive eating skill."

The IFOCE sponsors more than 100 international eating contests per year. The IFOCE keeps official eating records and maintains a list of the "Top 50" eaters. In 2008, Joey Chestnut was ranked number one. Chestnut holds eating records in a number of categories including: asparagus (8.8 pounds in 10 minutes); chicken wings (7.5 lbs in 12 minutes); grilled cheese sandwiches (47 in 10 minutes); Jalapeno Poppers (118 in 10 minutes); and pork ribs (8.4 lbs in 12 minutes). However, it is his hot dog eating prowess that has led to his greatest fame. In 2008, Chestnut successfully defended his Nathan's Hot Dog Eating Contest "mustard belt" (given to the hot dog eating champion) when he beat the former six-time champion Takeru Kobayashi.

Nathan's annual July 4th hot dog eating contest, held in New York City's Coney Island, is the most prestigious of all competitive eating contests and dates back to July 4, 1916 (Nerz, 2006). For the past few years, ESPN has dedicated a full hour of coverage to this eating event. In 2008, Chestnut and Kobayashi tied for first place, with each consuming 59 hot dogs in 10 minutes

(the contest used to last for 12 minutes but the IFOCE is trying to standardized all sanctioned eating contests to 10 minutes). Rather than having co-
champions, both eaters were pitted against one another in a "5 dog eat off."
During this extra time, Chestnut was able to squeeze out a victory. After the
competition Chestnut was asked about how he felt beating Kobayashi for the
second straight year. "He wanted it, but I needed it" (Goldman, 2008). Ah!
Spoken like a true athlete!

Considering that a billion people around the world are starving to death, the
concept of competitive eating hardly seems sporting. In addition, competitive
eating may involve a degree of physicality but it certainly does not qualify as
a sport. Furthermore, we would not consider competitive eaters as athletes.
(Note: We will discuss the criteria of being an athlete later in this chapter.)

Sports

As defined earlier, sports are institutionalized, structured competitive activities
that go beyond the realm of play that involve physical exertion and/or the use
of relatively complex athletic skills. Sports are competitive physical activities
that go beyond contests. They are highly structured, involve institutionally defined rules, and are far removed from the realm of play. Physical competition
in-and-of-itself is not a sufficient criterion, as the need for complex athletic
skills is of crucial importance. Generally, such skills take years of cultivation,
so that an added component is the necessity of proper training, guided physical exertion, and often the need for coaches and other means of support. Perhaps in today's world, where competition often becomes the most important
attribute in sports (who has the most records; which athlete has contributed the
most to his/her team, etc.) one can overlook the personal development aspect
of sport. Learning the proper rules, adapting (or at times alerting) them, and
engaging in intense physical exertions can be both a way to accomplish one's
best within the sport as well as a preparation for related activities outside of
the particular sport (learning how to cooperate and appreciating proper rules,
for instance). Still, it is also clear that what constitutes a "sport" is itself an al-
ways-changing phenomenon. Perhaps even more remarkable is the sheer number of activities that fall within the definition given above.

SPORTS, SPORTS, SPORTS, EVERYWHERE THERE ARE SPORTS!

Even the novice to the world of sport is certainly aware of the large number of
sports that exist in the United States and elsewhere. In the U.S. there are popu-

lar participating sports, such as bowling and running; popular commercial sports, such as football, auto racing, baseball, basketball, and hockey; there are sports popular in specific regions such as lacrosse and surfing; and there are a number of universal sports, such as tennis, soccer, and ping pong (table tennis).

The Most Popular Sports in the United States

Any discussion about the "most popular" sports in the U.S. (or in the world, for that matter) must begin with a clarification of what "most popular" means. In other words, when determining popularity it is necessary to distinguish between participatory popularity and responses to the question, "What is your favorite sport?" For example, if a representative sample of the entire United States were asked, "What is your favorite sport?" the largest number of people would say, "football." However, claiming football as a favorite sport does not mean that the respondents actually play (or played) football; instead, they like the game of football and/or they like to watch football being played.

The authors examined numerous studies (See, for example: Thomsen, 2006) and have concluded that the most popular participatory sports are: bowling (approximately 54 million participants); running/jogging (38 million); fitness walking (36 million); basketball (32 million); golf (26 million); tennis (18 million); and inline skating (17 million).

When Americans are asked to identify their most favorite sport to *watch* the overwhelming top response is professional football (close to 30%). College football and baseball are a close second and third, both around 14 percent. Auto racing, especially NASCAR, is fourth with about 9 percent, followed by professional basketball (7%) and college basketball (5%). Professional hockey and golf follow basketball's popularity with about 4 percent each.

If attendance figures were combined with sports fans' identification of their favorite sport, baseball would rank as the top sport in the United States and football would rank as number two. Baseball, however, has higher attendance figures because there are nearly ten times as many games played by each team as in football. Basketball and hockey follow baseball and football in this measurement of popularity. However, if auto racing had anywhere near the total venues of basketball and hockey, its popularity would rank even higher. Interestingly, in the United States, unlike in many other countries, stock car racing (NASCAR) is far more popular than open wheel racing (e.g., Formula 1).

The Most Popular Sports in the World

In some ways, Americans are quite unique in their sporting preferences. As mentioned above, we greatly prefer stock racing (NASCAR) while the rest of the world prefers open-wheel, especially Formula 1. In fact, most world-wide connoisseurs of auto racing consider stock car racing as an inferior form of auto racing. This belief has not deterred some of the world's best drivers (e.g., Juan Pablo Montoya and Dario Franchitti) from trying their luck with NASCAR, however. We Americans also prefer our hard-hitting, full contact, running, kicking, and passing offensive-oriented version of football while the rest of the world prefers the low-scoring, kicking a ball back-and-forth, defensive-minded *futbol* (soccer). On the other hand, Americans do play soccer—there's an adage that states, "American youth play soccer, but they watch football." We also participate in many other universal sports such as running, swimming, volleyball, tennis, golf, basketball, and rugby.

Determining a ranking of the world's most popular sports presents a more daunting challenge than attempting a ranking of the U.S. top sports positions, as data from countries across the globe must be tallied and totaled. Although some of the studies we reviewed showed slight differences in the middle of the "Top 10" ranking order, the listed sports themselves were consistent. Furthermore, there appears to be a universal agreement over the world's top two most popular sports. It should be noted that this ranking combines participation with viewership.

Undoubtedly, most readers already know that soccer, or *futbol*, is the most popular sport in the world. The game is played in more than 100 nations around the world and is especially big in Europe, South America, Mexico, China, and Africa. Soccer's World Cup, played every four years, is the most watched sporting event in the world, drawing nearly a billion viewers for the championship game alone. The two authors were in Europe during the 2006 World Cup events and can attest to the passionate involvement throughout the continent, with countless people wearing their teams' colors and cheering madly for their favorite athletes.

Have you thought about the second most popular sport in the world? The answer may surprise you. It is cricket. Yes, *cricket*, a sport that very few Americans have ever played or watched. Cricket's popularity is due to its distinction as the number one sport in the populous India, as well as the smaller nations of Pakistan, Bangladesh, Nepal, Australia, and parts of the Caribbean and Africa. Tennis and field hockey are generally ranked as the third and fourth most popular sports, followed by baseball, basketball, and volleyball. Rounding out the top 10 are table tennis (ping pong), rugby and golf. It should be noted that auto racing (primarily Formula 1) ranks higher than many of these sports when the participation factor (few people actually race cars) is eliminated from the ranking formula.

Box 1.1. *Rambo III* and Buzkashi

One sport which is relatively unknown outside its native land, but incredibly popular within, is the ancient sport of "Buzkashi." Buzkashi—a term meaning "goat-grabbing" is a widely popular sort in the country of Afghanistan. It is a contest between two teams of horsemen over the possession of a dead calf or goat carcass, with the object being for one talented and fearless rider to gain control of the slippery carcass and then separate from the pack of horsemen vying for the same prize. "'Buzkashi' means goat, but a calf carcass is often used because it reportedly stays intact longer. The animal is beheaded, bled, and behooved before being used. It can be either gutted or not" (Craig, 2002:154-155). It is a high-contact combative event, with horsemen often plowing into each other as well as into the crowds of spectators. "Gashes and broken bones are common; spills commonly send riders and horses alike tumbling. Being a spectator at a buzkashi match isn't all that much safer" (King, 2001:B-3).

Most Americans, it can be assumed, had never heard of this "game" until they were introduced to it through the venue of popular culture, in the 1998 movie *Rambo III*. In it, Sylvester Stallone's character John J. Rambo is in Afghanistan to help rebel forces against the Russian "aggressors." To bond with the native forces, he plays a vigorous game of buzkashi with them, and quickly dominates, earning the praise of the Afghan rebels.

Ironically enough, those same rebels would later become identified with the Taliban, who would become America's enemy after the 9/11/2001 attacks for sheltering Osama bin Laden. Even more ironically, when they came to power after defeating the Russians, one of the first things the Taliban did was outlaw buzkashi! But since the fall of the Taliban, it has made a comeback (one of the authors recently had a student from Afghanistan who attested to its continuing popularity there). Ulam Siddiq, "a grizzled fan," was quoted as saying, "It's part of our culture, and we're very happy to have it back again" (King, 2001:B-3).

Buzkashi—sport or not a sport? Perhaps only John J. Rambo knows for sure.

ATHLETES AND SPORTS ADHERENTS

People do not agree on everything and sports fans will argue over just about anything that is sports-related. For example, are race car drivers, golfers, bowlers, and football players athletes? Maybe you think football players are athletes but race car drivers are not. Most likely, sports fans are ready to "discuss" such a topic! Furthermore, some readers may have disagreed with our definition of sport and others may steadfastly believe that poker *is* a sport. With this reality in mind, we turn our attention to defining an athlete. Once again, in order to define something, parameters must be established.

We believe that the most important parameter involves distinguishing between participating in physical activity versus participating in athletics.

Athletes

Sport sociologists have traditionally argued that an athlete is someone who
participates in school athletics (high school and/or college), plays professionally, or is in training for some specific sporting event such as the Olympics.
But how do we categorize a person who works out on a regular basis? Is he
or she an athlete? Technically, such an individual is labeled a physically active person. Let's examine this more carefully. A *physically active* person is
someone who exerts physical energy while participating in some sort of activity, such as walking, hiking, skiing, volunteering, and so on, but he or she
does so for the enjoyment and/or health benefits such activities provide. An
athlete, by contrast, is exerting energy for a specific sporting activity, such as
playing football, baseball, basketball, or lacrosse. In this regard, athletes compete in sports while physically active persons do not. Harry Edwards (1973)
explains this quite clearly. "It is only in sports that the participant can accu-
rately be termed an 'athlete'" (p.55). When distinguishing between physically
active people and athletes it is also important to highlight the importance of
competition build into athletics/sports. When one plays sports, he or she is in
competition with other athletes or previous records. Physically active people
are not in competition with others, although they may try to beat their own
personal best.

Sports Adherents

If athletes did not compete sport would not exist. Thus, their importance to
the world of sport is self-evident. However, there exists another key ingredient to sport—the fans. Although chapter 7 will focus on sports fans in greater
detail, we find it important to introduce those most responsible for the world-
wide popularity of sports here, in this introductory chapter.

There are literally millions of sport adherents (fans) in the United States,
and billions throughout the world. Most of us are first exposed to sports during our childhood. As children we played sports, watched sports on television,
and/or attended sporting events at various venues. For most adherents, early
childhood experiences with sports fostered a life-long love for sports throughout their lives.

Sports fans may be categorized a number of ways, ranging from those who
attend games on a regular basis to those who consume sports via the media,
and those who are highly identified with a particular team or athlete and those

who are mildly or lowly identified. Some are ardent supporters of their favorite teams, regardless of how well that team is doing and will root for them "come hell or high water"; others are "fair-weather fans" who lose interest when their team is doing poorly or is not in competition for the highest honors.

Sport sociologists have categorized fans by a number of criteria. Borrowing (and revising) a distinction of sports fans from Wann and associates (2001) we have established the following distinctions:

1. *Sports Fans – Sport Spectators.* "Sport fans" are those individuals who are interested in and follow a sport, team, and/or athlete. They have a love for the game and a particular rooting interest in a specific player(s) or team(s). Unlike sport spectators, however, many sports fans may not have ever witnessed their favorite athlete or team perform in person. "Sport spectators" are those individuals who witness a sporting event in person. In many cases, the sport spectator represents the most loyal of all fans because he or she has dedicated time and money to watch a game in person. A season ticket holder, for example, often represents the most dedicated of all sports fans because he or she regularly attends games. However, in other cases, sport spectators may also include the casual fan, or people who attend a sporting event out of curiosity or because he or she was a part of a group (e.g., company employees) that has tickets for a game.

2. *Direct and Indirect Sport Consumers.* A sport consumer is someone who purchases sport-related products. Sport consumers can be divided into two sub-groups: direct and indirect. "Direct sport consumers" are those who purchase sporting event tickets and/or purchase sport-related merchandise, including pay-per-view television events. "Indirect sport consumers" are those people exposed to sport through some form of the mass media, merchandizing, or advertising. In this regard, sports have entered their world through interaction with others rather than through self-initiated contact with sport.

3. *Lowly and Highly Identified Sport Fans.* "Highly identified fans" outwardly show their allegiance by wearing team apparel, face painting, and other visible signs of association. These fans "live" for the game and their lives are heavily influenced by sporting events and especially, the outcome. A favorite player's or team's defeat can leave the highly identified fan feeling devastated; while a victory can lead to feelings of extreme happiness and joy. "Lowly identified fans" rarely outwardly display their allegiance to an athlete or team. They are similar to "band-wagon" fans in that only when their favorite team or athlete wins do they reveal their allegiance.

In the United States, a nation of consumers, sports consumerism is strongly encouraged because it helps to stimulate the economy. It is not a mere accident that the sports-related industry (sports, leisure, and recreation combined) represents a trillion dollar enterprise. For sports fans, however, the consumption of sport is done voluntarily because of their love for the game. And although most sports fans are (reluctantly) aware that sport, especially at the professional and collegiate levels, is a business, it is the game aspect that excites us the most. While not begrudging the right of owners and players to earn a profit, fans focus more upon physical competition than upon economic aspects.

SPORT AS A MICROCOSM OF SOCIETY

For most fans, sports are what they are—games played by amateurs and professionals alike. Sports provide us with opportunities to cheer and boo; they motivate and deflate us; and they bring joy and sorrow. Sports fans realize that there are multiple layers of sport. Athletes have personal lives and sometimes their off-the-field endeavors affect their game performance. Owners of professional sports teams make decisions that are often based on economics and such decisions may lead to an inevitable trading away of fan favorite players or the signing of players that will help to bring a championship to the community that plays host to the team. And these two examples merely represent the tip of the iceberg of sports' complexity. In other words, sports possess multiple layers that allow for analysis from a variety of sport talk show hosts and from fans themselves. In fact, sports are so multi-faceted and so ingrained in society, it has often been said that sports are a microcosm of society itself.

You may be asking yourself, "What does it mean to say that sports are a microcosm of society?" We say that sport is a microcosm of society because it reflects, or mirrors, the cultural principles of a society. For example, as society has grown more corporate and materialistic over the years, so too have sports. In the United States, the ideals of capitalism and consumerism dominate both society and sport. Just as Americans are encouraged to purchase commodities of any sort (remember receiving "stimulus" checks in 2008?), sports fans are encouraged to buy a wide variety of sports merchandise, including team jerseys, ball caps, autographed memorabilia, and so on. In this regard, the consumerism aspect that dominates capitalistic societies is reflected in the world of sports as well. Because of this mirroring affect, social researchers, and especially sport sociologists, have found that sport is an appropriate institution to examine the basic tenets of a society's ideology. Sport serves as a useful microcosm because it reflects both the negative and positive aspects of society.

Among the negative aspects of sport are elitism, racism, sexism, extreme competitiveness, a willingness to cheat in order to win, and illegal drug use. But why would anyone be surprised that these elements exist in sport when they exist in society as well? Studying the negative (as well as the positive) aspects of sport helps us to understand why these behaviors exist in society's other social institutions.

Of course, sports also reveal many of the positive aspects of society, including the provision of opportunities to achieve and succeed; promoting hard work as a means of getting ahead in life; and the value of teamwork and cooperation.

That the sport pages often resemble the news pages—filled with stories of crime and deviance as well as articles praising the positive exploits of individual athletes and sports teams for their hard work successes—is a testament to the reality that sport serves as a "natural laboratory" for the analysis of society. Furthermore, the institution of sport is relatively precise in its parameters and thus provides us with an opportunity to understand the greater society by concentrating our research in one specific area, sport. As the prominent sport sociologists D. Stanley Eitzen and George H. Sage stated two decades ago, the institution of sport provides scientific observers with a convenient laboratory within which to examine values, socialization, stratification, bureaucracy, and so on, that also exist at the societal level (outside of sport). "The types of games people choose to play, the degree of competitiveness, the types of rules, the constraints on the participants, the groups that do and do not benefit under the existing arrangements, the rate and type of change, and the reward system in sport provide us with a microcosm of the society in which sport is embedded" (Eitzen and Sage, 1989:14).

The idea that sport is a microcosm of society has a long history in sport sociology. However, only recently has the value of sport sociology as a discipline gained increased credibility. Nixon and Frey (1996) state, "If sport can be a mirror of society, then the sociology *of* sport actually is sociology *through* sport" (p.3). Sport sociologists provide insights on the social aspects of the sports world that are applicable in the greater society as well. An examination of sports' values and ethics is fruitful in the further understanding of culture. It is the idea that sport is a microcosm of society that gives the field one of its best valid claims of legitimacy.

Ethics and Sports

Ethical issues are predominant in any society. (Note: Ethics and civility will be discussed in further detail in chapter 8 in our discussion on sportsmanship.)

Once again, sport serves as a "window," or microcosm, of the world of ethics. Morality is a key aspect of ethics. Ethics is the study of morality (how people act and how they justify their actions to themselves and to others). Values cherished by citizens often vary tremendously from one society to the next, and within specific societies. "It is widely believed that moral judgments made within one cultural tradition are contradicted by moral judgments made within other cultural traditions. Moral judgments also conflict within cultures, frequently along religious, ethnic and socioeconomic lines" (Simon, 1985:4). In contemporary society cultural pluralism, or diversity, is highly promoted as a social policy designed to integrate varied groups. Those who promote such an ideology believe that people from different backgrounds will learn to agree on moral issues. Issues of morality are learned, after all, and therefore, it is believed that people can learn to be tolerant of others. However, there are researchers who argue that ethics and morality are rigidly tied to specific beliefs of what constitutes "proper" and "right" behavior. As Simon (1985:6) points out:

1. People from different cultural, religious, and socioeconomic backgrounds make conflicting moral judgments.
2. Therefore, there is no correct resolution of their disagreement; each group is bound only by its own morality.
3. Therefore, rational inquiry designed to rationally resolve such disagreement is pointless.

Rationality does, however, play a big role in ethics and morality, in the form of politics. Most laws passed by legislative bodies reflect issues of morality and proper behavior. Certain segments of a society may not agree on the "ethical validity" of such legislation, but in civil societies the law of the land supercedes special interest groups' wants and desires.

One of the main debates amongst ethicists, therefore, is whether ethical norms are universal (which is to say, moral rules should transcend cultural, religious or temporal differences and be the same for all people) or relative (i.e. moral rules arise and are justified precisely because of their specific connections to unique cultural, religious or temporal conditions and cannot be applied across the board). The study of sports ethics is itself connected with this longstanding debate. For instance, in many Latin American countries bullfighting is considered a national sport, and the matadors are cultural heroes. Yet there are many who consider bullfighting not to be a sport at all, but rather a barbaric and cruel abuse of animals. In Great Britain in 2004 fox hunting was abolished by the Labour government of Prime Minister Tony Blair, on the grounds that it was immoral, even though there were many professional fox hunters who strenuously argued that it was a time-honored and morally acceptable sport of the British upper classes.

There are two critical elements that make ethical issues especially relevant to the sports world: the "ethics of competition" and the concept that "sport builds character." The primary goal of sport is to win. The late Vince Lombardi, former coach of the Green Bay Packers has often been attributed (perhaps falsely) as having said, "Winning is not the most important thing; it's the only thing." Whether Lombardi actually made this comment or not, the idea is ingrained in nearly all athletes' attitudes toward sports. As Al Davis, owner of the Oakland Raiders, once famously proclaimed, "Just win, baby." The Oakland Raiders have a motto of "A commitment to excellence." Despite the fact that the Raiders often fall far short of excellence, the motif is still relevant. Competition in any endeavor implies a winner(s) and loser(s). "Fair competition" is about fair play, abiding by the rules, and generally adopts a philosophy of "May the best person win." The authors define "ethical sport competition" as sports played within the rules established by governing bodies while pursuing victory. It is important to note that sport often "imposes its own set or moral standards and requirements on those who participate in it . . . These standards and requirements [involve] 'fair play' and 'being a good sport'" (Morgan, Meier and Schneider, 2001:1–2). Fair play involves playing by the rules, respect for the rules, respect for the game, and a slew of virtues determined within the sports world.

The "ethics of competition" involves an analysis of the negative and positive consequences of sport competition. Some may wonder whether it is necessary to morally evaluate competition in sport. "Isn't it enough to say simply that participants and spectators alike enjoy such competition? To critics of competition in sports, that is not enough. They argue that such competition is either inherently immoral or that it has the effect of reinforcing other social values that are undesirable. Many persons, including some professional athletes, have criticized competition and the overemphasis on winning that they claim it breeds and have proposed a more relaxed attitude toward sports, at least at most levels of amateur play, than sanctioned by the competitive creed" (Simon, 1991:15). Other criticisms of sport competition involve claims that competition is selfish and egoistic. The primary goal of winning makes "losers" out of the remaining competitors. "The goal of competition is enhancement of the position of one competitor at the expense of others. Thus, by its very nature, the goal of competition is selfish. But since selfish concern for oneself at the expense of others is immoral, it follows that competition is immoral as well" (Simon, 1985:19). The statement "selfish concern for oneself at the expense of others is immoral" reflects a moralistic bias itself. Herbert Spencer (1820–1903), an English sociologist who coined the term "survival of the fittest," demonstrated long ago the validity of the idea that we are in constant competition with others (and with the environment) at all times (Delaney, 2004A). Those who do not take care of their own needs risk dissolution (losing). The egotistical aspect of competition is revealed when some winners have an elevated sense of self worth and think and act as though they are superior to others (both those in the sports world and those who are not).

Proponents of competition often cite (usually unknowingly) Spencer's "survival of the fittest" concept. Every social institution is filled with competition. All members of society are in competition on a daily basis. Competition extends to the workplace, the search for dating and mating partners, research grants, and so on. Advocates of sports competition argue that sport participation prepares youth for the "real world"—one that is filled with cutthroat competition. And yet, one of the most cited benefits of sport participation is that it builds moral character. Athletes that lose on the playing field will learn to overcome adversity and compete another day. Hard work and determination are cornerstone values of American society. Being a member of a sports team can cultivate one's leadership abilities as well as encourage learning the importance of teamwork and cooperation. These values are the basic building blocks of sport competition.

The concept of "sport builds character" is debated in the sports world—does sport build character, or does it build characters? Morgan, Meier and Schneider (2001:3-4) identify six categories of sport characters:

1. The Good Sport—The good sport respects the game and is primarily concerned with a well-played game between competitors who gave their all and played within the rules of the game. The "good sport" is the type of player most of us would like to have as a teammate. Conversely, the "poor sport" is someone we would not like to have as a teammate—unless of course, he or she possesses great talent and contributes to a team victory.
2. The Poor Sport—"The poor sport tends not to take responsibility for his or her own poor play and does not credit opponents' good play . . . The poor sport may abandon fairness and turn to cheating. He or she might give up if the game is going badly; in such a case the poor sport might adopt the stance of the spoilsport" (p.3). The poor sport is the type of person who will pout and blame others when things do not go his or her way. The poor sport often brings down the morale of the entire team.
3. The Gamesperson—"The gamesperson plays to the letter, not the spirit of the rules. The gamesperson considers anything permitted that is not explicitly forbidden and sees penalties as costs of doing business" (p.4). The television show *Seinfeld* provides an excellent example of the gamesperson. In the episode "The Big Salad" Kramer explains his displeasure with

his golfing partner, Steve Gendason, with Jerry and Elaine. On the 15th hole, Steve is about to hit his second shot, when he picks up the ball and cleans it. Kramer goes ballistic and penalizes him a stroke because the rules clearly state you cannot clean the ball unless it's on the green. He explains that the rules are very clear about that, and Kramer feels the need to enforce such a peculiar rule even while playing with a friend. Gendason reacts angrily with Kramer. The episode ends with Kramer and Gendason reenacting the famous O.J. Simpson "car chase" in a white Ford Bronco (Delaney, 2006A).

4. The Cheat—"The cheat is not concerned about fairness. The cheat will break the rules (often hoping that no one notices) when he or she thinks it is to his or her advantage. The cheat is concerned only with the score, not the playing of the game" (p.4). Interestingly, a great deal of cheating is tolerated in sports; for example, it said that "holding" occurs on nearly every down of professional football; and yet, it is penalized relatively sparingly. In many cases, athletes are actually taught how to cheat and get away with it. Soccer players and basketball players who take "dives" pretending to be hit by an opponent in an effort to gain a favorable call are guilty of cheating and yet this is often considered "part of the game." In this regard, cheating has become institutionalized.

5. The Spoilsport—"The spoilsport intentionally destroys the game for others" (p.4). A child may knock the game board over or unplug a computer game, take the equipment and go home; and adults find ways to subvert the game, making it impossible for others to play. Spoilsports are immature and have been socialized improperly.

6. The Trifler—"The trifler does not care about the game and does not try to play. He or she may be on the field but makes no effort to perform the actions the game requires. This situation differs from one in which a player is unskilled in a particular game but at least is trying' (p.4). The trifler then is simply going through the motions. His or her heart is not in the game and as a result, this person should not be playing.

Which of these character traits bests describes your favorite athlete? Which type of character best describes you as an athlete or sports fan?

FINAL THOUGHTS

As demonstrated in this introductory chapter, sports are competitive activities that go beyond the realm of play and leisure. There are a wide variety of sports including individual sports and team sports; amateur and professional sports; regional and universal sports; and sports with great world-wide appeal. Sports provide adherents with opportunities for joy and happiness and sorrow and pain. But sport is also a major social institution that reflects the values, norms, and ideology of the greater society. In that regard, we can look at sports as a microcosm of society, consisting of both positive and negative aspects.

Sport teaches participants to be competitive, physically active, emotionally and mentally prepared to perform, and pushes them to limits they may have never achieved otherwise. Some athletes interpret these lessons to become good sports; while other athletes learn to value winning even at the cost of fair play and may cheat in order to attain victory.

Most of all, sport—both in participation and in appreciation—gives individuals a sense of meaning in their lives. In the following chapters, we will look in more detail at the origins of various sports, how people have learned about them, and the benefits of taking part in and becoming identified with various sporting activities and organizations. The game is on!

Chapter Two

Our Love Affair with Sports throughout History

From ancient times through the present, one sport has been a part of every culture. Among the present day stars of this eternal sport are Emmitt Smith and Jason Taylor. What sport are we talking about — Football? No, not really. It is dance. Yes, that's right, dance! The earliest known sporting activities of Africa and Asia included dance. Dance was valued because it involved physical movement and strength and because it had religious or spiritual meaning. Dance, of course, still exists today and although it remains a physical endeavor and can be competitive, it is generally not acknowledged as an example of sport.

Although most people today do not consider dancing a sport, one former (Smith) and one present day (Taylor) National Football League stars have gained notoriety for their participation in the television show *Dancing with the Stars*. Smith and professional dancing partner Cheryl Burke won the 2006 competition and Taylor and his dancing partner Edyta Sliwinska were the 2008 runner-ups.

For the unacquainted, *Dancing with the Stars* involves twelve celebrities (6 males and 6 females) and their professional dancing partners competing against one another in elimination round format. The professional dancer is responsible for teaching the celebrity how to perform specific dances, which the pair then performs live on the weekly show. Three judges score the dancers' performances. Viewers of the show are also allowed to vote by phone, text message, or through online methods. In this manner, viewers (fans) play an interactive role with the show and help to determine its outcome. This is something that fans of football, and other sports, are not allowed to do!

Although Smith and Taylor have made inroads with regard to the public's perception of football players who dance, there are still "old-school" folks who are not so accepting. Among these old-school types is Bill Parcells. Parcells is a long-time NFL coach known for being strict and authoritarian. And while Taylor was dancing with stars, Parcells was solidifying his role as the new head coach of the Miami Dolphins (Taylor's team). It became public knowledge that Parcells was not happy with Taylor spending so much time dancing instead of concentrating on football. By the time Taylor reached the finals of *Dancing*, Parcells had reached a boiling point. Taylor claimed that he was in top shape because dancing required a great deal of physical exercise. Perhaps predictably, Parcells traded Taylor (to the Washington Redskins) a couple of months after the dancing competition and a couple of months prior to the start of the 2008 NFL season. It seems as though some people just want to see their football players only play football!

In this chapter, we will take a brief look at sport throughout history. We will discover that many of today's games and sports have long histories. We will also find that many sports reflect the climate of their times and the adaptations to these sports reflect the changing nature of culture.

AN INTRODUCTION TO THE EVOLUTION AND DEVELOPMENT OF SPORT

When did sport first emerge? The problem in answering this question is underscored by the debate over when humans first appeared on earth. "Scientists have difficulty determining where humans originated; that is, whether life began in a single area of the world. Scholars theorize that humans evolved from simpler forms of life, but they have been unable to find concrete examples of all stages of the evolutionary process. Traces of early humans have been found scattered across Africa, Asia, and Europe" (Freeman, 1997:59). Many social thinkers believe that human life originated in Africa one or two million years ago. According to Turner (2003), our most direct ancestor evolved from Africa, around 150,000 years ago. "The order to which humans belong—termed *primates*—has been around for perhaps as long as 60 million years, but these distant ancestors looked more like a modern tree shrew or rodent than a human . . . The ancestral lines of present-day primates like chimpanzees, with whom we share 99% of our genes, and the immediate ancestors of humans, whom we call *hominids*, split apart around five million years ago" (p.1). Although faced with innumerable predators, humans, through cooperation with one another and the development of basic survival techniques (e.g., tools and intellect), learned to compete with and survive against the many dangers found in the natural environment. "Primitive people lived in a harsh environment. To survive constant battles with nature, they gradually developed crude tools, such as axes, knives, and bows and arrows, that elevated them above other forms of animal life. The primitive human's cranial capacity (which is larger than that of other creatures in relation to their body size) permitted the full development of their capacity to reason, improving their chances of survival" (Freeman, 1997:59–60).

After millions of years, the evolutionary process and the survival instinct eventually led to humans dominating the physical environment. "In fact, it was not until a few thousand years ago that humans abandoned hunting and gathering as their basic mode of survival and began an entirely new chapter in their evolution. Biological evolution was increasingly replaced by the evolution of culture and social structure" (Turner, 2003:2). Thus, throughout most of its history, humanity has been concerned primarily with basic survival; every day was filled with the challenge of securing the basic necessities of life: food, clothing and shelter. It is doubtful that there was much leisure time for hunters and gatherers constantly foraging for food and protecting themselves from wild animals and natural threats. There was little time for sport as we know it today.

As stated in Chapter 1, play has seemingly always existed. "Archaeologists have produced evidence of physical play in prehistoric societies, but signs of organized sport remain elusive" (Nixon and Frey, 1996:18). Children have always found time to play, even if it involved such elementary activities as skipping rocks on a river or lake, challenging a friend to a contest of throwing some objects for distance, or testing playmates' strengths through playful wrestling. Mandell (1984) argues that play precedes humanity because animals also play. Dogs and cats wrestle and chase each other, fish and birds dance, and the apes have simple, pleasurable games. But sport is different from play. Sport is an organized activity consumed with rules and specific roles. Ancient man had little time for sport. Even so, the roots of many sports can be traced to antiquity.

Early human survival was tied to the development of physical skills. Hunters and gatherers had to be especially adept at running distances and using spears.

> To become good at using the spear, one had to practice. The would-be, confident spear tosser had to master and perform a here-there kind of thinking that was sharply different from the hunting techniques of non-tool using beings whose play, relaxation, and exercise was not much different from that of the beasts. According to the Marxist, sport separates men from beasts. Sport is a cultural manifestation but it is not play. Sport is only preparation for work and a reflection of the needs of a creative animal to survive and progress (Mandell, 1984:2).

The skilled spear tosser was valued in hunting and gathering societies, for such a person could kill an animal and feed the clan. By the time of the ancient Greeks, throwing a spear for purely survival purposes would be replaced by throwing a javelin for sporting purposes. (The spear was, however, still a valued weapon of war during the time of the Greeks.)

In short, the evolution of man parallels the evolution and development of sport. "Sports games are human creations that have not only a basic structure but also a long evolutionary history. Like most societies they have evolved over long periods of time to fit various needs" (Bell, 1987:11).

ANCIENT SPORTS (CIRCA 1400 BCE–800 BCE)

The "Ancient World" "is a term that, by common usage in Europe and America, encompasses a considerable period of time, from the Neolithic agricultural revolution at about 7,000 B.C. to the fall of the Roman Empire" (McIntosh, 1993:19). However, when discussing ancient sports, the implied time frame is the beginning of human history to the time of the ancient Greeks. The first variations of sports and games of the ancient world would emerge out of a combination of physical survival and religious ritualistic significance.

Physical Survival ✓

As described earlier in this chapter, developing survival skills was critical for the survival of humanity. Survival skills not only included the ability to defend oneself and others, the ability to provide food, clothing and shelter; it also involved physical activities such as hunting skills (e.g., archery, spear and rock throwing, and stalking animals). Survival was also dependent upon such physical capabilities as running, jumping, swimming, and hand-to-hand combat (primarily wrestling).

> The essential characteristic of primitive physical activities was survival skills, practicing the skills needed for defense against natural enemies. Similarly, sport was essentially 'survival sports,' or 'natural sports,' for many of the sporting activities had their source in the same basic skills as the physical activities . . . When we look at the early forms of sport used by primitive people in Western culture (European prehistory), we often see a warlike basis for the activities. Success in sport required a mastery of the basic skills of war. We have traditionally considered this warlike basis of sport to be a common trait, but it is not true for all primitive societies. However, even though primitive sport was not always warlike, or war oriented, it was taken seriously (Freeman, 1997:61–62).

Games of dexterity and skill were also found in ancient cultures. Archery, for example, was an especially valued sporting and warring skill. Dance was viewed as an activity of physical and religious value.

Religious Significance of Ancient Sport ✓

Dance was significant in some primitive societies as a form of prayer, or as a way to communicate with forces that could not be clarified. "Because they tried to influence what they could neither understand nor explain, they gradually developed religious beliefs and customs. Primitive people used dance for religious communication and experience" (Freeman, 1997:61). Evolved to the point where it had survived millions of years of predators, humankind had yet to develop the intellect to explain everyday phenomena (e.g., a solar eclipse). As a result, it turned to creating gods that were held responsible for the ways of nature and humanity itself. The philosopher Friedrich Nietzsche would later wryly note that "I would believe only in a god who could dance" (Nietzsche, 1979:153). For him, dance was the perfect way to harmonize the rational and the emotional aspects of human life: it demanded order and practice while also allowing for spontaneous movement. The combination of these often-warring elements can bring a peculiar sort of joy, related to the concept of "ecstasy," meaning to get outside of one's self. In addition, for many, dance was a way of getting in touch with the divine. As Nixon and Frey (1996) explain, "The ceremonial, symbolic, and ritualistic aspects of the earliest sports tended to give them a sacred quality associating them with the spiritual or supernatural realm. Early sports participation became an expression of religious worship, designed to appease or please the gods" (p.18). The ritualistic, albeit secular, behavior of athletics today can be traced back to ancient sport—as Emmitt Smith and Jason Taylor can attest!

Sports in Ancient Africa

The early Africans participated in archery and dance. Archery was valued because of the warring skills involved, while dance was revered because it was viewed as a physical interpretation of religious spirituality. Beyond archery, a number of games that required dexterity and skill, (e.g., wrestling) were popular throughout Africa. While wrestling practices differed throughout Africa, there were some common themes, such as competition within age groups and by size (weight). Festival victors were often rewarded and publicly celebrated (Craig, 2002).

There are other sports beyond archery and wrestling that exist today which were practiced by the ancient Egyptians, including: dancing; running; boxing;

swimming (especially in the Nile River); and *senet* (also called *senat*), a tabletop game. The ancient Egyptian sport of *pankration*—which involves contestants boxing, kicking, wrestling, and applying pressure holds and locks—is very similar to today's "ultimate fighting."

Sports in Ancient Asia

Sports in ancient Asia, like those in Africa, were tied to physical survival. However, ancient Asian sport also possessed a philosophical quality. As sport historian Steve Craig (2002) explains: "Sports and games have long histories on the rich and diverse Asian continent, and ancient scholars and artists have left many records of these games . . . They, like all ancient cultures, had sports that were born from the activities of being a warrior or soldier, but these were often tempered with a philosophical approach that tried to humanize the sport—be it archery, wrestling, or sword-and-stick fighting—in such a way that it took on elements of an art form" (p.39).

While some sports were common throughout Asia, its great diversity led to the development of many geographical distinct sports and games. The Chinese played many board games including chess. They played a game called *t'su chu* (an early version of soccer); *pula*, or polo, a game believed to have its origins in Tibet; archery; wrestling; and martial arts. The Japanese played board games including their own version of chess called *shio-ghi* (Falkener, 1961). Sumo wrestling was quite popular in Japan. It does not appear as though sports were as common in India as they were in other parts of Asia. A few recreational sports and games were played, and dance was used for ceremonial purposes and religious observances.

SPORTS IN ANCIENT GREECE (800 BCE–100 BCE)

Every civilization is influenced by those that preceded it. Ancient Greece is no exception. Greek culture and sport were shaped by "outside" forces beginning nearly four thousand years ago. "The first Greek-speaking people were the Achaeans. They were invaders who settled in the northern areas of the Greek peninsula about 1900 B.C.E. and replaced the society and culture of the Minoan civilization of Crete. By about 1500 B.C.E. the Achaeans controlled most of the peninsula and had established Mycenae as their capital" (Freeman, 1997:65). The Achaeans formed alliances with such other powerful cities and states in eastern Mediterranean as Troy, Cyprus, Palestine and Egypt. "After several hundred years, however, prolonged warfare and a declining economy allowed another invasion of the Greek peninsula. Those northern invaders, the Dorians, referred to themselves as Hellenes and to the area they had invaded (the peninsula of modern Greece) as Hellas" (Freeman, 1997:65). The early era of the Dorian reign (1100 B.C.E.-900 B.C.E.) is known as the "dark age" of Greece of which little is known (McIntosh, 1993; Mandell, 1984). History of ancient Greek sport begins with epic poems dating around 800 B.C.E.

The Greeks would introduce technology to ancient sports. For example, recognizing the value of horses in warfare, the ancient Greeks established horse racing and chariot racing. Horse racing first appeared in the Olympics in 624 BCE. The Minoan influence on Greek sports led to the development of boxing wherein the boxers wore gloves and bull vaulting (a contestant would stand in front of charging bull and try to catch it by the horns in attempt to swing himself on the bull). The expression, "Take the bull by the horns" most likely dates back to ancient Greece. The Egyptian sport of pankration was also popular in Greek society. The Spartans used this sport to train their warriors.

Ancient Greece was a culture that highly valued athletics and competition. Sports heroes were routinely honored in poem and statue. But Greek culture was also characterized by a belief in gods, and thus Greek sports took on a religious flair symbolized through rituals and symbolic gestures. As a result, as one might suspect, dance was a popular sporting activity in Greek society.

The Ancient Olympics

The Greeks were known for putting on elaborate panhellenic festivals and organized sporting events. The oldest of the panhellenic festivals were: the Pythian Games at Delphi, held in honor of Apollo; the Isthmian Games held in Corinth in honor of Poseidon; the Games of Nemea and the Olympics, both which were held in honor of Zeus (Swaddling, 1980). The Olympics, of course, were the most famous of these games. It is interesting to note that some scholars trace the religious significance of the Greek games to the Irish funeral festival, Aonach Tailteann, which is older than the Olympic games, Thus, the Irish claim that *they* were the inspiration for the Greek games (Freeman, 1997).

The first recorded Olympic Games took place in 776 BCE in Olympia, a small village that existed for the purpose of hosting Greek sport spectacles. Among the original sports performed at the ancient Olympics were a number of running competitions; discus throw; the javelin; wrestling; pankration; chariot racing; horse racing; boxing; and the pentathlon, a competition that included five events (a sprint, the long jump, the discuss and javelin throws, and wrestling). Because of its warrior nature, boxing was a favorite sport among the Greeks. In ancient boxing, the two combatants stood toe-to-toe with one another and they were not allowed to move backwards, as such a move violated the code of warriors. Furthermore, any attempt to avoid the opponent's punches by moving out of the way was considered shameful behavior. Clearly, this form of boxing is much different and far more violent from today's version.

Women were not allowed to participate and the male contestants performed in the nude—reflecting the love of the physical body that the Greeks possessed. The women would eventually establish their own games and dedicated them to the goddess Hera, sister-wife of Zeus. Originally, only Greek citizens from wealthy families were allowed to compete. Clearly, the original Olympic Games were not about equality (they were elitist, racist, and sexist)! Nonetheless, the Olympics represent the first step toward sports as a spectacle deserving of national, and eventually, international standing.

SPORTS IN ANCIENT ROME (100 BCE–500 CE)

The defeat of the city of Corinth by Mummius and his army in 146 B.C.E. marks the end of the Greek empire and the beginning of the Roman. The Roman Empire is usually said to have begun around 27 BC when Julius Caesar's great-nephew Gaius Octavius was given the name "Augustus" by the Roman Senate as a sign that he was now the undisputed ruler after years of bitter civil war. The Roman Empire was to incorporate the entire ancient Greek world and would take over the civil and religious life of that region. The Greek Games, however, survived. From as early as the first century B.C.E. victors in the four panhellenic festivals (at least one occurred every year) enjoyed a fixed grant from the public treasury for life. These four festivals were known as the "circuit" during the Roman era. The athletes belonged to a guild (similar to a player's union today) which had its worldwide headquarters in Rome. Thus, these athletes were "professional" (McIntosh, 1993). Unlike the Greeks, the Romans allowed participants from all social classes; thus, Roman sports provided an opportunity for a limited number of people to attain social mobility through athletics. (This same limited opportunity for upward mobility via sport exists today.) The Romans also objected to the games being performed in the nude "and suspected homosexuality and degeneracy" as the reasons behind the nudity requirement (McIntosh, 1993:31).

As the festivals continued to flourish in Greece, the games eventually found there way to the city of Rome itself. Emperor Augustus, in 30 B.C.E., introduced the games to modest reviews and acceptance. In 67 A.D., the Emperor Nero competed in the Olympic Games, having them postponed from 65

A.D. so that he could participate in the Pythian and Isthmian festivals first. These games were a "joke" as no participant was allowed to beat Nero. No other Emperor followed this absurd course of action (McIntosh, 1993). Nero's influence on Roman sports, however, extended beyond his participation as an athlete. In 60 A.D., Nero established the Neronia games, where knights and senators were encouraged to fight in the arena as gladiators — much to the delight of the spectators. Imagine if today's Congressional Representatives and Senators were forced to engage in "ultimate fighting" — would ESPN cover it?

Around the time of the birth of Jesus, the city of Rome had well over 1 million inhabitants, most of whom lived in horrific slum conditions; many were unemployed and over half of them were supported by the state (similar to welfare) (Baker, 1982). During the reign of Claudius (41–54 A.D.) there were 159 official holidays in the Roman calendar, a reality that is not conducive for productivity. Idle time and poverty are two ingredients that fuel crime. As a result, the emperors sought ways to keep the masses entertained. They turned increasingly to sport. Roman leaders used sport activities to train soldiers and to provide the masses with entertainment spectacles. For the Romans sports became a show, a dramatic event staged for the purpose of diversion.

Roman Games and Sports

The Romans, especially the wealthy, enjoyed a variety of sporting events before the introduction of the infamous gladiator games. Among the favorite games of the Romans was *harpastum* (construed as an early form of rugby, or keep-away), a physically active game designed to assure that participants exerted a great deal of energy. The Romans also played *trigon*, a stripped down version of harpastum that included three-person teams instead of the larger teams associated with harpastum. Harpastum, trigon and hoop bowling (a type of game that involved participants throwing a spear, or stick, threw a rolling hoop) were never popular spectator sports. Roman emperors, realizing the need to placate the growing masses, decided to create games that would entertain the public. Roman leaders also wanted to incorporate military training with sports training. These two desires led to the formation of gladiator games. Gladiator games (which first appeared in Rome in 264 B.C.E.) involved many physical traits necessary for military service including, pace training, weapons proficiency (especially swordsmanship and the ability to throw spears), and weight-lifting.

Over the centuries, the Roman Empire continued to grow. The Romans themselves became lazy and dependent on the state for food and social services (a type of welfare system). They hired armies to fight their battles and protect Rome from possible invasion. The Romans also commandeered "undesirables" to fight against trained gladiators. These "undesirables" included slaves, criminals, captured soldiers, and Christians (during the time it was an outlawed religion). The concept of sportsmanship and fair play became distant memories during the gladiator era. The gladiators entered the arena with the intent to kill their opponent in order to appease Roman leaders and the bloodthrist of the spectators. After generations of this type of gladiator fighting the masses once again became bored. In response, the Roman leaders had gladiators fight animals, including lions, crocodiles, bears, and elephants. Public executions occurred during "half-time" (lunch break) of gladiator games.

While the Greeks had attempted to place sports and leisure on a lofty quasi religious-philosophical plane, the Romans sought to drown in it. The Roman over-indulgence of leisure pursuits, moral decay, and a lack of a work ethic would ultimately lead to the demise of the Empire. The Romans had succeeded in transforming Greek festivals into spectacles. In short, Roman sports represent a regression into barbarism (Dunning, 1999) and it is questionable whether or not Roman gladiator games even qualify as sports.

By 500 C.E. waves of "barbarians" (e.g. the Goths, Huns, and Avars) succeeded in raiding Europe and destroyed the Roman Empire. The Romans themselves were now the "undesirables" who fell victim to the newest gladiators.

SPORTS DURING THE MIDDLE AGES (500 CE–1500 CE)

The Middle Ages are sometimes referred to as the "Dark Ages," but this term has fallen from favor to avoid the entrenched stereotypes associated with the phrase. However, it *was* a period of great migration (and thus, some scholars use the term "the Migration Period"), with little scientific or cultural advancement, and the feudal system did limit opportunities for advancement among the poor. During the 5th–8th centuries C.E. trade was difficult. Pirates dominated the seas and land travel was dangerous because of barbarian raiders. Muslims began to gain power in the Middle East and parts of Europe, and a rivalry between them and the Christians hampered socio-economic development. Between 900 C.E. and 1100 C.E. signs of stability began to emerge. Trade slowly developed. Large towns sprung up around the Mediterranean which were capable of protecting local citizens. However, between 1096 and 1270 a series of eight crusades (religious-based wars) occurred, which further hampered cultural development.

The "darkness" of this period was also manifested by the fact that education was limited to nobility. Religious dogmatic thinking emphasized the afterlife—an idea that left people to accept things as they were in the present life. By the 15th century, kings and queens would consolidate power and nation states would form—thus changing the character of society.

Sports Played

Grandiose sporting events that characterized the Greek and Roman era were replaced by secular, local folk games, hunts, and tournaments during the Medieval times. These categories of sports were mostly class-restricted. For example, participation in tournaments was restricted to the upper class; although members from all social classes could serve as spectators. The primary sport of tournaments was *jousting*. Jousting involved knights of rival nobility fighting under the ideal of chivalry. Chivalry ended however if a knight was killed in battle as it was common for people to strip him of his possessions. Defeated knights often fell victim of hostage demands placed on the rival kingdom for his safe return.

The Medieval sport of jousting is a popular attraction at Renaissance Faires. (Courtesy Tim Delaney)

Folk games, hunts and other *blood sports* (most of which still exist today) were common among the peasants. Folk games included dancing at local festivals; a type of ancient rugby (*soule*); field hockey; handball; bowling; and by the late Middle Ages, futbol. Hunts involved the killing of animals for sport, cockfighting, and dog-fighting. (Atlanta Falcons football star Michael Vick attempted to keep the "sport" of dog-fighting alive, much to the horror of his fans.)

Box 2.1.   Cockfighting: "The Little Jerry Seinfeld Way"

Cockfighting is a brutal sport that has existed since, at least, the Middle Ages. In some cultures, this blood sport is still culturally acceptable. In the United States, it is not. (In 2008, Louisiana became the last state to make it illegal.) The *Seinfeld* episode "The Little Jerry" shed light on the fact that this "sport" exists primarily as a wagering activity in the back rooms and dark alleys of deviant America. In this episode, Jerry has bounced a check at a bodega owned and operated by Marcelino. As a form of public shaming, Marcelino has done what many merchants do when a customer tries to pay by check with insufficient funds—he tapes it to his cash register along with the other bad checks. Jerry attempts to make amends to Marcelino by covering the $40 check with cash and offering him an extra $20 for the inconvenience. Marcelino accepts; however, citing the store's policy, he does not take the check off the register. Jerry is upset and reminds Marcelino that he owns the bodega. In a classic petty bureaucratic response, Marcelino states, "Even *I* am not above the policy."

Meanwhile, Kramer is disgusted by the quality of the breakfast eggs served to him at Monk's diner. Desiring fresh eggs, Kramer decides to go "cage free" and purchases a chicken. At sunrise, Kramer's "chicken" loudly crows. Jerry is awakened and walks next door to Kramer's apartment to ask about all the noise. Kramer informs Jerry that, "Oh, Jerry loves the morning." Confused by this statement, Jerry asks, who is "Jerry"? Kramer informs his buddy that he has named his chicken "Little Jerry Seinfeld" in his honor. Jerry provides a courtesy acknowledgment, but informs Kramer that he has actually purchased a rooster! Kramer responds, "Well, that would explain Little Jerry's poor egg production."

Later that day, Kramer, with his pet rooster on his side, pleads to Marcelino to take Jerry's check off the cash register. Another customer walks into the bodega with a dog. Little Jerry quickly and violently pecks at the dog, forcing his retreat. Marcelino is impressed. He invites Kramer to pit Little Jerry in a cockfight that he holds in the back room of his bodega late at night. Kramer agrees to the challenge, but only if Marcelino takes Jerry's check off the register.

Kramer begins to "train" his rooster for the fight. He envisions that the roosters will be wearing such protective gear as gloves and helmets, like in *American Gladiators* (a TV show) and agrees to let Marcelino borrow Little Jerry. When Jerry explains the brutality of the sport, Kramer wants to back out of the cockfight and rushes to the bodega. But he is too late—the fight is over and Little Jerry is the victor. Marcelino takes the check off the register. Later, however he places it back on the cash register and demands that Little Jerry fight one more time. Further, he wants Little Jerry to take a "dive." A sporting event fixed? Yes, it happens, apparently, even in cockfighting. However, as Jerry proclaims to Marcelino, "I don't think you can make a rooster take a dive." Kramer is convinced that Little Jerry can win the fight so he agrees to have his rooster fight one more time. Jerry, Kramer, Elaine, and George are all at the bodega at 3:00 AM to watch Little Jerry fight. They are stunned to discover that Marcelino has brought in a "ringer" rooster from Ecuador. This rooster has a 68-0 record. Fearing for Little Jerry's life against this much larger bird, Kramer runs into the ring, only to be violently pecked several times by the Ecuadorian champion.

As *Seinfeld* teaches us, cockfighting is a violent and cruel "sport"!

SPORTS DURING THE PRE-INDUSTRIAL AND INDUSTRIAL ERAS (1500 CE–1900 CE)

The Pre-industrial Age includes the Renaissance, the Reformation and the Enlightenment. Collectively, this was a time when aspiring philosophical and scientific thought began to emerge. During the Renaissance, which is usually said to have begun in the late 1400s in Florence, Italy, there was a reawakening of interest in the pre-Christian worlds of the ancient Greeks and Romans and a renewed interest in depicting human activities in the here-and-now rather than focusing on the afterlife or the lives of saints. The Reformation, begun in 1517 in Wittenburg, Germany by the monk Martin Luther, marked the point at which the religious harmony of the European continent was split asunder into rival Christian forces, Catholic and Protestant. The Enlightenment, said to have begun in the mid-1600s, was a period which focused on science and critical thinking as a means of overcoming doctrinal differences, and freeing human beings from superstition.

The universities established in the major European cities (e.g., Paris, Bologna, Oxford, and Cambridge) during the Middle Ages were partly responsible for this period of rebirth and transition in Europe. New ideas were being explored. Intellectuals attempted to change the course of humanity. The masses and nobility, however, were not quite ready for such a transformation—it would take the socio-economic force of industrialization to radically change society. In addition, the invention of the printing press helped to increase the literacy of the masses, and encouraged a growing thirst for knowledge.

Sports Played

During the early stages of Pre-industrialization, many of the Medieval sports remained popular. By the end of this period, however, Calvinism and Puritanism were taking hold as dominant cultural influences in both Europe and colonial America. Among the cultural ideals were working hard and avoiding sports and leisure as they were deemed frivolous and profane. The Puritans forbade sports on Sundays, a cultural custom that would influence American society through most of the twentieth century. The occasional farm festival was allowed in colonial America, but activities were functional (post-barn raising celebrations, quilting bees, and cornhusking contests) rather than sporting. Fishing and hunting were also conducted for functional purposes (to eat) rather than for sport. By the end of the Pre-industrial era a wealthy class had emerged in many of the larger Northeastern cities. Horse racing and crude form of yachting were relatively common among the social elite.

SPORTS DURING EARLY INDUSTRIALIZATION
(1750 CE–1900 CE)

In the mid 1700s, a very profound socio-economic and political force, known as industrialization, arose first in Western Europe and then in the United States and Canada. These nations experienced great social change as a number of interrelated developments culminated in the transformation of the Western world from a mainly agricultural to an overwhelmingly industrial system. Among the relevant aspects of the Industrial Revolution (to the discussion of sport) was the introduction of machinery and mass production. This increased productivity caused a ripple effect that included the development of more machinery, the need for instructions on how to operate the machinery (and thus, literate people), the further development of technology, and an overall increase in the number of people with disposable income and time to spend on leisure and sport pursuits. The mass production of products spilled over into the sports world, including bats, gloves, uniforms, golf clubs, bicycles, and balls. Furthermore, increased leisure time would eventually fuel the development of numerous sports and the number of participants, spectators, and consumers.

Sports Played

The sport of boxing became quite popular during the Industrial era. However, as the cultural civilizing process was beginning to enter many social realms, sports being one of them, a number of refined rules as dictated by the Marquis of Queensbury characterized boxing. In fact, the attempt to standardized and establish governing sport bodies—a feature so common with present day sports—began to intrude in most sports during the Industrial era.

The indoor sports of basketball and volleyball were created in the late 1800s in an attempt to keep young people who resided in cold wintry areas physically active and fit year around. During times of warmer weather, many people began to ride bicycles as a means of keeping fit. Rowing and cricket were among the popular sports at the growing number of European and American colleges. Horse racing was becoming a profitable sporting business. All of the sports to emerge during the Industrial era, it was baseball that had the most impact on American culture.

Baseball: America's First Great Sports Pastime

Baseball, a sport derived from the English game "rounders," has been played in the United States for more than 150 years. There is a controversy as to the origins of American baseball. According to Major League Baseball (based on the 1905 A. G. Mills commission's report headed by Al Spalding), the sport was founded in Cooperstown, New York by Abner Doubleday in 1839. Unfortunately, Doubleday was a cadet at West Point at the time he supposedly invented the game. Furthermore, he never claimed to have invented baseball. The most likely inventor of baseball was Alexander Joy Cartwright, head of the Knickerbocker baseball club of New York City. Cartwright established the basic rules of baseball (e.g., nine contestants at a time for each team during play and a regulation size and use of an infield diamond) that serve as the foundation of the sport today. Cartwright established a permanent site for the Knickerbockers to play at Elysian Fields in Hoboken, New Jersey (1845). This explains why Hoboken challenges Cooperstown's claim. Furthermore, city officials and historians in Pittsfield, Massachusetts assert that a version of baseball was played in their city in the late 1700s. They cite a 1791 bylaw that banned anyone from playing ball within 80 yards of town's new meeting house. It appears as though many windows were broken in Pittsfield because of people playing ball.

Perhaps it does not really matter where the game of baseball was invented; after all, we do not know the precise origin of many of our sports but that does not interfere with our play, or love for the game. As far as MLB is concerned, Cooperstown is the home of baseball and it serves as the host city for the Baseball Hall of Fame.

A two hour drive to the west of Cooperstown is Auburn, New York. Auburn plays host to the Toronto Blue Jays' New York-Pennsylvania

"Abner Doubleday" is the mascot of the Auburn Doubledays baseball team. (Courtesy Tim Delaney)

(NY-P) minor league affiliate. The Auburn franchise is nicknamed the "Doubledays" in honor of the "founder" of baseball. Their mascot consists of a character named Abner Doubleday, including a handlebar mustache.

There is much more to baseball than a debate over its origins. Baseball represents America's first sports pastime. It was America's sport, rarely making any claim to be descended from the game "rounders". It was the sport of summer, the time of year that best afforded leisure pursuits. Baseball games were generally followed by postgame festivities filled with food and alcohol—much in the way that pregame tailgating at football games dominates today (see chapter 7 for a detailed description of tailgating). The momentum of passion for baseball in the early Industrial era would only get stronger during the twentieth century.

The Rebirth of the Olympics

By the time of the Industrial era, geographies of people were bordered with the firm establishment of nations. Early nomads, agricultural societies, and

---

Narrative 2.1.   An Interview with Thomas E. Ganey, CEO of the Auburn Doubledays of Auburn, New York.

1. How long have the Auburn Doubledays existed?

   Auburn has been a franchise since 1958 in the NYP League. The Doubledays were named in January of 1995.

2. What MLB franchise are the Doubledays affiliated with? How does the relationship between the Auburn franchise and the parent franchise work?

   The Toronto Blue Jays are the present affiliate, after the 19 year affiliation with the Houston Astros. The Blue Jays provide the players, manager, coaches and trainer, paying their salaries and benefits. The Doubledays General Manager provides the day to day operations of the team. I personally meet 4 to 5 times a year and our General Manager has weekly contact with representatives from the Blue Jays.

3. Why is the Auburn franchise nicknamed the "Doubledays"? How was this decision made?

   During the Fall of 1994, the new ballpark was under construction and it was decided to have a contest to name the team. We received several hundred entries and a committee of local fans and board members selected the name the Doubledays effective in the 1995 season.

4. Officially, MLB recognizes that Abner Doubleday created baseball in Cooperstown, New York. There is some debate among baseball scholars as to whether or not he actually deserves credit for "creating" baseball. What is your reaction to this "controversy"?

   The Board of Directors and fans of the Auburn community believe in and supports that Abner Doubleday is the creator of baseball as it is known today.

5. Your mascot is dressed as Abner Doubleday. How do spectators react to him (e.g. positively or negatively)?

   Abner makes several appearances throughout the year and is well received by both the younger and older fans of the Doubledays. First time younger fans are overcome by the size and appearance of Abner; however, once mom or dad befriend him, the younger fans line up to high five Abner.

---

scattered kingdoms were replaced by nation-states. The developed nations were already competing against one another in a variety of sports. The idea of revitalizing the Olympics had been tossed around by various world leaders. However, it took a Frenchman, Baron de Coubertin, to establish the formation of the Modern Olympics.

A well-educated, upper crust member of society, as well as an accomplished sportsman, Coubertin was inspired by the structured sports organization in England and the United States and instilled the passion of sports to his countrymen. He also felt that sport participation would help to keep his countrymen physical fit. (Coubertin blamed France's defeat by the Germans in the Franco-German War [1870–71] on the French soldiers' physical inferiority.)

Committed to the ideals of amateurism, the first modern Olympic took place in Athens in 1896. There were no national teams at these Games. Instead, athletes simply signed up for events, paid an entry fee, and competed. It was also decided that the host country would decide which events would be held (Marshall, 2008). The events of the 1896 Olympics would be considered the norm today and including various sprints, throwing sports (discuss, hammer, shot put), and field events (e.g., hurdles and high jump). However, until the policy of the host city determining the events to be played was changed after World War I (due to the formation of the International Olympic Committee which took over the selection process for host cities, qualification standards, and sports played) a number of odd sports characterized the Olympics. Here is a sampling:

• Paris 1900—Live pigeon shooting, which led to the death of nearly 300 birds; a form of diving, wherein participants were judged based on how far they could get without taking a stroke; the diving plunge, an underwater race, where swimmers earned points based on how long they could hold their breath and how far they could get before grasping for air; croquet; and the tug-a-war.
• St. Louis 1904—Club swinging; roque (a variation of croquet—the U.S. was the only team to compete); and the tug-a-war.
• Athens 1906 Summer Olympics—Dueling pistols (the participants actually shot at mannequins, not each other!) and the tug-a-war.

A number of sports have been added (for example, beach volleyball in 1996) and others deleted (e.g., baseball and softball beginning in 2012) from Olympic competition over the years. As a rule, the Summer Olympic Games are played every four years during the leap year; initially the Winter Games were played during the same year, but since 1996 they are played two years after each Summer game.

SPORTS IN THE TWENTIETH CENTURY

As the twentieth century began, sports and leisure activities enjoyed a valued status in the Western world. Games that had been played for centuries had been refined and standardized with rules and governing bodies to over-see the operation of university and professional sports. International com-petitions (e.g., the Modern Olympics) fostered nationalistic pride and in-dustrialization provided the means (via equipment, etc.) for the masses to participate in numerous forms of sports and recreation. Despite the new-found appeal of sports and the variety of activities available for children and adults to participate in, the United States, as a nation, was embarrassed to learn that nearly one-third of the men called to military service in 1916 (for World War I) failed the physical examination. The 1920s is a decade known as the "Golden Age of Sport" because of "the adulation, interest, and naïve wild enthusiasm for sport probably reached a peak at that time" (Curry and Jiobu, 1984:40). The "Golden Age" involved a peak level of sports mania; increased leisure time; increased number of sports leagues, both amateur and professional; advances in technology, making sport more exciting; dramatic publicity and promotion; greater possibilities for fame, fortune and money; and a time when an athlete could emerge as a national hero—a celebrity (Leonard, 1988). The "baby boom" that followed World War II would lead to huge numbers of youth participating in sport. A dra-matic increase in the number of sports leagues followed. "Big-time" college sports programs gained in status. Unfortunately, due primary to budget cuts and a lack of money, many physical education programs and sports pro-grams were cut toward the end of the twentieth century. The increased num-ber of obese children (and adults), along with the ever-present need for peo-ple to serve in the military, should be a strong enough signal to policy makers that cutting sports and physical education programs in schools may have disastrous results.

Sports Played

Sport's refinement and standardization continued throughout the twentieth century. Along with the popular sports of the Industrial Age, other sports played were billiards, or pool; bowling (the number one participatory sport in the United States); basketball; volleyball; and track and field. Tennis and golf, two sports once reserved for the upper class, were now far more accessible and available as team sports at most high schools. Baseball continued as America's favorite pastime through much of the twentieth century. However, as American culture changed and continued to evolve, so too did its taste in sports. Many Americans grew tired of baseball and its slow, almost mechan-ical pace. Despite it many moments of excitement, baseball was increasingly perceived as a boring game. The American public yearned for a more excit-ing, hard-hitting, contact sport that also involved intelligence, cunning, and brute strength. They found their desired sport on college campuses across the United States. This sport was football.

Football: America's Second Great Sports Pastime

Football represents the desired qualities of the American public because it mirrors contemporary society. Football is controlled violence and it is poetry in motion. It is chaotic and it is planned precision. In many respects it is very primal and yet quite evolved in sophistication and technology. It *is* America's sport and it generates the most passion. Football dominates the American sports world at both the professional and collegiate levels. As baseball has its Little League, football has its Pop Warner youth indoctrination program. "Named after famous college coach Glenn 'Pop' Warner, the Pop Warner Football League started in 1927 in Philadelphia as a program to keep young men off the streets. Like Little League, its real expansion came after World War II as young families moved to the suburbs" (Jay, 2004:53).

Football is a game derived from English football (soccer) and rugby. The first intercollegiate game of football in the United States pitted teams from Princeton and Rutgers against one another in 1869. Initially, football was an elitist sport and a popular pastime on eastern college campuses. Football was also originally student-controlled. From the start, football was a violent and virile sport played by gentlemen who wanted to prove their manhood. "By the early 1890s, football had replaced baseball as the most popular intercollegiate sport" (Carroll,1999:25). By the beginning of the twentieth century, football was being played at most major colleges and universities throughout the United States. A 1905 study of 555 cities showed that 432 of them had football teams at the collegiate and secondary school levels (Carroll, 1999). Football, because of its brutality, did have its detractors. A number of college presidents, trustees, professors and others questioned the legitimacy of such a game being played in an academic setting. Football, obviously, survived these protests and continued to thrive at the college level. It remained, however, as mostly an urban sport in the early 1900s. With the onset of World War I, physical educators promoted football as a means of toughening up the youth and preparing them for war.

During the "Golden Age of Sport" (1920s), college football became increasingly popular and economically significant. Huge college stadiums were built for the first time in order to benefit economically from football's immense popularity. Simply building stadiums was an economic benefit for a country fresh off a world war. "A massive football stadium not only became a symbol of big-time intercollegiate athletics in the 1920s but also put more pressure on coaches, athletic directors, and college presidents to produce

competitive if not winning teams" (Carroll, 1999:63). The assembly-line production of automobiles and expansive road system provided opportunities for
many Americans to attend college football games. Radio broadcasts delivered
football to millions of Americans far removed from college campuses. Many
football heroes emerged during this "Golden Age". Among them was Red
Grange. Grange (University of Illinois) has been described as a great football
player, folk hero and sociological phenomenon (Carroll, 1999). When
Grange's college football career ended, he had to weigh his future options. A
number of people wanted him to run for political office or go into business;
others wanted him to play professional football.

Despite the huge success of college football, professional football was not
in vogue. Grange noted how all the college coaches and athletic directors
were 100 percent against professional football. The primary reason for their
opposition was due to the fact that college officials wanted to maintain control over the sport. The Big Ten Conference passed a rule that no person could
coach in their conference if they had coached as at the professional level.
Grange decided to play professional football, alienating many with his decision. He created further controversy when he left college (after his last playing season) before graduation. Grange would ultimately help give professional football credibility and sparked the public's interest and acceptance of
it.

Professional football began as the American Professional Football Association (APFA) in 1920. A number of franchises folded and emerged the first
few years of the APFA. There were 10 teams the first season. In 1922 the
APFA revised its name to the National Football League. The NFL fielded 18
teams in 1922. Franchises would continue to come and go and change their
nicknames throughout the 1920s. In 1926, Grange joined the New York Yankees of the American Football League. The league folded after one season
and merged with the NFL. Throughout its history, professional football has
witnessed franchises that came and went, and periodically it would be chal-
lenged by rival leagues. Through it all, the NFL would continue to grow and
flourish. Today, it is the premiere sports league of North America. Furthermore, as stated in chapter 1, the most popular sports in the United States are
professional football and college football.

SPORTS IN THE TWENTY-FIRST CENTURY

The dominant and popular sports of American culture continue to persevere
throughout the twenty-first century. However, many youth have become frustrated with the overly-specialized, highly competitive and selective participation

character of most traditional sports. As a result, they seek sports alternatives that they can call their own. Collectively, these sports are known as "alternative" sports or "extreme" sports.

Sports Played

The point should be re-emphasized: most of the traditional sports of the twentieth century remain popular today. But new types of sports have grown in popularity in the 2000s. As a result, we would like to mention a number of extreme sports that have grown relatively popular in this millennium. Extreme sports are generally risky, adrenaline-inducing forms of activities that are not governed by sanctioned bodies and therefore possess amendable rules of procedure. (Note: Most of these examples of extreme sports were influenced by surfing. Surfing will be discussed in detail in chapter 3.) Examples of extreme sports include:

- Skateboarding—A California-origin sport that dates back to the 1950s became a symbol for "rebels" in the late 1980s. Skateboarding is viewed as surfing on land. Skateboarders are known for their jumping ability and their habit of skating in public areas where such behavior is forbidden. Matt Groening chose to have Bart Simpson as a skateboarder when *The Simpsons* debuted in an attempt to demonstrate what a rebel he was. Today, skateboarding is much more popular and has lost its "edginess."
- Snowboarding—Snowboarders are really the skateboarders of the slopes. Seemingly more dangerous than skiing, snowboarders were viewed as rebels a decade ago. Today, snowboarding, much like skateboarding, has become popularized and as a result has lost its charm as an extreme sport. It is after all, an Olympic sport. Furthermore, skiing is a faster, more dangerous sport than snowboarding!
- Sky surfing—This sport still qualifies as an extreme sport. Participants must first jump out of plane with a board attached to their feet and then surf the atmosphere by performing any number of aerobatics. Not everyone is cut out for this sport.
- Elevator surfing—A type of indoor surfing wherein individuals ride on top of elevators. These daredevils go through the emergency hatch in order to climb atop the elevator. Among the inherent dangers of elevator surfing are being crushed between the elevator and the top of the elevator shaft and falling off the elevator, possible to one's death. Elevator surfing usually takes place on college campuses or on tall skyscrapers.
- Street luge—A combination of ice luge and skateboarding, this sport is illegal when lugers grab a hold of a car and ride around city streets. Because

of the limited capacity of the driver to control the board, street luge is a potentially dangerous activity.

• BASE jumping—BASE jumping involves parachuting off buildings, antennae, spans and earth (therefore the acronym "BASE"). Because of the risk involved, this sport is not for everyone.

Remember, the people attracted to extreme sports find the freedom from rules and regulations as a primary draw. Unfortunately for these participants, many extreme sports have become commercialized and standardized. The "X Games," created by ESPN in 1995, represent an example of the bureaucratization of extremes sports. Sporting activities such as skateboarding, bicycle stunt riding, snowboarding, street luge, and so on, are regularly featured sports. Records and rankings are kept and participants have become consumed by commercialization. What other sports activities lie out there for thrill seekers?

The answer is simple. There are many sports that already exist and possess an element of risk; they include, climbing rocks, mountains and ice glaciers; running with the bulls in Pamplona, Spain; surfing mavericks in California (see chapter 3); rugby; football. Although (at present) it is more popular as a spectator sport than as a participant sport, many younger people enjoy Mixed Marital Arts (MMA), or ultimate fighting. The popularity and spectacle of MMA has soared through the early part of twenty-first century. MMA combines such traditional sports as marital arts, wrestling, boxing, and kickboxing. The goal(s) of MMA competition is simple—dominate and overwhelm an opponent. There are multi-million dollar purses available at the elite level of MMA and pay-per-view (PPV) events have totaled nearly a quarter of a billion dollars. Its popularity has been fueled by YouTube videos and PPV events that glorify ultimate fighting. MMA is in the process of replacing the popularity of marital arts courses, once popular with young and old alike. As with other extreme sports, a number of young people are turning to MMA instead of the traditional sports of football, baseball, basketball, and so on. The growing popularity of MMA has extended to youth sport as well. In this regard, MMA has become relatively mainstreamed.

However, there are plenty of detractors who worry about children, as young as 3-4 years-old, fighting one another in an extreme manner and being taught to brutalize an opponent at any cost. Certain acts that are legal at the adult level, such as blows to the head and throwing elbows, are not allowed at the youth level. Then again, at many tournaments these watered down rules (for youth) are poorly enforced. Psychologists worry about the impact of promoting fighting among youth; especially when parents encourage this behavior. It could be argued that MMA is little more than gang warfare, only with referees enforcing rules and parents cheering their children's participation. Proponents of youth MMA point to the great physical workouts involved; claiming this as an important element of the sport when considering the growing rate of obesity among American youth. In this manner, any type of workout—even pummeling other children—is viewed as a more positive alternative to playing video games and drinking sugared drinks and eating fatty foods. In addition, MMA teaches youth, as well as adults, how to protect themselves from predators. What do you think?

It should be pointed out that the perception of MMA as a new sport is inaccurate, as it resembles the ancient sport of pankration (discussed earlier in this chapter). It seems our desire for violent sports, whether it is football or the extreme ultimate fighting, reflects the violent world we live in. The United States is confronted with violence domestically as well as internationally in two on-going wars. Here is a question to ponder: if the world were ever to enjoy peace, what type of sports would be played?

FINAL THOUGHTS

As this brief review of sports throughout history reveals, Americans, like people around the world, have always enjoyed sports. Sports both reflect culture and represent a major social institution of society. Although organized sports as we know them today have not always existed, some form of play and games have existed throughout humanity. It seems apparent that sports will remain popular in the future.

Many ancient sports—or at least variations of them—continue to be popular today. Baseball and football (although the origins of each remain debatable) dominate in the interests of most of today's American athletes and fans. But since the beginning of the twenty-first century many young people have become upset by the overt commercialization and obsessive rule-orientation of many sports, and have begun to experiment with more spontaneous types of activities. Only time will tell if these "extreme sports" will themselves become overly marketed and rule-bound. At the very least, it is clear that both old and new types of sports remain as important aspects of the majority of people's daily lives in America and throughout the rest of the world. In the following chapter, we'll examine the ways in which sports connect with, and sometimes symbolize, cultures in general.

Chapter Three

Sports as a Cultural Phenomenon

As described in chapter 2, many "extreme" sports, such as skateboarding, snowboarding, sky surfing, and elevator surfing, are variations of water surfing. Another variation of surfing—although not really a sport—is crowd surfing. Crowd surfing is popular at rock concerts and involves an individual(s) being carried over the crowd by the hands of the audience. When the crowd is cooperative, the person being carried experiences a sensation similar to surfing, wherein the audience is like the ocean and their hands are like the waves. Your body is the board.

Although some crowd surfers make their decision to surf at the last moment—perhaps because they are swept away with the fun and excitement of live, outdoor concerts—it is best to plan ahead. People who go to concerts with crowd surfing in mind generally prepare themselves by following a number of simple rules, or suggestions. First, it is a good idea to wear tight clothing and avoid sharp buckles, zippers, and snaps. Also, make sure your shoes are tied tight, as some audience members will try to snag them from you—especially if you inadvertently, or purposely, kick them. Next, common sense should tell you that carrying your wallet, cell phone, or any other important personal items is ill-advised, as any of these materials may fall out of your pockets or, once again, serve as a temptation for others to steal while they are passing you around.

When water surfing, one paddles out into the ocean, sits atop his board, waits for a "good" wave, and hops atop the board in a slouching upright manner, and rides the wave toward shore. With crowd surfing, the routine is altered right from the beginning. When allowed (by security), the easiest way to get started involves standing on the edge of the stage, signaling your intentions to the crowd, and leaping onto them. Hopefully, they will catch you in-air and glide you on your journey. However, security guards at most concerts do not allow this and, as a result, a crowd surfer needs to begin by climbing atop near-by cooperative audience members. On some occasions people will give you a boost. (For obvious reasons, the heavier you are, the more difficult it will be to start and successfully surf.) After the initial hand-off, surfers are advised to keep their legs and arms in the air and let people pass their bodies along.

There are a number of potential dangers with crowd surfing, beginning with the obvious: you may be dropped and injured. Even a successful ride to the front of the audience is likely to lead you over a security fence where guards may kick you out of the concert, or at the very least, assist you to the back of the audience. As already mentioned, you may fall victim to theft. Furthermore, although it is illegal to grope, females are especially vulnerable to being touched inappropriately while being passed around. Male crowd surfers, on the other hand, may be punched in vulnerable areas by mean-spirited concert goers. Finally, don't assume the audience wants to spend its time "working" by passing surfers around during a show that they paid money to watch and hear.

Crowd surfers, skateboarders, snowboarders and all other surfers have, at least, one characteristic in common: they belong to subcultural groups. There are numerous examples of subcultures, some which involve sports, many others which do not. Subcultures are smaller groups of people found within a larger, more dominant culture. And, as this introductory story indicates, there are a number of social expectations and rules that members are expected to abide by within the subculture. This fact provides a glimpse into the reality that subcultures are like mini cultures within a greater culture.

Sports play an important role in nearly all cultures and have done so since ancient times. In some cases, sports are shaped by culture; and in other cases, sports influence culture.

SPORTS AND LEISURE: A CHARACTERISTIC OF CULTURE

The types of sports played, the encouragement or discouragement of sport participation, along with the importance placed on sports are all aspects of a society's culture. Because the word "society" will be used quite a bit here, let's explain what we mean by the term. A society is a group of people who interact with one another as members of a collectivity within a defined boundary. A society also consists of a number of highly structured systems of human organization and this organized system helps to influence cultural standards of ideal behaviors.

Culture

All societies possess a culture. Culture reveals the important aspects of a society, including its shared knowledge, values, language, norms, behavioral patterns that are handed down from one generation to the next and form a way of life, and the social institutions designed to meet the needs of its members. The United States, as with other cultures of the West, values education, hard work, attempts among individuals to "better" themselves, and entertainment. For many Americans, entertainment comes in the form of sports and various leisure pursuits.

The creation of a large leisure class that accompanied industrialization during the nineteenth and twentieth centuries afforded many Americans the time and means to pursue non-productive activities such as sports. If we look at this piece of history from a sociological standpoint, we will see how culture itself was transformed. After all, now that people had more leisure time, cultural norms and values would have to be adjusted. Pursuing leisure and following sports were no longer viewed as a crude snub at the work ethic, but rather, a deserved reward for a job well done. Before long, cultural idealism included the belief that people who had time to enjoy sports and leisure deserved it because they must have worked hard enough to produce a surplus income. Thus, a culture consumed by sports and leisure is equated as a culture that is productive enough to enjoy the fruits of its labor. The United States, and other societies consumed by sport participation and spectatorship, should heed the cause of the collapse of the Roman Empire (discussed in the previous chapter)! That is, enjoy the benefits that come with disposable income, but never neglect the work ethic that created that excess.

Culture's Impact on Sport

Culture has a strong impact on sport. Luschen (1981) states, "Sport is indeed an expression of that sociocultural system in which occurs . . . American football was changed through the American culture from rugby to a completely different game. It is now well integrated and quite obviously shows in its vigor, hard contact and a greater centrality on the individual, the basic traits of the culture of American society" (pp. 288–289). Thus, American culture transformed the European sport of rugby into a game (football) that was more reflective of its values and norms. The development of American football reflects the development of the United States itself, and serves as another example of the concept of sport as a microcosm of society. "The nature of sport, its organization, values, goals, functions, and structure, provide revealing clues about society" (Leonard, 1988:58). As a reflection of society, sport *is* culture.

In some societies, sports play an important role in shaping, modifying, and/or creating culture. Sports are such an integral aspect of that society that it appears *culture* mirrors sport. That is, a sport becomes so symbolic of that culture that culture itself becomes identified with the specific sports. The surf culture of Hawaii and the surf subculture of California serve as a good example.

Subculture

As indicated in this chapter's introductory story, subcultures consist of members from the greater society identifying with one another based on a characteristic that they have in common. Subcultural members usually form a social group and display characteristic patterns of behavior that allow them to be distinguished from others in the greater society. By implication, subcultures are smaller groups of people found within the larger, dominant culture. They accept most of the cultural ideals of the greater society, but abide by certain social expectations and rules that dominate the subcultural group. Belonging to a subculture helps individuals form a sense of identity; albeit there are often stereotyped beliefs about all members of the subculture. Thus, a person who regularly skateboards may embrace the "skateboarder" label because he has come to view himself as a skateboarder first, and anything else second. However, once identified as a "skateboarder," he may endure negative stereotypes the greater culture has regarding skateboarders, such as, underachievers, devious, and Bart Simpson-like in character.

SURFING: ELEMENTS OF CULTURE AND SUBCULTURE

As means of illustrating how sport is both an aspect of culture and a subculture itself, we turn our attention to water surfing; or more simply, surfing. The sport of surfing was chosen to serve as the exemplar because references to this sport were made previously in this chapter, but more importantly, because it is a sport rich in cultural and subcultural significance.

Early Surfing and Polynesian and Hawaiian Culture

It is nearly impossible to determine the exact origins of surfing; although most would agree that it has Polynesian roots. As Steve Craig (2002) explains, petroglyphs—or rock carvings—found in Hawaiian lava rock resemble that of a person surfing, but only go back to circa 1500 C.E. Most historians do not believe that surfing predates this period. By the eighteenth century, "surfing was a central part of Polynesian culture, especially in the areas of modern Hawaii and Tahiti. There were also reported instances of surfing in a few Melanesian territories and a traditional pastime in Australia that has strong similarities to surfing" (Craig, 2002: 246). Ben Finney and James D. Houston (1996), in their history of surfing in Hawaii, note that "early sources tell how the sport was bound up with the traditional religion, sexual practices, and the system of social classes. Surfing feats and romantic encounters in the surf were celebrated in song and legend. Board builders followed sacred rituals, and at least one temple was solely dedicated to surfing. The privileged chiefs as well as people from all levels of society took part" (p.13).

By the time European explorer Captain James Cook navigated the Polynesian waters, surfing was an integral aspect of culture and was endorsed by royalty. Cook detailed surfing activities in Tahiti in 1777 and on the island of Oahu (in modern Hawaii) in 1778. Cook wrote in his journals that "the Hawaiians, including their lovely bare-breasted women, came out on surfboards to meet his ships" (Redondo Beach Chamber, 2008). Cook also noted that surfers were expected to be able to stand on their boards as a sign of respect to chiefs and princes.

Men and women alike surfed the big waves on long wooden boards—an accomplishment that few European sailors could master. As Shane Nelson (2007) explains, "Surfing was a vital part of the Hawaiian culture when the first Europeans arrived. Enjoyed by men and women of all ages, the sport was a significant part of their spiritual bond with nature, a highly social activity . . . Many European accounts describe entire villages that would empty completely on days when the waves were good" (p.51). Records taken from Cook's voyages reveal that surfing competitions had greater meaning for Hawaiians than the Olympics did for the ancient Greeks. Hawaiians would cease to participate in war, and even work, for a three month period to honor Lono, the god of sport and fertility. These sporting competitions had over 100 games; including, of course, surfing. Prowess in surfing held great importance with the ruling class in Hawaii. A commoner who was especially good at surfing was respected among the cultural elite. As implied, social class distinctions were clearly established in Hawaii.

A major characteristic of social class in Hawaiian culture was revealed in surfing. "Hawaiian royalty used surfing, particularly with their huge boards known as *olo*, as a means of proving their physical superiority while improving their own strength and agility" (Craig, 2002: 247). The boards used by royalty were generally 14 to 18 feet long, made from a buoyant wood from the wiliwili tree and could weigh as much as 175 pounds. The commoners used a shorter, 10–12 foot board called *alai* that was lighter and made from the denser koa wood (Craig, 2002).

   The pattern established by European explorers in the Americas (e.g., forcing their culture and religion on an indigenous people) was preceded by a Hawaiian custom that would accelerate the cultural downfall of the native people. Banks (1997) explains, "The propensity of Hawaiians to share eventually helped to seal their demise. Besides providing provisions for ships, Hawaiians were quite willing to share their women, and Whites were eager to become intimate with them. These casual contacts over a long period of time had a decimating effect on the islands' population. The venereal diseases introduced by European and American sailors found little natural resistance among the Hawaiians and, along with measles, cholera, and alcoholism, took a deadly toll" (Banks, 1997: 181–182). Historians generally estimate that were approximately 600,000 - 800,000 Hawaiians on the islands before European contact. By the end of the nineteenth century there were fewer than 40,000 remaining.

   The natives that survived the deadly diseases introduced by the Europeans were forced to embrace a foreign culture. The communal way of life that had dominated Hawaii before European contact was replaced by a plantation system. This plantation system was designed to maximize profits for foreign investors and as a way of keeping the natives a race/ethnicity of laborers (Banks, 1997). In 1820, the first Calvinist missionaries, most from Puritan New England, were brought to Hawaii to teach the indigenous people a foreign religion. The missionaries frowned upon the happy hedonistic (women routinely went topless and men wore loose loin clothes while surfing) lifestyle enjoyed by the natives. Surfing was among the activities banned by the missionaries. Nelson (2007) explains, "The spread of Christianity took a tremendous toll on the culture, and beliefs about elevating work and prayer above all other pursuits didn't leave much time for surfing" (p.51). By the late 1800s, surfing had nearly disappeared from the Hawaiian culture.

The Rebirth of Surfing, and the Corresponding Rebirth of Native Culture

In 1898, Hawaii was annexed as a United States territory. The cultural influence of conservative Calvinism was replaced by American economic and political interests. An increasing number of American tourists began to travel to Hawaii, looking for sun, sandy beaches, and something a little exotic. At this same time, an early "traditionalist" movement began in Hawaii. This movement represented the first of many forthcoming attempts among native Hawaiians to revitalize the traditional Hawaiian culture. (Note: presently, there is a strong movement in Hawaii to embrace old customs and culture

among native people and a "setting to right of wrongs"—known as *Ho'o-
ponopono* [*Teaching Tolerance*, 2003]. Ho'oponopono is a native Hawaiian
tradition emphasizing forgiveness to resolve conflicts.)

Inspired by the ways of their ancestors, in the traditionalist ideal, Hawaiian
royal youth began to surf. American businessmen saw the rebirth of surfing
as a way of promoting tourism in Hawaii. Tourists were amazed by the
surfers. As Willard (2002) explains, the very sight of bare-chested surfers
"became the object of desire for white men who sought to step outside the
bounds of civilization and the convention of western dress" (p.18). The two
social forces of American economic opportunism and native Hawaiians' desire to embrace surfing were more than enough to stimulate surfing's rebirth.

Hawaiians cite the formation of the Waikiki Outrigger Canoe Club in 1908
and one of its earliest members, Duke Paoa Kahanamoku (known as the
"Duke"), as a major influence on the native desire to reestablish surfing on
the Hawaiian Islands.

Preceding the "Duke," and of greater relevance for us, however, is the story
of George Freeth, the man responsible for bringing surfing to California.
Freeth was born in Honolulu on November 8, 1883. His father was an Irish
sailor and his mother a descendant from a local prince, making her royal. As
a child, Freeth saw an old Polynesian painting that showed his ancestors surfing. (Remember, surfing had been banned in the era preceding Freeth's childhood.) His uncle showed him a 16 foot surfboard that was hidden away for
safe keeping. Freeth decided to cut the board in half so that he could carry it
to the ocean. As a gifted athlete, and using a shorter board, Freeth quickly
mastered the sport of his Hawaiian ancestors. In Hawaii, Freeth was chal-
lenged by some of the most impressive waves on the planet. Watching someone successfully ride the giant waves of Hawaii is enough to impress anyone;
and it certainly caught the eye of one specific wealthy American, land baron
Henry Huntington.

Huntington witnessed Freeth's surfing in the early 1900s and was so impressed that he was able to convince the surfer to move to California to promote tourism and real estate development in Redondo Beach (a Los Angeles
suburb). In 1907, Freeth arrived to the mainland. Freeth was billed as "the
man who could walk on water." George rode an 8-foot board made of solid
wood and weighing about 200 pounds. Freeth gave regular demonstrations to
the amazement and grand delight of all in attendance. As a result of these
surfing demonstrations, Freeth influenced many locals to start surfing; his influence would later lead to his distinction as the "Founder of American Surfing." By all accounts, he certainly appears to be the first surfer in the United
States. His Redondo Beach dives into the ocean were legendary. His ability
to seemingly walk on water continued to baffle spectators. The California

This statue of Duke Paoa Kahanamoku (known as the "Duke") adorns Waikiki Beach in Honolulu. Surfers are upset that the "Duke's" back is to the ocean—something surfers would never do because turning one's back to the ocean may lead to physical harm. (Courtesy Tim Delaney)

A bust of George Freeth, the man credited with bring surfing to the U.S. mainland, is displayed at the Redondo Beach; an area where he once performed many surfing feats. (Courtesy Tim Delaney)

beach boys idolized Freeth and the women wanted to be with him. Freeth was, indeed, influencing culture; and little did he realize at the time, he was setting the groundwork for the future California surfer subculture.

Residents of Redondo Beach, as one of these authors once was, have heard the stories of George Freeth and his impact on California surfing. A monument to George Freeth inhabits the Redondo Beach Pier highlighting the many accomplishments of this first American surfer.

Freeth did much more than introduce the sport of surfing to Southern California. He also introduced the game of water polo to the West Coast. Freeth trained many champion swimmers and divers, he invented the torpedo-shaped rescue buoy (that is now used worldwide), and he is also known as the "first official lifeguard." Freeth saved countless lives on the Southern California beaches while serving as a lifeguard, including seven Japanese fishermen whose boat was being swept to sea during a winter storm in Santa Monica (December 12, 1908). In recognition of his bravery, Freeth was awarded the Congressional Medal of Honor, the Carnegie Medal for Bravery and the U.S. Life Saving Corps Gold Medal. His bravery would indirectly lead to his untimely death. After several rescues during a winter storm in Oceanside in 1919, he contracted influenza and died at the young age of 35 (Borte, 2000).

The Growth of Surfing During the Twentieth Century

While surfing was enjoying a rebirth in Hawaii and the surrounding islands, witnessing a birth in California, it was also spreading to Australia, an area that today plays host to some of the world's best surfers and most challenging waves. Australia's beach-front, especially the popular tourist areas, reflects the surfing subculture identity, known by many around the world that is attached to this island nation.

During the 1930s, the shape of the surf board was revolutionized by the development of the narrow-tailed hot curl board. The design of this board allowed the rider to maintain a tighter angle across the wave (Young, 1987). Armed with this new and improved weapon, confident surfers sought out larger and more challenging waves to ride. The threat of enemy invasion via the West Coast put a brief end to surfing during World War II as the beaches were barbed wired for security purposes. After the war ended, surfers took to the waves. Among the more popular places was Malibu. The interest in surfing grew during the ban; especially because it had been banned by society. Those who tried to surf during this era were viewed as deviants. This "bad boy" persona often accompanies surfers today.

Interestingly, because a number of service personnel were stationed in Hawaii during World War II (there are still numerous bases in Hawaii), many mainland-bound service men returned, or moved to southern California. They brought with them the interest in surfing they acquired while in Hawaii. During the 1950s and 60s a number of surf shops opened up and down the California coast. The 1957 film *Gidget* introduced the general public to the surfer lifestyle of California. The short-lived television show, of the same name, reinforced the idea to many across the nation that California culture was all about surfing and beach parties. The introduction of surfer magazines and upbeat music of the Beach Boys helped to spread the surfer culture image around the world. Obviously, all of California was not consumed with beach blanket bingo, but a highly-identifiable subculture of surfing had taken grip.

Surfing Today

Surfing innovations continued throughout the late twentieth and early twenty-first centuries. Better board design, the surf leash (a tethered leash connecting the surf board to the surfer's ankle), wet suits, and the introduction of the boogie board. Boogie boarding is to surfing as training wheels are to bicycle racing. Surfing is popular in Florida and all the way north to Long Island, New York. Surf competitions net champion-caliber surfers large sums of money. And although it would seem rather obvious that surfing has geographic restrictions—an ocean is almost always necessary—the influence of this sport extends beyond coastal areas. According to Surf Industry Manufacturers Association, surfing is a $7.5 billion industry and every state is home to at least one surf shop (Crowe, 2007).

Elements of the surf subculture, such as language, have found their way into the larger society. Expressions such as "hanging ten," "hang loose" and "dude" are among those with cross-over appeal. According to linguist Scott Kiesling, the word "dude" is so popular that it has multiple uses: in greetings ("What's up, dude?"); as an expression ("Whoa, Dude!"); commiseration ("Dude, I'm so sorry."); to one-up someone ("That's so lame, dude."); as well as agreement, surprise and disgust ("Dude.") (Crissey, 2004: A-1). Kiesling argues that the word "dude" derives its power from something he calls "cool solidarity"—an effortless kinship that's not too intimate (Crissey, 2004: A-1).

The popularity of surfing is demonstrated by the rather unusual places that the sport has appeared. When there are gale-force storms over the Great Lakes, it is very likely that particularly brave surfers from Cleveland to Detroit to Chicago will be found battling the elements. Magilla Schaus, a firefighter in Buffalo, New York, braves the waves every winter by organizing a surf contest on chilly Lake Erie. The gales of November can never come too soon for him. "The winter is the best time for me," he claims. "When the

---

Narrative 3.1.   An Interview with Gary Sahagen, Chairman of the International Surfing Museum located in Huntington Beach, California-Surf City USA.

1. How long have you been a surfer?

    I started surfing at 12 when I moved to Huntington Beach. It was the greatest feeling when I caught my first wave. After that I was hooked. I have been surfing since 1966 and competed in hundreds of surfing events, I spent most of the 1970s living in Hawaii, where I really had the surfer lifestyle going on. I recently had back surgery, and just got back out surfing after a year off.

2. What impact do you think surfing has had on American Culture?

    Surfing interest has increased primarily due to media's use of surfing images I believe.

3. In what ways do you consider surfers to be a "subculture"?

    The impact on American Culture from music to fashion has been far-reaching. The lifestyle depicted by surfers is desired by people worldwide. The extreme sports so popular today are a direct offspring from surfing. As a sub-culture surfing enthusiasts are typically going against the grain. This is their history. Going forward I see this sub-culture fading to a more mainstream acceptance of a more even-keeled surfer who can blend in with mainstream culture.

4. How important do you think George Freeth was to the history of surfing in America?

    George was more important to lifeguard history. His exhibitions of surfing were more of a performance than an invitation to paddle out. Duke Kahanamoku and Tom Blake came later and invited spectators to join in.

---

weather starts changing, then the fair-weathered surfers go away . . . On the ocean they say, 'A surfer leaves nothing behind but his footprints in the sand. A Great Lake surfer leaves nothing behind in the sand—or the snow" (Higgins, 2005: B-21).

In Galveston, Texas, "super tanker surfing" is the current rage. The Houston ship channel in Galveston is the busiest in the United States, with 20 super tankers traveling through the waters daily. These 95,000-plus ton tankers (e.g., oil tankers, car carriers, storage container ships) create waves, the bigger the ship, the bigger the wave. Unlike reef surfing with shore breaks that last 4 or 5 seconds, tanker waves last as long as 10 minutes. Utilizing precision timing, surfers follow the tankers in motorized boats, leap off and catch a wave. There are even man-made wave machines that allow surfers to ride waves indefinitely. Royal Caribbean advertises cruise ships

**Narrative 3.2.   An Interview with Magilla Schaus, President
of the Wyldewood Surf Club, Buffalo Firefighter, and a
surfer on all 5 Great Lakes**

1. When did you start surfing, and why?

   Surfing in the Great Lakes is an activity that is like being in a third party in the U.S. Presidential Elections debate. We Great Lakes surfers are out riding waves on every storm that comes through the Great Lakes. It is a habitual practice that comes from love of the riding. Some surfers come to surfing to join a group and create a self identity they lack, while others come to wave riding because they know no better thrill or experience. There is a surfing heritage that connects the Great Lakes with the Hawaiian culture. The icon of Hawaiian surfing Duke Kahanamoku attempted to advance the greatness of the Hawaiian culture, which was the sharing of waves and a friendship across this planet. He went out like a surfing missionary after the Olympic Games to places like Australia and New Jersey. He met heads of state, authors and actors of his day. The Duke met Great Lakes and ocean Legend Tom Blake in a movie theatre in Detroit, Michigan. Blake moved to California from Wisconsin and went on to invent the rescue paddle board, the wind board, place a stabilizing fin on the bottom of the surfboard (which was a breakthrough in surfing technology) and many other innovations. Now how in the world does this connect me to surfing one might ask? I got into surfing because of a family named O'Hear who found this rustic and under developed place along the Canadian shores of Lake Erie at Wyldewood Beach in the early Fifties. It was by sheer luck that I ever became exposed to surfing culture through the O'Hear family.

   It was in the 1964 late summer gale that I first saw John O'Hear and Tom Christopher paddle out into Lake Erie into over head waves.

2. What are the main differences between lake surfing and ocean surfing?

   It depends on the day that one surfs. There are days on the Great Lakes when the waves are small and comparable to that on a perfect small day in the ocean. However Lake Superior for its depth and size mimics the ocean for it waves and their strength. The main difference in lake and ocean surfing or surfing in general is the people one meets and the waves one encounters. The lakes get offshore waves that can sink ships. The shipping lore of the lakes and diving opportunities confirm this fact. However the waves we ride in in the lower four lakes range to head high or better. The waves in Superior get much higher and do break surfboards and spit out like a serpent's tongue. The biggest waves in the ocean are the alphas of surfing and are wonders of nature on this planet.

3. Can you describe some of your most memorable experiences surfing Lake Erie?

   Here are a few of many, many stories that are good, bad and ugly. My most memorable experiences are from taking road trips with Canadian and U.S. surfers in the sixties to New Jersey to find waves. What most significantly

(continued)

Narrative 3.2.   (*continued*)

comes to mind is the relationships that I have developed across local and far away distances with surfers over an expanse of time that stretches over decades. I have known hundreds of Great Lakes surfers. Surfing in this part of the world is like living at the bottom of a trap door. Some surfer new or old is always showing up at the beach and I learn their stories and consider myself to be lucky to meet and ride with them. I know surfers from across the planet and the Great Lakes. What countless memories this has been like a blessing on my life. Recently when I learned that I had a tumor in my head Great Lakes surfers rallied to help me. Some of the surfers that came to my aid were ones that did not see eye to eye with me but nevertheless showed class and a humanistic compassion and true aloha. I only have one eye. I lost my left eye to a rare cancer/tumor behind my eye in 2006. I have become the half blind turtle catching the waves.

---

with wave machines that allow "surfers" the opportunity to ride waves while on a ship that is riding natural waves.

For the serious surfer, surfing represents a spiritual communion with nature. Such cultural idealism reminds one of the ancient Greeks and their attitude toward sport. Like the Greeks, surfers enjoy the challenge of competition. The most experienced surfers—the "big wave" surfers—live for an opportunity to ride the largest and most challenging waves. Among the more impressive places to surf are "Mavericks" and the "Pipeline." Mavericks is located at Half Moon Bay (San Francisco), California, an area of off-shore ocean filled with large rock formations, sharks, and waves that can reach 50 feet in height during the fall and winter months (October – March). The gnarly waves reach such impressive loftiness because of an unimpeded eastbound jet stream that glides across the vast Pacific Ocean.

The North Shore of Oahu represents the "Mecca" of surfing. The North Shore is home to the famous "Pipeline" where waves regularly reach and exceed 20 feet in height. When the waves are at their peak, the Pipeline is restricted to experienced big wave surfers. The risk factor is evident by the realization that more surfers have died at Pipeline than all other places in the world combined.

Technological innovation, an element responsible for changing cultures around the world throughout the history of humanity is also evident with surfing, especially big wave surfing. Modern surfers, besides keeping in top physical shape, study weather patterns, listen to radio broadcasts by the National Oceanic and Atmospheric Administration, and chart wave swell heights and wave characteristics in logbooks (McHugh, 2008). Armed with this valuable information, big wave surfers are known to pack up their boards and head off

---

Box 3.1. The Pipeline and *Blue Crush*

While surfing has traditionally been identified as a male activity, much is chang-ing in that regard. Bethany Hamilton, for instance, is a Hawaiian native and avid surfer who drew international attention in 2003 when—at the tender age of 13— she was attacked by a tiger shark while out for a morning surf. The shark ripped off her left arm just below the shoulder. Undaunted, Bethany returned to her board just three weeks later, and in July 2004 won the ESPN "Best Comeback Athlete of the Year" Award. Her life story was depicted in the 2007 documentary film *Heart of a Soul Surfer*.

A fictional film that vividly captures the female side of surfing is 2002's *Blue Crush*. Based on a article by journalist Susan Orlean entitled "Surfer Girls of Maiui," the film deals with the adventures of Anne Marie Chadwick (played by Kate Bosworth), a surfer who had been traumatized early by a near-drowning ex-perience, and her friends Eden (Michelle Rodriguez) and Lena (Sanoe Lake). Filmed mainly on the island of Oahu, the highlight of the movie is a dramatic surf competition near the famous North Shore Pipeline. Overcoming her fear, Anne Marie enters the competition. While initially "wiping out," she undauntedly re-turns and completes the course. While not winning, she regains her confidence (and, more importantly, receives the notice of a commercial sponsor).

Blue Crush deals with such themes as friendship, female camaraderie, and per-sonal empowerment. More importantly, it has spectacular surfing scenes, many featuring actual professional female surfers. Best of all, the film made it clear that the fight for female equality is as much a part of the surfing culture as it is for the rest of the broader culture—something Bethany Hamilton can attest to as well.

---

to areas where the waves are the knarliest. And to think, in the old days, surfers simply jumped on their big wooden boards and paddled out to sea whenever the waves were visibly large. Anyway, here's to all surfers who en-joy tubular sandwiches!

SPORTS IN OTHER CULTURES

As this rather lengthy discussion of surfing reveals, sport can both mirror so-ciety, influence culture, be influenced by culture, and lead to subcultural for-mations. Nearly all sports share these same characteristics. After all, there is certainly a subculture of NASCAR fans, football fans, rodeo fans, and so on. And certainly, the United States is not alone in its admiration for sports. Sports are popular around the world and most popular in societies where peo-ple have leisure time.

Obviously, it would be impossible to discuss the role of sport in all cultures, or to provide a comprehensive review of any number of them. Furthermore, providing an all-inclusive analysis of sports around the world is not the scope of this book. However, it should prove interesting to take a brief look at a select number of cultures and a sampling of sports played in that society.

Argentina

Argentina is the world's eighth largest country, comprising almost the entire southern half of South America. Colonization by Spain began in the early 1500s, but in 1816 Jose de San Martin led the movement for Argentine independence. Since that time, the political situation has fluctuated between those who desire a strong central government (the "Unitarists"), and those who advocate more local control (the "Federalists"). The culture of Argentina has been greatly influenced by the massive European migration in the late nineteenth and early twentieth centuries, primarily from Spain and Italy. The majority of people are at least nominally Catholic, and the country has the largest Jewish population (about 300,000) in South America. From 1880 to 1930, thanks to its agricultural development, Argentina was one of the world's top ten wealthiest nations. Unlike many other South American countries, it developed a large middle class, and a leisure economy that strongly supported sports. It also has a high literacy rate.

Until shortly after the World War II Argentina was an economic powerhouse, but in recent decades it has struggled for economic stability. The Peronista party, founded by Juan Peron and his wife Eva, aggressively attempted to empower the working class, and exacerbated class hostilities which continue to exist to the present day. In 2001, Argentina suffered a major economic downfall. Hard times inevitably lead to increased levels of crime. Kidnappings are very popular in Argentina. Criminals target sport stars and celebrities. Generally, it is the family members of these wealthy people who are targeted. Although sport-related kidnappings are fairly common in Russia and the former republics of the Soviet Union, over 75 percent of the world's kidnappings occur in Latin America. Soccer stars and their families are often targets in such countries as Columbia, Bolivia and Brazil. Kidnapped family members are held for a ransom. The common occurrence of kidnappings in certain nations reflects the poor economic conditions found there.

The highest paid athlete in Argentina is Manu Ginobili. Ginobili is an Olympic Gold Medalist, NBA champion (as a member of the San Antonio Spurs), hero, and role model. ESPN sports anchor Stuart Scott referred to Ginobili as an "icon for a country." Although soccer is the dominant sport in Argentina, in Ginobili's coastal hometown of Bahia Blanca, basketball reigns supreme. Ginobili's family members are protected by guards 24 hours a day. When his mother goes shopping, she has a guard. When his father goes to work, he has a guard. There are guards outside his Bahia Blanca home continuously. The Ginobili family, although uncomfortable with the constant security and threat of kidnapping, simply go about their business. They are proud of their son and his humility in victory (ESPN, 2005).

Like most South Americans, the people of Argentina are obsessed with soccer. The origin of the game there has been traced to the British influence in the early 1800s. Guttmann (2004) notes: "British sailors on shore leave had played some kind of football as early as 1840, at which time the local newspaper, *La Razón,* informed its readers that this odd pastime 'consisted of running around after a ball' . . . Employees of British-owned railroads were also active in the diffusion of Argentine soccer" (p.169). But the native Argentines soon made the game their own. The Asociación del Fútbol Argentino (AFA), was founded in January 1893. Guttmann (2004) adds, "By 1928, no one quarreled with *El Grafico's* conclusion that football was 'the collective sport of the *criollo,*' as deeply embedded in his psyche as the tango . . . Football mattered. Defeat in the World Cup Final—like the humiliating 6-1 loss to Czechoslovakia in 1958—threw Argentine fans into a depression" (p.170). But World Cup victories in 1978 and 1986 were causes for national celebration, and the Argentine team has been a top contender in most of the recent World Cup competitions.

The 1986 World Cup quarterfinals were particularly significant. Argentina faced England for the first time since the Falkland War between the two countries four years earlier. Argentines looked upon the 2-1 victory as vindication for the humiliating loss they had suffered in the war, although the British complained that Argentine star player and team captain Diego Maradona had cheated by scoring his first goal using his hand rather than his head. Maradona denied that his hand had touched the ball, famously saying "the hand of God" had sent it into the net. In 2005, however, he acknowledged on Argentine television that he deliberately used his fist to score the goal, but was unrepentant, feeling that, since in the view of Argentines the English had stolen the Malvides (Falkland) Islands, he was only stealing from a thief. His second goal in the 1986 game is undisputed, and has been called the "Feet of God" goal. The Fédération Internationale de Football Association (FIFA), sponsor of the World Cup, declared it to be the greatest goal ever in World Cup competition and in 2000 named Maradona and Brazilian star Pelé as the best players in soccer history. Maradona, a true anti-hero known for his drug use and wild private life (in 1991 he failed a drug test and was banned from soccer for 15 months) remains one of Argentina's most beloved figures, is much in the news, and hosted a popular television talk show. Tributes to this beloved sports star abound in Argentina. The authors' visit to Buenos Aires in 2005 confirmed this fact first-hand.

Brazil

Both the largest and most populous country in South America, Brazil was colonized by Portugal, which ruled it for three centuries, until 1822. Thanks to its industrial and agricultural growth, it is today South America's leading economic power, but unequal distribution of wealth remains a great problem. For most of its history Brazil was ruled by military dictators, but since 1985 it has had a democratic form of government. Most Brazilians are nominally Catholic, but Protestant fundamentalism is a growing movement throughout the country. In addition, Brazilians are multi-ethnic, and consider their culture to be one of mixed unity. Most of the people are a mixture of Indian, African and European bloodlines.

Arguably the most famous Brazilian of all is Pelé (Edson Arantes do Nascimento), the charismatic former soccer player often considered to be the greatest player of all time. Famed for his lightning speed and total control of the ball, he scored over 1,000 goals in his career, and led Brazil to three World Cup championships. Since retiring in 1977, he has become an international spokesperson for the game. Pelé is an example of a skilled performer hero, famed for his exceptional abilities as well as his winning personality. In the world of soccer, he is "the good guy", often contrasted to the "bad boy" Maradona. Growing up in great poverty, his natural abilities were first noted by Waldemar de Brito, who predicted that the young Pelé would become the greatest player of the game. He was voted athlete of the century by the International Olympic Committee (IOC) in 1999.

Like Argentines, Brazilians are ardent soccer fans. The Brazilian national football team is the most successful soccer team in the world, with five World Cup victories, including the most recent tournament in 2002. In fact, it is the only country to have qualified for *every* World Cup final since the tournaments began in 1930.

One interesting point made by Allen Guttmann (2004) is that *futbol* is looked upon differently in Latin American cultures than it is in the United States. Guttmann (2004) notes that:

> Throughout Latin America, soccer is a popular theater of macho masculinity. In the United States, it has become a showcase for female athleticism. At American colleges, women's soccer teams outnumber men's teams. In American high schools, over a quarter of a million girls play soccer. The final game of the 1999 Women's World Cup—the United States versus the People's Republic of

China—was played in Pasadena's Rose Bowl before 90,185 hysterically enthusiastic spectators. The photograph of an exuberantly celebrating Brandi Chastain—in a black sports bra, with some remarkable abdominal muscles—is likely to remain one of the most widely recognized images of the twentieth century. The contrast between soccer in Latin America and in the United States proves conclusively that no sport is intrinsically masculine or feminine. Sports mean whatever they are made to mean (p. 173).

Guttmann is indicating, of course, the role of culture in interpreting the meaning of sport. In Brazil, futbol is a sport wherein men can display their masculinity in a culturally accepted manner. In the United States, males display their masculinity via American football and females display their athleticism most notably through soccer.

In addition to soccer, South America (especially the Dominican Republic, Cuba, and Mexico) produces a large number of baseball players, many of whom come to the United States to play. This is a way out of the ghetto and a chance for a good life. The obsession with *béisbol* transcends many cultural boundaries, as rich and poor, radical and conservative, all seem to be fascinated by this *Norteamerican* game. There is even an urban legend that Fidel Castro, the Cuban revolutionary leader, once tried out for the Washington Senators baseball team. Even though many of the best players end up coming to the United States, the passion for *béisbol* continues to grow throughout all of South America.

Brazilians are interested in many sports, including auto racing, volleyball, surfing and tennis. One sport, in particular, which is quite popular in Brazil is *capoeria,* a type of martial arts similar to breakdancing, which has roots going back to Angola. This is indicative of the strong African origins of much of Brazilian culture. In capoeria, two contestants move in a series of swift cartwheels and whirling handstands on the floor. Each one tries to deliver blows to the other without using one's hands—only legs, feet, heels and heads are allowed. It combines dance, song, and martial arts, and is highly coordinated. In recent years interest in capoeria has spread to other countries, including the United States, Canada, and Austria, and there is now a capoeria community on the internet (www.capoeira.com) with over 30,000 registered members.

Canada

Canada became a self-governing dominion in 1867, maintaining close ties with its motherland of Great Britain while forging economic and social connections with its neighbor to the south, the United States, with whom it shares the world's largest undefended border. Canada (over 9.9 million square kilometers) is the second largest country geographically, after Russia (over 17 million square kilometers), and has two official languages, English and French. (Note: The United States and China are the third and fourth largest nations in the world, respectively.) The province of Quebec remains an uneasy member of the federation, and there is still an active movement within it to secede and form an independent country. A technologically advanced and prosperous nation, Canada is a multicultural society, with an awareness of its Anglo-European roots, an appreciation of its native cultures, and a sensitivity to its large number of immigrants from Asia and Africa. All of these aspects play a role in Canadian sports.

Considering its northern geography and corresponding cold and snowy climate, it is probably not surprising that winter sports such as hockey, skiing, snowboarding and figure-skating are the favorite sports of Canada. It is hockey that provides Canada with its most notably cultural identity. Canadian passion with ice hockey is akin to an obsession. Canadians play hockey in indoor arenas and outdoors on frozen lakes and rivers. "Hockey Night" on Saturdays remains a national television treasure. Canadian youth dream of emulating the success of national hockey greats that preceded them. In 2008, Canada won the World's Junior Hockey Championship for the fourth straight year. In 2004, both the men's and women's Canadian national teams were world champions in hockey. For the men, the 2004 victory over Sweden marked Canada's 21st World Hockey Championship. As of 2008, Canada has 24 total world titles in hockey.

Another winter favorite sport of Canada is curling. Often called "chess on ice," curling involves two teams of four players each sliding heavy stones toward a goal. It became an Olympic sport in 1998, and interest in it has spread to the United States, Japan, and Europe. Interestingly enough, the sport itself can be traced back to 15th century Scotland. Curling places special emphasis on proper etiquette—a game is always preceded by a handshake and the expression "Good Curling."

It may come as a surprise to many that Canada's official national sport is not hockey, nor is it a winter sport. Instead, it is a summer sport that holds the distinction: lacrosse. Lacrosse is considered by many to be the best amalgamation of the various elements of the "Canadian Identity," as can be seen in the following statement by Mike Mitchell, Director, North American Indian Traveling College:

> The roots of our country lay in many cultural soils, and Canadian society has grown and benefited from the contributions of people of many cultural backgrounds. The English and French are recognized as the dominant influences in the creation of this country and the foundation of our nation. Before the English,

French and many other immigrants to this continent strove and competed to build Canada, the aboriginal societies and cultures dominated North America. Unfortunately today there is little common knowledge among Canadians of the nature and complexity of the societies of the First Nations. There is even less understanding or appreciation of the rituals and activities of those cultures. Lacrosse, because of its unique history, exists as a link between these disparate components of Canadian society. It is one of the rare examples of the culture of the First Nations being accepted and embraced by Canadian society (www.lacrosse.ca).

Lacrosse was first declared the National Game of Canada in 1859, and it is now one of the fastest-growing and most popular sports not only in Canada but throughout the world. Unlike the winter sports of ice hockey or curling, it is not dependent on climate, and can be played anywhere. However, hockey advocates took offense to the claim that lacrosse was the "official" national game, and petitioned the Canadian Parliament to finally settle the matter. Therefore, on May 12, 1994, Bill C-212, Canada's National Sport Act, became law. It recognized hockey as Canada's National Winter Sport and lacrosse as Canada's National Summer Sport. This ably demonstrates the Canadian gift for compromise and pragmatic resolutions of problems. Instead of an either/or solution, the government came up with an elegant both/and resolution.

Canada, like the United States, has passed a great deal of legislation (e.g., gender equity) governing the sports world. Canadian sports are also becoming increasingly influenced by corporations. As Harvey, Thibault and Rail (1995) found over a decade ago, "Strong corporatist tendencies, if not always explicit, are evident in the recent developments surrounding both fitness and amateur sport in Canada. The initiatives undertaken by the state favoring representation from various interest groups are leading to a corporatist structure" (p.259). The corporatist trend in Canadian sports has paralleled that of the United States and continues today. There is a continuing fear among many Canadians that hockey, a sport traditionally identified with their country, is ceasing to be so. Miller, Lawrence, McKay and Rowe (2001) note: "'Canada's game,' long driven by American corporate interests . . . has become even more Americanized during the past two decades. . . Virtually every aspect of hockey—the form and content of games, broadcasting style, personnel, franchise selections, and TV contracts—has been marketed to American audiences, advertisers, and sponsors" (p.74–75). Franchises in many Canadian cities have ceased to exist (some of them having moved south to the U.S.), whereas such warm-weather U.S. cities as Anaheim, Dallas, Phoenix, and San Jose now have professional teams. The long-term national identification of Canada with hockey remains a problematic issue.

England

For the English football (or soccer) is a passion. This passion, unfortunately, often leads to an extreme form of fan violence known as soccer hooliganism. Indeed, the English have had an ambivalent relationship with soccer from its earliest days. During the Puritan era, soccer was seen as frivolous.

> In *The Anatomy of Abuses* (1581), an eloquent Puritan divine, Philip Stubbes, joined the establishment chorus in denouncing football as 'a friendly kind of fight [rather] than play or recreation, a bloody and murdering practice [rather] than a fellowly sport or pastime.' When he continued to assault football, however, Stubbes set himself apart from its non-Puritan critics. The Puritans objected to football, as they did to most popular sports and games, less from humanitarian, social, or legal motives than from a religious concern. 'Any exercise,' Stubbes continued, 'which draws us from godliness, either upon the Sabbath or any other day, is wicked, and to be forbidden' (Baker, 1982:75).

But such Puritanical objections have proven to be inadequate in halting the love for the game. Today, soccer fuels the passion of the English, even if the national team generally fails to fulfill the lofty expectations of a nation. Perhaps one of the most revered recent English athletes is soccer star David Beckham. Beckham, the former national team captain, inspired a movie named in his honor and as a tribute to his unique ability to control the direction of a kicked ball. In the film *Bend it Like Beckham*, a British Sikh girl idolizes Beckham so much that she is motivated to become a soccer star. So powerful is his influence that there are many who consider him to have been instrumental in convincing the International Olympic authorities to hold the 2012 Summer Games in London. In addition, the U.S. soccer club, Los Angeles Galaxy of the Major League Soccer (MLS) association hired Beckham for an extraordinarily high salary of $250 million (for five years) primarily to promote soccer to uninterested Americans. But after two years with the MLS, the aging soccer star has done little to change the perception of soccer in the United States.

One of the strangest current crazes in England is for a rather unique form of Extreme sport—"Extreme Ironing." Taking a battery-powered iron, an ironing board and unpressed clothing to mountain tops, forests, and even under water, athletes risk life and limb in order to remove creases from clothing in the most dangerous locations possible. The sport was started by Leicester resident Phil Shaw (known as "Steam") in 1997, who said it "combines the thrill of outdoor activity with the satisfaction of a well-pressed shirt." BBC News has referred to Extreme Ironing as "possibly the most bizarre extreme sport on Earth," and there have been many who point out that this sport is connected with the tradition of the English love for "irony" and eccentricity.

While it may have begun as a farce, it does seem that there are now actual participants, and websites devoted to their exploits. It will be interesting to see if Extreme Ironing is just a "flash-in-the-pan" or if it actually becomes an accepted and time-honored sporting activity. If nothing else, its athletes should have very nice looking uniforms!

Russia

While the game of chess can be traced back to ancient times, in the twentieth century it was dominated by Russian chessmasters. J. C. Hallman (2003) writes: "Russia is not the birthplace of chess, but it is the heart, a transplanted critical organ. . . . Even if India or China was the home of chess, Russia, by the early eighteenth century, was a kind of focal center, a boiling stew of chess ingredients from all over the world" (p. 43).

During the period of the Soviet Union, such domination became politicized, and a vital part of the Cold War atmosphere. The Soviet government gave state support to chess, and saw it more as a form of politics than a sport or game. The 1972 World Championship match in Reykjavik, Iceland between champion Boris Spassky and the American challenger Bobby Fischer was a legendary contest. While it is still debated whether or not chess is a sport, coverage of the Fisher/Spassky matches dominated the sports pages for much of 1972. American interest in the game grew tremendously, and Fischer—whose bizarre antics and unpleasant personality made him a true anti-hero—became a symbol of American exceptionalism when he defeated Spassky. Interesting enough, as David Edmonds and John Eidinow point out in their 2004 book *Bobby Fischer Goes to War,* such symbolism was misplaced. Fischer had no overriding love for his country, and in fact later renounced his citizenship, whereas Spassky was something of a dissident and had no love for the Soviet authorities. And the match itself might have had some ultimate effect on cooling Cold War passions:

> On the one hand, Fischer and Spassky represented their countries, and the match, according to the broadsheets, embodied East-West confrontation, particularly given the Soviet claim that its chess supremacy was the outcome of its superior ideology. On the other hand, no nationalist rivalry had been sparked off. Many Americans had supported Spassky, and many Russians had quietly rooted for Fischer. All in all, concluded *The New York Times,* the match had a unique political importance in terms of improved U.S.-USSR relations (Edmonds and Eidinow, 2004: 279).

When Fischer refused to defend his championship in 1975 the title was won by the Russian Anatoli Karpov, who in turn lost it to Garry Kasparov in

1984. Born in Baku, Azerbaijan (which was then a part of the Soviet Union) to Armenian-Jewish parents, Kasparov was the dominant world chess player until his defeat in 2000 by Vladimir Kramnick, and has gotten international attention with his matches against the computer "Big Blue." In 2005 he announced his retirement from the world of chess, and has entered politics, where he has become a prominent opponent of former Russian President Vladimir Putin, going so far as to attempt (unsuccessfully) to run for President himself in 2008.

During the days of the Soviet Union, Russia was noted for its emphasis on winning Olympic gold medals. While still priding themselves on such victories, Russians today are participating in many other international sporting events. Russian athletes are becoming noted for their prowess in volleyball, basketball, soccer, and other sports not normally connected with their culture. In recent years, female tennis stars such as Anna Kournikova, Anastacia Myskina, Elena Bovina, Svetlana Kuznetsova and Maria Sharapova have become international celebrities.

Soccer has also become an increasingly popular sport in Russia. The authors were in Moscow when Russia's CSKA soccer team recorded a stunning victory over Portugal's Sporting Lisbon to win the UEFA. Russians proclaimed the victory as a sign of a rebirth of the once proud Russian sports history. CSKA coach Valery Gazzayev proclaimed his players as heroes to every child in Russia (*The Moscow Times*, 2005). Similar to the American tradition of champion teams being invited to the White House to meet with the president; the CSKA team met with Russian President Vladimir Putin at his Moscow residence. The front page of Russian newspapers showed Putin kicking a soccer ball to the approval of the CSKA team standing in the background. Many of the Russians we spoke with expressed hope that this major soccer championship would encourage the government to start funding more sports programs.

In 2008, the Russian soccer team once again revived a sense of nationalism with its stunning quarterfinal victory over the Netherlands in the 2008 Euro Cup. For the unacquainted, the Euro Cup is the second most important sporting event in Europe; the World Cup, of course, is the most popular. The Euro Cup is played two years after each World Cup. At the conclusion of the Russia – Netherlands game an estimated 700,000 Muscovites took to the streets chanting jubilant slogans of victory. Russia had not enjoyed such a sports victory since the days of the old USSR. The breakdown of the former Soviet Republic and the lack of financial riches available to Russian athletes led to a decade (1990s) widely viewed by Russians as time of national depression and disgrace as most of Russia's greatest athletes went abroad to find success.

But this gloom and doom has been replaced with great optimism over the past few years. Consider, Former Russian President Vladimir Putin was able to secure the 2014 Winter Olympics for Sochi, Russia (a Black Sea resort center) and, in May 2008, the Russian hockey team beat its traditional rival Canada to win the 2008 Ice Hockey World Championship (Weir, 2008). The Men's hockey championship tied Russia with Canada with 24 world titles (Russian News & Information Agency, 2008). Despite all this sanguinity, the Russian soccer team lost in the Euro 2008 semifinals to eventual Cup winner Spain.

Similar to the situation previously described with Argentina, such growing sports popularity has had some unfortunate consequences in a society where economic inequality is a growing concern, and where modern-day gangsters (the so-called "Russian Mafia") prey upon the powerless with impunity. In his study of the Russian Mafia's influence in the United States, Tim Delaney points out how Russian players in the National Hockey League, including Alexei Zhitnik, have been harassed by this criminal element:

> Zhitnik admitted that he was a victim of extortion stating that family members back in Russia were kidnapped by the Russian Mafia and would be released if he paid a certain sum of money. Zhitnik refused and instead went to a more powerful criminal group who "took care" of the problem for him (assumingly for a lower fee than the original group). In January 1996 defenseman Oleg Tverdovsky's mother was kidnapped by Russian criminals who demanded ransom and protection money. He refused and she was later released unharmed. In 1994, a Russian gangster confessed to trying to extort $150,000 form then Buffalo Sabres forward Alexander Mogilny (Delaney, 2004B:14).

As Russian athletes continue to become major players in the lucrative world of international sports it will be interesting to see if such trends continue. Due to the recent crackdown of the Russian mafia, we feel that Russia will have fewer problems with family members of superstar athletes being kidnapped and held for ransom than compared to South American countries.

THE CULTURAL ICONIC STATUS OF SPORT HEROES

Have you have wondered about your impact on society? Will people remember you 25, 50, or 100 years after you die? Yeah, that second question is a bit gloomy, but think about it—what does it take to be remembered and admired by complete strangers long after we are gone? There are historic figures that most of us know by name: Plato, Aristotle, Joan of Arc, Galileo, Lincoln, Susan B. Anthony, Einstein, and Martin Luther King, Jr., to mention a few. We know who these people are because of their influence on culture. These people have been immortalized in print and lasting monumental statues. The legacies of people who make positive contributions to society are generally revered in heroic fashion.

Intellect alone is not a criterion for hero status. A person who saves the life of another is often considered a hero. The 9/11 terrorist attacks on the World Trade Towers and the Pentagon energized citizens to deem firefighters and police officers who risk their own lives to save others as heroes. Saving someone's life is certainly admirable and worthy of heroic praise. But, must one save the life of another in order to qualify as a hero? Many athletes are thought of as heroes, but they rarely save the lives of the adoring fans that bequeath such a label onto them. Thus, can an athlete really serve as a hero?

Just as any discussion on what constitutes a "sport" or an "athlete" requires a definition of such terms, so too is it necessary to define the term "hero" in order to ascertain whether or not athletes can be labeled as heroes. Let's examine the Greek origin of the word "hero" and compare with today's conception. The ancient Greeks believed that a hero was a half god and half mortal who performed admirably in given situations. Citizens of the modern world no longer believe in the Greek gods so this interpretation has fallen by the wayside.

Today's heroes are mortals and usually reflect the cultural idealism of a society. The cultural ideals of American society include acting altruistically, which may or may not involve saving someone's life; hard work and dedication; service to others; being entertained; and so on. Thus, a contemporary definition of a hero would be a person of distinguished courage or ability, who is admired for brave deeds, noble qualities, achievement, dedication, courage, dedication, integrity, and/or skill. Because Americans love to be entertained and appreciate skill, there is little wonder that many athletes serve as heroes to adoring fans. Just as the legacy of iconic intellectual figures such as Plato and Einstein live on, so too have many past athletes such as Jim Thorpe, Bath Ruth, Ty Cobb, Carl Feller, Honus Wagner, Babe Zaharias, and Jesse Owens become immortalized through sport.

Following the Greek tradition of honoring its heroes and legends in poems and statues, many contemporary athletes have been honored in print and in bronze at various sports Halls of Fame and sports stadiums. These stadium statues are everywhere. Here are a few examples: Hank Aaron in both Atlanta and Milwaukee; Willie Mays in San Francisco; Babe Ruth in Baltimore (his hometown); Michael Jordan in Chicago; Tony Gwynn in San Diego's Petco Park; Frank White in Kansas City; and Ernie Banks in Chicago. There are many other statues at many other stadiums. Being honored in statue form not only allows the athlete a chance to become "immortal"; it also provides a link from one generation of sports fans to the next. Furthermore, as a member of one generation explains to a member of a younger generation the qualities and virtues that led to a particular athlete being honored as a hero, this can help to reinforce the cultural values and idealism that athlete exemplified.

Types of Heroes

In other publications, the authors have described the role of heroes in society. Here, we will briefly mention the primary groupings of heroes and provide examples of each type. Each of these categories represents a value component of culture. Clearly, there is room for a great deal of debate as to which athlete should appear in what category. But once again, that is the beauty of sport, as such topics as who qualifies as a hero often leads to great discussions—and arguments. Let the debate begin!

- The Winner—This type of hero is determined by outcome assessment (e.g., winning a championship or individual sport), and not necessarily by any high level of skill. The winner may not be the most graceful or skilled player, but they somehow find a way to win. Examples include Michael Phelps, Robert Horry and Eli Manning.
- Skilled Performers—This type of athletic hero possesses extraordinary skill. Skilled performers give off an aura of invincibility and have usually psyched out the opposition by their mere presence. Present day examples include Kelly Slater, Tiger Woods, and Roger Federer.
- Social Acceptability—This category of hero upholds the values of society through efforts on the playing field/court and displays good sportsmanship. Peyton Manning, Wayne Gretzky, and Jesse Owens are examples of heroes of social acceptability.
- Group Servant—This hero is similar to a "martyr" in that he or she is willing to put the needs of the team above personal needs, wants and desires. The group servant is more concerned about a team victory than individual statistics. Examples include David Robinson, Pat Tillman, and Daniel "Rudy" Ruettiger.
- Risk Takers—American society values triumphant risk takers. This category of hero is applied to athletes who are willing to place themselves in harm's way in order to gain success. Daredevils, such as Evel Knievel; race car drivers, such as Jeff Gordon; and many extreme sport athletes, such as Danny Way and Shaun White, qualify as risk takers.
- Reluctant Heroes—This type of hero leads by example (on the playing field) rather than by trying to inspire teammates with a rousing speech, pep talk, or some other indirect method of leadership. Many people consider

Marvin Harrison, Eric Heiden and Tim Duncan as examples of reluctant heroes.

- Charismatic Hero—The category of hero possesses charm, wit, or some other unique characteristic that sets him or her apart from other athletes. This athlete is likely to give the rousing, inspirational speech that reluctant heroes shy away from, and is also likely to be the captain on a team sport. Examples include Derek Jeter, Ray Lewis, and Shaquille O'Neal.

- The Anti-Hero—The primary reason heroes exist rests with the realization that they uphold the cherished values and cultural norms of society. However, there are people who are admired because of their rebel spirit and their willingness to buck the rules and fly by their own set of standards. Fans who enjoy the "rebel" tend to cheer for the anti-hero. The anti-hero, then, is an enigma, in that, he or she does not demonstrate the desired values or norms of society and yet, still possesses a fan base. The anti-hero is the opposite of the "group servant." There are plenty of examples of anti-heroes including Bode Miller, Barry Bonds, Randy Moss, Terrell Owens, Kyle Busch, and Allen Iverson.

The study of heroes is quite revealing as every category of hero—except the anti-hero—reflects an important aspect of culture. In this regard, a society's heroes reveals the aspects of society deemed important by its citizens. The presence of anti-heroes indicates that currents of counter-culturalism exist within a given society. When a society has more anti-heroes than heroes, there is surely a great deal of social discontent. Once again, we see that sport is indeed a microcosm of society.

FINAL THOUGHTS

Sport has a tremendous impact on culture. Culture provides people with a "script" for what is acceptable behavior, and puts order into our lives. Sports usually have tangible elements such as uniforms, stadiums and equipment, as well as nonmaterial elements such as attachment to locations, values of fair play, and preferences for specific teams. In addition, symbols are used to represent meanings within a society. In sport, rings and trophies are symbols of achievement.

Cultures can vary a great deal, and such differences are often reflected in sport. For instance, cultural values, such as fair play or competitiveness, can be reflected in a country's most popular sports, such as soccer or baseball. Subcultures are groups within a culture who share beliefs and behaviors which distinguish them from the larger society. They do so through the use of clothing, mannerisms, and language (although such symbols often become popular throughout the general culture). Many sports are a type of subculture, such as surfing, which is specific to certain geographical areas.

Heroes were once thought to be semi-divine, and they still have a legendary status in societies. Such criteria as achievement, courage, dedication, integrity, and responsibility are admired by most societies, and athletes often demonstrate these qualities. There is a great deal of evidence to show that, whether they wish it or not, athletes are among societies' leading heroes. However, the media has had a tremendous impact on the demise of the hero in today's society, and the mythical status of sports' heroes is no longer so evident.

In the next chapter, we'll focus on the ways in which popular culture helps to make people aware of sport and sports' personalities, through the socialization process. As the surfers would say, "Hang Ten!"

Chapter Four

Sport Socialization through Popular Culture

Over the course of a lifetime, each of us will receive numerous messages from a variety of sources. Some messages, such as those provided by parents and significant others, are direct and require immediate attention. For example, when your mother says, "Wash your hands before dinner" she means precisely that—wash your hands! A message such as this is meant to serve another purpose as well. Namely, the mother is hoping that her child will eventually learn to wash his or her hands without being *told* to do so. In this regard, the child has embraced a valuable lesson of hygiene that should carry through his or her lifetime. This is just one of many lessons each of us is expected to learn. When you think about it, we are bombarded by a never-ending array of direct requests, or orders: "No parking," "Don't walk on the grass," "No smoking," "Clean up your room," "You're not wearing that," "Run 5 more laps," and so on and so on.

We also receive a great number of understated messages from a variety of sources—especially the media. Most obviously, we are constantly bombarded with a barrage of media commercials that are designed to directly influence our purchasing behaviors. But there are times when the media is more subtle. The mass media, which includes newspapers, radio, television, the film industry and, now, the internet, often presents us with sociological and philosophical ponderings that manage to bypass our conscious awareness and reach into our subconscious. How many of us have tried, in vain, to erase inane jingles and advertising slogans from our long-term memories? Films have played a very important role in promoting sports' themes. Most likely these classic lines from sport films will conjure images in your mind: "There's no crying in baseball," "If you built it, he will come," "Cut me Mickey," "I coulda been a contender," "Yo, Adrian," and

"Show me the money!" We'll explore the powerful ways in which the mass media make us aware of the rules and importance of sports.

THE SOCIALIZATION PROCESS AND SPORTS

The direct and indirect messages we receive from others are a part of the socialization process. Socialization is the life-long process of social development and learning that transpires as individuals intermingle with one another and learn about society's expectations of appropriate behavior. When we are young, we are taught the values and norms of the family. As we age, we are expected to learn how to behave properly in public (including school). When we tried out for a sports team we were expected to learn the rules of the game and the rules of the coach. By the time we reach adulthood, we are expected to abide by the rules and laws of the greater society. We are taught all these social expectations through the socialization process by significant others.

Significant others, or agents of socialization, include our immediate family members, peers, close friends, teachers, and the media. The agents of socialization teach us to accept cultural customs, values, and norms. Learning takes place when individuals internalize the messages being delivered to them. When people respond properly to given stimuli, they have successfully internalized a society's social expectations. For example, in football, the offensive line is taught to maintain their position until the ball is hiked; otherwise, if they move ever so slightly, the team will be penalized. Defensive players have been taught to try a number of tactics, including pretending to blitz the quarterback or talking trash in an attempt to cause premature movement from the offensive players. The offensive line coach (an agent of socialization) will teach his players to keep an eye on the ball and not move until it is hiked. When the offensive line players reach a point where they are nearly rock-solid in formation until the ball is hiked, learning has occurred.

Furthermore, once any learned behavior becomes routine, it has been added to the script of acceptable behavior of individuals. In this manner, a college offensive lineman does not need to be taught to remain still during formation because he has already learned this in high school, if not Pop Warner football. Professional players, of course, should not have to be taught fundamentals of the game; the basics of the sport should already be a part of their script. This reality helps to explain why football fans become so angry with players who make elementary mistakes like lining up off-sides. How can any professional player (let alone a high school or college player) line up off-sides? Look at the location of the damn ball!

It is understood that people with normal, or relatively normal, brain functioning capabilities have the ability to learn. Thus, when we are taught certain things by the agents of socialization, we are capable of comprehending the messages and heeding them. We also learn through past experience and modeling the behaviors of others. That people model themselves after significant others reveals the importance of heroes.

Agents of Socialization

Agents of socialization are sources of culture and social expectations. They are people, groups, or institutions that teach us what we need to know in order to perform properly in any given situation, including on the playing field or court, or in society in general. The most important agents of socialization for any individual are those people whom we revere and trust the most. The agents of socialization include:

- Parents and Immediate Family Members—Upon birth, each of us were completely dependent upon our immediate caregivers; generally, one's parents. Parents and other close family members provide us with the early preparation for life; they teach us the fundamental requirements of how to function in the social world.
- Schools (including day care)—When youngsters start school they interact with a number of other adult authority figures, including teachers, counselors, principals, and even the "lunch lady." All of these people will attempt to teach children various rules. Teachers are especially in a position to bond with children and therefore exert influence over their behavior.
- Peer groups—The term "peer" is used to refer to a grouping of people of about the same age. Around the time children reach third grade, parental influence begins to wane and the opinions, values and norms of peers because quite important.
- The community—The community at large in which a person resides may have great influence over individuals. Whether or not one's community is "safe" or "crime ridden" will have an impact on the social services provided to its citizens and will influence the mind-set of community members.
- The mass media—The mass media refers to the forms of communication that have a wide appeal and influence in a society. Among the primary examples of the mass media are television, radio, the music industry, motion pictures, magazines and newspapers, video games and the Internet. Most people consume large portions of the media which allows for potential significant influence.

- Religion—Religion was created by humans for the specific purpose of influencing human behavior. Most people adhere to one religion or another and as a result, religion represents a significant spiritual presence in their lives; for others, religion has less importance.
- Employment—Sooner or later, the vast majority of people will have to find work in order to pay their bills and maintain a certain lifestyle. Because most people have to work, employers have a relatively high level of influence on our behavior.
- The Government—Although the role and power of the government may be rather subtle at times, the type of socio-political structure found in a society either hampers, or provides for, opportunities for individuals to pursue chosen paths in lives.

The agents of socialization impact the lives of individuals in varying degree, but collectively, they exert a great deal of influence on us all. The agents of socialization then, also impact our involvement with sport.

Communities across the nation often proclaim their pride with the sports accomplishments of members from the local community. In this photo, the small city of Oswego, New York, erected many signs in honor of Erik Cole, a member of the 2006 NHL champion Carolina Hurricanes. (Courtesy Tim Delaney)

SOCIALIZED INTO SPORT

Why is it that some people play sports and love to watch sports, while others have little or nothing to do with sports? Socialization and past experience provide the two most fundamental explanations.

Each of us can examine the role and impact of the agents of socialization on our relationship to sport. Let's begin with the primary agents of socialization, parents and immediate family members. A child raised in a home already enthusiastic toward sport is more likely to develop an interest in sport than a family that has little or nothing to do with it. Some parents are so passionate about sports that they may start to socialize their newborn child into sport by dressing the baby in sports outfits and decorating the baby's room in a sports motif. A parent who places a miniature football in the crib of a baby boy is sending a direct message, even if this gesture is beyond the comprehension of the newborn. Parents who interact with their children by such simple means as tossing a ball back and forth are positively reinforcing sport participation. Parents that watch ballgames on television with their children, or take their children to ballgames, are not only forging a bond with one another, they are positively reinforcing the role of sport in the everyday life of the child. A child who has an older sibling that plays sports is more likely to be drawn to sports. In short, children raised in an environment where sports are viewed as a normal and necessary aspect of life are more likely to develop their own passion for sport.

Conversely, children raised in an environment where sports are not a part of the everyday miss out on the socialization into sport aspect. Furthermore, parents who attempt to force sport participation onto their children, or attempt to live vicariously through their children, are likely to foster negative reinforcement patterns. That is, if a child associates sport with being yelled at by his or her parents because of poor sport performances, the sports world will quickly lose its appeal and most likely be considered something to avoid rather than appreciate or participate in.

Historically, boys have been far more active at playing organized sports than girls. This can be attributed, in part, to the patriarchal nature of society wherein it was deemed that boys should play sports so that they can learn how to be part of team—a necessary ingredient in the employment sector. Girls, meanwhile, were encouraged to participate in passive activities, such as "playing house" with their dolls, in order to learn how to become better home makers. Over the past few decades, however, much has changed in regards to gender expectations and gender roles. Today, girls are equally encouraged to play sports by their parents and family members as well as at school. Most schools, especially since the advent of Title IX of the Education Amendments of 1972, provide ample sports teams for females and males. Young women and girls today have no idea how drastically different sporting opportunities were just decades ago. Girls today, like boys throughout recent history, assume that it is okay to play sports. And the schools reinforce this conviction.

The mandate that females must be allowed to play sports in schools paved the way for increased participation, but the acceptance among peers is what assured its success. Boys have long been encouraged to play sports by other their male friends. In fact, many boys who did not play sports or did show an interest in sports were victims of teasing at school. When girls started playing sports they were teased as "tomboys" by their female peers. Today, they are generally encouraged to play sports. Furthermore, having close friends who play sports, or enjoy sports, also increases the likelihood that an individual will also share this interest in sports.

The role of community and socialization into sport is multi-faceted. For one, the geographic location of the community may have great influence on sport participation. Children raised near a beach are more likely to surf than children raised in Lincoln, Nebraska (or Buffalo, New York!). Children raised in wintry communities with nearby mountains or large hills are more likely to ski, snowboard, and snowmobile, than children raised in the Deep South who are more likely to play football and baseball. The examples go on and on. As the number one sport of the United States, participation in football is encouraged in nearly every community. However, some communities take football more seriously than others. For example, in Massillon, Ohio, located about an hour south of Cleveland, football is so important that parents do not have to place a tiny football in the crips of their boys because the local hospitals do it for them! That's right a football is placed in the crip of every newborn baby boy. No pressure there! This small city of 30,000 residents is home to a stadium that holds (and regularly fills) 20,000 people. Massillon is home to football legend Paul Brown (who formed the NFL's Cleveland Browns and the Cincinnati Bengals) and 22 state championships and nine national championships in football. To the west of Massillon is Canton, Ohio, home to the NFL's Hall of Fame. Every year Massillon and Canton participate in a grudge rival game. The intensity of this long-time rivalry dates back to a time when both of these cities played host to professional football teams—the Massillon Tigers and the Canton Bulldogs—that would eventually serve as the fore-runners to the modern NFL.

Communities that provide sports programs after school or in the summer also play a role in socializing youth into sports. Some communities may provide ballparks and public pools, others may provide a hockey rink or skateboard parks. Economically poor communities have a harder time coming up with the funds to support sport programs.

Perhaps nothing has had a bigger influence on the perception of sports as the mass media. To a large extent, much of what we know about how various sports are played, what the proper rules for each game are, and who the most important players are, comes to us from the media. "The mass media and the sports world have a symbiotic relationship; they are partners in creating the most marketable product possible. They cooperate with one another but are not dependent on each other. Nearly all American households have a least one television set, and many have more than one. The social institutions of sport and media would like those viewers watching a sports-related program. Both sport and media could survive without the other. . . However, these two powerful social institutions remain loyal partners" (Delaney and Wilcox, 2002:203).

The role of the mass media in sport is still growing. Once upon a time (long before cable television), sports fans had to settle for the "Game of the Week," whether this was baseball on Saturdays in the summer, or football on Sundays. Today, with the advent of cable, satellite television, and streamlined Internet broadcasts, nearly all major professional and college ball games are available on television. Alternative sports have become mainstreamed through such entities as ESPN's "X Games." Sports video games are very popular (See Box 4.1). Sports highlight shows are regularly aired on television. The sports section of newspapers remains a staple for older sports fans, and sports magazines appeal to multiple generations. Later in this chapter we will see how sport films play a major role in socializing the masses into sports. In short, the mass media provides us with access to sports games and information 24 hours a day.

Box 4.1.   "Madden Madness": The Xbox Phenomenon

While the general economy may be showing definite signs of a recession, one item continues to be a hot seller regardless of financial distress: video games. In 2008 sales of consoles and software jumped 53% (*Sports Illustrated*, 7/28/08:19). And one of the most popular sellers, celebrating its 20th anniversary, is *Madden NFL*. It's not too much of an exaggeration to say that millions of sports fan go mad for Madden every year, standing in lines for hours—sometimes days—to be the first to purchase the latest version. *Madden NFL 09* marks the 20th anniversary of the incredibly successful video game franchise.

Originally developed by Electronic Arts Tiburon, the game is named after the Football Hall of Fame coach John Madden. A former National League player (with the Philadelphia Eagles), Madden began his coaching career at Buffalo State College. He became head coach of the Oakland Raiders in 1969 and led them to a Super Bowl championship in 1977. He retired from coaching after the 1978 season, and began a highly successful career as a football color commentator. Madden's larger-than-life personality (including a famed fear of flying, which necessitates his traveling around the country in a customized coach-bus) and enthusiastic mannerisms (such as a propensity for filling television screens with computerized "chalk" marks from his patented "telestrator") have made him one of the most beloved sports broadcasters of all time. He has a host of pet phrases, such as "BOOM" and "Here's a guy . . .", which are often parodied by comics such as Frank Caliendo, and which have come to be known as "Maddenisms." One of his best-known traits is a fondness for former Green Bay Packer quarterback Brett Favre. Ironically enough, after Favre's announced retirement in 2008, he was the first non-active player ever to appear on the game cover of the *Madden NFL* game. By the time the game was released in August of 2008, however, Favre had dramatically come out of retirement and was acquired by the New York Jets. Instead of re-issuing the cover, EA Sports offered an alternative cover, with Favre in a Jets uniform, for free downloading.

Every year the Madden game gets more complicated, with added features such as voice commentary performed by Madden himself; online play, a fictional radio show that interviews players and coaches; and the "Truck Stick," which allows offensive players to lower their shoulders to break a tackle. In 2006 the *QB Vision* was introduced—it simulates a quarterback's field of vision, directly corresponding to the actual player's Awareness and Passer Accuracy rating. It was a controversial feature, and has been dropped from the 2009 version. But the increasing authenticity of the game, including its new "Total Control Animation System," makes it ever-more realistic.

One of the most talked about aspects related to the game is the so-called "Madden Curse." Before 1999 Madden himself was featured on every cover, but for that year Garrison Hearst of the San Francisco 49ers was chosen to appear on the cover, and every year since a player designated by Madden as the top player of the year is selected. Not unlike the so-called "Sports Illustrated Cover" curse, there are those who claim that appearing on the Madden game cover is usually connected with a decline in performance, even though statistics don't bear this out.

Perhaps most importantly, the Madden video game has changed the way millions of fans experience the game of football. Critics have argued that video games in general, and the Madden game in particular, are increasing the passivity and isolation of people: instead of playing actual football or going out to watch real players perform, they are staying at home glued to their game boards. However, exponents claim that the virtual real experience is actually increasing people's physical dexterity and mental abilities, and helping to create vast networks of people sharing information and playing together, in ways that would never before have been possible. For the millions of *Madden* players, the various levels of skill, the dazzling graphics, the realistic images, and the authentic football knowledge makes it as close to participating in an actual NFL game as possible. Perhaps the next version will allow players to actually experience the pain that real players receive when they are tackled—that would really be a cause of Madden to yell out "BOOM!"

The other important agents of socialization, such as religion, employment, and the government, have a less direct influence on sport—although, as previously mentioned, it took government legislation (Title IX) to drastically impact female participation in sport. Still, it is the government that pays for community-based sports programs (through tax revenue) and offers professional sports teams "sweetheart" deals in an attempt to attract franchises to relocate, or remain, at specific geographic locations. In an attempt to forge a bond among workers (and with management/ownership) many businesses provide an "employee night" wherein the employer purchases tickets, and provides transportation and refreshments, to its employees at a ball game. And although many employers strongly discourage betting "office pools" others turn a blind eye to such activities as they know this is another way to forge a bond between employees. (At the very least it gives the employees a reason to look forward to work!) At one time, many religions discouraged sport participation because it represented a frivolous distraction from the spiritual world. Today, the secular world of sports has reached congruence with religion as many church-based institutions find it valuable to win on the sports field.

SPORT AND POPULAR CULTURE

The term "popular culture" has different meanings for different people, not unlike the term "sport." It generally is used to describe areas of the culture that people choose to participate in, or have a positive feeling about. It tends to relate to the everyday activities that people engage in. It is often contrasted with both folk and high culture: the former represents the simpler lifestyle characteristic of rural life, where traditions hold forth and change is discouraged. It tends to be local in its orientation, and promotes stability and distrust of outside agents. High culture tends to connote a level of sophistication based upon extensive experience, training, or reflection and is usually connected to a social elite which frowns upon the masses. Popular culture, on the other hand, is receptive to change, usually open to large number of people, and is far more diverse in its orientation. It is usually identified with urbanization, industrialization, the rise of the mass media, and the continuous growth of technology.

Popular culture may be defined as "the products and forms of expression and identity that are frequently encountered or widely accepted, commonly liked or approved, and characteristic of a particular society at a given time" (Delaney, 2007B: 6). There are many examples of popular culture, including music, print, entertainment, leisure, fads, advertising, and television. In recent years, video games and "cyber culture" have become important components. And sport is certainly one of the most all-pervading examples.

Sports are played and watched by members of all social classes, and tautologically the masses are responsible for the huge popularity of sports. Some sporting events, such as the World Cup and the Olympics, are consumed by a world community. Sports are pervasive in most societies and represent a major part of many people's lives. Many people watch numerous hours of television everyday. It is such a powerful influence that, paradoxically, it is often taken for granted. For four generations now, almost all members of the civilized world have experienced television's images and sounds from their earliest days. Such images, however, do not remain stable, but continue to change, often in a bewildering way. For instance, viewers of television in the early twenty first century are often astonished to see clips of programs from the mid to late twentieth century where almost everyone has a cigarette in his or her hand. The Surgeon General's warning that cigarettes are hazardous to one's health was not issued until the mid Sixties and didn't enter into popular consciousness until well after that time. It would be almost impossible to imagine a prominent athlete puffing away on a cigarette while being interviewed after a big game today, but such an image was by no means rare until relatively recently.

Advertising goes hand-in-hand with television. Popular athletes not only engage in sporting events—most of them endorse products, and not always products associated with the sport they participated in. Perhaps the most infamous example was "Broadway" Joe Namath's ad for pantyhose. To what extent such ads actually encourage people to buy the product is debatable, but the connection between athletes and specific products is one most people have become accustomed to over several decades of constant juxtapositions.

SPORT FILMS: ENTERTAINMENT AND A METHOD OF INDOCTRINATION INTO SPORT

We have briefly discussed the importance of many significant others and their influence on our socialization into sport. The remainder of this chapter will focus on a particular aspect of the media, sports films. Beyond playing sports and watching sports (whether one watches it in person or on television), sport films represent one of the more entertaining modes of socializing people into sport. As Randy Williams writes, "From passion (*The Cup*) to cynicism (*North Dallas Forty*), from fantasy (*Field of Dreams*) to culture clashes (*Mr. Baseball*) and racism (*The Jackie Robinson Story*), and from celebrating our need for heroes (*Knute Rockne: All-American*) to questioning it (*Cobb*), sports movies have covered a broad range of topics as an allegory of the human condition, an insightful window on society, and we are passionate about them" (Williams, 2006: xi).

ESPN.com (2005) came up with a list of the "25 Best Sports Movies, 1979–2004," as determined by a panel of experts. Here is the list—how many have you seen, and do you agree or disagree that these are the best sports movies of recent times?

1. *Hoosiers*
2. *Raging Bull*
3. *Field of Dreams*
4. *Bull Durham*
5. *Caddyshack*
6. *The Natural*
7. *Chariots of Fire*
8. *Jerry Maguire*
9. *Seabiscuit*
10. *Remember the Titans*
11. *A League of Their Own*
12. *Eight Men Out*
13. *White Men Can't Jump*
14. *Major League*
15. *Tin Cup*
16. *61**
17. *The Hurricane*
18. *The Color of Money*
19. *Finding Forrester*
20. *The Rookie*
21. *Ali*
22. *Bend It Like Beckham*
23. *Cobb*
24. *Rudy*
25. *Searching for Bobby Fischer*

Such lists are bound to cause arguments, if not serious fights! Interesting enough, even though football is the number one most popular American sport, films about baseball dominate the list.

Below is an interview with George Grella, Associate Professor of English and Film Studies at the University of Rochester. He has published widely on the topic of sports and film, and is a weekly film critic. He is also a regular participant in the annual Cooperstown Symposium on Base-

Narrative 4.1.   An Interview with George Grella, Associate Professor of English and Film Studies at the University of Rochester

1. What do you consider to be the best films made about sports and/or athletes?

   I think the two best films about sports (neither a baseball film, by the way) are *Chariots of Fire* and *Raging Bull*. Both are terrific films of course, simply as films, but they also use sports as a context, a metaphor, a way of exploring character, society, manners, sociology, etc., which distinguishes them from all those inspiring, heartwarming, uplifting sports flicks. Although several baseball movies display beautiful images and some great sense of the emotionalism that surrounds much of the sport—*The Natural*, *Field of Dreams*, for example—and a lot of others attain some level of value, significance, and interest, probably the best of the lot is *Bull Durham*, because it shows some of the gritty reality and irony of the game.

2. What difficulties are there in dealing with athletics in feature films?

   To begin with, one must avoid the sentimentality that surrounds most of them, all that stuff about winning the big game, luck and pluck rewarded, good guys finishing first, etcetera, etcetera. Another thing is the difficulty of showing the sport as it really is, without the fakery and slickness of so many films—*This Sporting Life* captures some of that, as does *Bull Durham*; sometimes it's also difficult simply to film the field of play, the constant individual motion, the grand sweep of a game, which explains why boxing movies outnumber all the other sports movies—the arena is small and defined, the contest is controllable, the side and back stories are fascinating, the violence is undeniably vigorous and entertaining. Another point is that it's hard to find actors coordinated and convincing enough to pass as professional athletes, too, despite the magic of the cinema—Robert DeNiro in *Bang the Drum Slowly* is a good example of an utterly unconvincing portrayal of a ballplayer, no matter how good an actor he is. Plus all the difficulties inherent in making a feature film, a task akin to running a small country.

3. Can you describe the annual conference at the National Baseball Hall of Fame and Museum, where you give a presentation every year on baseball and American culture?

   Yes, it is a truly interdisciplinary conference, representing more areas of study cohering around baseball than any other conference I have ever heard of. It attracts historians, musicologists, architects, sociologists, economists, engineers, physicists, statisticians, urban design experts, journalists, etc., and even a few literary and film types, like me. The Cooperstown Symposium on Baseball and American Culture deals not with the game in the sense of how to play it, but in all sorts of aspects of its place in the culture, its history, and its ongoing significance.

ball and American Culture, held every summer at the National Baseball
Hall of Fame and Museum.

Given the important role which the mass media has played in making people aware of sports, it is not surprising that major sociological themes have
been addressed in some of the most popular films of recent years. Topics such
as the role of sport in the community; gender; participation in school sport;
religion and sport; sports heroes; and race and ethnicity are all major themes.
Films often allow people to watch controversial themes and discuss them in
a relatively dispassionate way. Here are a few examples.

Sport in the Community

The 1989 film *Major League* (written and directed by David Ward) dealt
with the ways that major league sport franchises can both unite and divide
a community. In the movie, Rachel Phelps (played by Margaret Whitton),
the owner of the Cleveland Indians (a former Las Vegas showgirl whose
late husband, the original owner, had recently died) desires to move the
team to a warmer climate, in Miami, Florida. The movie begins with a depressing montage of images from the decaying industrial city of Cleveland,
coupled with scenes from the actual Cleveland Indians' last World Series
victory in 1948, and the mostly losing seasons since. Randy Newman's
acerbic song "Burn On"—about the night when the Cuyahoga River caught
on fire due to its polluted state—plays behind the melancholy scenes. When
Phelps is told she can't sell the team, she finds a loophole that would allow
her to do so if attendance drops below 800,000 paid customers. She comes
up with a scheme to field the most inept team of players possible, so that
even the hard-core Indian fans will stay away in droves. This includes a
self-centered third baseman (Corbin Bernsen), a burnt-out catcher (Tom
Berenger), a brash center fielder (Wesley Snipes), a voodoo-worshipping
hitter (Dennis Haysbert), and a recently-imprisoned out-of-control pitcher
(Charlie Sheen).

Not surprisingly, the team initially stinks up the joint, but a strange kind of
camaraderie begins to bring them all together. When the gruff manager (Lou
Gammon), a former tire salesman who had never managed in the big league
before, learns about Phelps' plan, he tells the team, which inspires them to
pull together. The highlight of the film is the one-game playoff between the
Indians and their hated rival the New York Yankees to see who will be first in
the division. After a series of comic misadventures, the Indians win the game
3-2 and head to the playoffs.

A successful—and outrageous—comedy, *Major League* is particularly good at capturing both the behind-the-scenes relationships among players and the ways in which fans rally around a team with spirit. For instance, Rick Vaughn, the struggling pitcher played by Sheen has been nicknamed "Wild Thing" because of his unpredictable throwing skills. The song of that name is played whenever he enters the field. When it is discovered that his problem is due to poor vision (which a pair of eyeglasses quickly solves) he quickly becomes the heart of the team and is embraced by the fans, who joyously sing "Wild Thing" in celebration. (Sheen's performance, by the way, is often considered one of the best in any sports film—he was an expert pitcher in real-life, noted for his 85-miles-per-hour fastball).

Another important theme is the role of diversity. The team itself is comprised of definite individuals from different economic backgrounds, belief systems, races, and work ethics. Berenger's catcher, for instance, is reaching the end of his career, and is initially disgusted with the prima donna antics of Sheen and Bernsen; Snipes' character is talented but brash, needing guidance to bring his running skills to their best effect; and Haysbert's character is a Cuban defector who violently debates the merits of his voodoo beliefs with various born-again Christian team members. While exaggerated for effect, such characters represent the disparate elements most major league teams are made of today, and the film does an excellent job of showing how a manager needs to inspire them (in this case by inflaming them against their common enemies the Yankees and Mrs. Phelps) in order to make them into a workable and effective team.

Best of all, the film give a realistic sense of how a team can equally inspire the community in which it resides. From its depressing opening scenes to its raucous affirmative conclusion, we see many images of the real city and citizens of Cleveland (although for financial reasons much of the movie was actually filmed in Milwaukee!), and we get a good sense of how a community facing its own economic and social hardships can come together to support a struggling but scrappy sports team. Ironically enough, while writer/director Ward chose the Indians precisely because of their long-standing losing tradition, shortly after the film's successful opening, the real Cleveland Indians took a dramatic turn for the better, winning seven division titles from 1995–2008 and two American League pennants. Unfortunately, just as the Indians of *Major League* never won the World Series, neither have the real Indians won baseball's championship since 1948. Nonetheless, the Cleveland fans have embraced the film, and often re-enact scenes from it, including having Rick Vaughn Glasses Night.

Gender

As mentioned earlier, while football may be the number-one favorite sport among fans, baseball continues to dominate as the theme of most sports films. One of the most popular recent movies was 1992's *A League of Their Own*. It deals with such important themes as economics (how to keep baseball itself alive during wartime), family (the sibling rivalry between two sisters on opposite teams), and class status (players from a rural setting coming into conflict with big city players). But it primarily deals with gender issues: *should* women play baseball and is their style of playing identical to or different from that of men?

The film is a fictionalized account of the real All-American Girls Professional Baseball League (AAGPBL), which was founded by chewing gum magnate and Chicago Cubs owner Philip K. Wrigley in 1943, and which lasted until 1954. Wrigley was deeply worried that, with most of the young men in America off to fight in World War II, baseball would fade from the public view until after the war's end, and might not be able to recoup its losses. Wrigley, along with other baseball executives, decided to found an all-female league in order to keep baseball in the public eye. *A League of Their Own* has a similar plot. Candy manufacturer Walter Harvey (Gary Marshall—the brother of the film's director Penny Marshall) starts an all-female league during the war and announces a national talent search with tryouts in Chicago. Two sisters from a farm in Oregon, Dottie (Geena Davis) and Kit (Lori Petty) become the star pitcher and catcher, respectively, of the Rockford Peaches. Dottie's husband is fighting overseas, and she is initially reluctant to leave the farm, but her baseball-loving sister convinces her to do so. Other recruits include a gruff third baseman (played by Rosie O'Donnell), a sexy center fielder (played by Madonna) known as "All the Way" Mae, and a second base player (Megan Cavanaugh) who is talented but not considered attractive enough by the scouts to initially be invited to play. When Dottie and Kit refuse to join the team because of this, an exception is made—but the importance of "sex sells" is brought home again later, when they all see the skimpy costumes they are expected to wear. "What do you think we are?", one of them exclaims, "ballplayers or ballerinas?" This is further hammered home when, in addition to team practice, they are also required to go to charm and beauty school.

Tom Hanks plays coach Jimmy Dugan, a former ballplayer who is initially opposed to the entire idea of the league, which he considers to be just a publicity stunt and not worthy of his expertise. In the most famous line of the film, he bawls out an outfielder (Bitty Schram), who breaks down in tears. "Are you crying?" he yells out. "There's no crying in baseball!" He is further disgusted when, in order to get publicity for the new league, the players are encouraged to perform antics such as catching balls while doing splits (which lands them on the cover of *Life* magazine). Sharing the sexism of the times, Dugan does not take the women players seriously, until he begins to see that their genuine talent and love for the game matches his own.

Another theme of the film is the ways in which the characters differ in the ways they see the game as central to their lives. While they all understand that being in the league is giving them new opportunities (a montage scene includes a newspaper headline about how they have traded "oven mitts for baseball mitts"), they are ambivalent about what this means to them. "Penny Marshall uses her baseball game sequences to show how sport, even for most of these women, was not all-encompassing. We see not only the women's relationships with each other, their manager, their owner, and the media but, more importantly, their confusion and internal struggles caused by suddenly finding themselves in transition. Now they have new roles, new opportunities that go against the images and principles fed to them all their lives about staying at home and caring for the family" (Williams, 2006:107).

Dottie, while both the star player and the "sex symbol" of the team, quits baseball as soon as her husband (played by Bill Pullman) comes back from the war. At the end of the movie, a now-aged Dottie is reunited with her sister (who earlier in the film had been traded to another team and became her great rival) at the opening of a women's section at the Cooperstown Baseball Hall of Fame and Museum. Dottie's daughter is proud of her mother's achievement, and the movie makes it clear that much has changed since the war era in terms of women's sports. (Many of the women shown in the final scene were actual members of the AAGPBL.) *A League of Their Own* is an entertaining film, but it nonetheless depicts a formerly little-known part of baseball's history, and connects it to the ongoing drive for women's equality in sports and society in general.

Participation in School Sport

When asked what their all-time favorite sport film is, many people—both men and women—will automatically say *Rudy*. This is not surprising, for the movie—based on the real-life story of Daniel "Rudy" Ruettinger—is the inspirational story of a young man whose dreams of playing football at Notre Dame were finally fulfilled. It is the ultimate "feel-good" film, but it also deals with some important sociological themes, such as religion (several of the main characters are priests, and the importance of the Catholic faith for Rudy is a constant theme), family (including the lack of support Rudy receives from his siblings), economics (such as Rudy's desire to escape the dead-end occupations he and his family and friends have to take in order to survive), race (after some initial hostility, Rudy becomes friends with an African American groundskeeper who admires his determination) and education (it is stressed to Rudy several times throughout the film that, whether or not he ever makes it as a Notre Dame football player, the excellent education he is receiving while a student will ultimately be more important to his career and personal possibilities).

Rudy (directed by David Anspaugh and starring Sean Austin in the lead role) came out in 1993 and deals primarily with events from 1972–1975. It is the story of a young man growing up in Joliet, Illinois, the third of fourteen children. Working in a steel mill, alongside his father and brothers, he dreams of going to Notre Dame and playing on their famed Fighting Irish football team. However, his blue-collar family does all it can to dissuade him, pointing out that his physical abilities (he is 5'7" and 165 pounds) and his academic record are inadequate to allow him to accomplish this goal. They encourage him to be realistic, and strive for a lifelong career in the steel mill. But when his best friend is killed in an explosion in the mill, Rudy resolves to escape. While rejected by Notre Dame, he is finally accepted by a small junior college in South Bend, Indiana, where he can at least be close to the Notre Dame campus. While there, he works hard as a student (and learns that his difficulties with studies are due to dyslexia, not lack of intelligence) and is finally accepted into Notre Dame in his junior year as a transfer student. He earns a place on the practice squad, helping the varsity team prepare for games, where his persistent and fierce determination gain the respect of both players and coaches. Finally, head coach Ara Parseghian (played by Jason Miller) promises to let him dress for one game before graduation.

Ironically, what should be the highlight of the film becomes one more crisis, when Rudy learns that Parseghian has unexpectedly stepped down as head coach, and been replaced by Dan Devine, who knows nothing about the promise and is unconvinced that Rudy deserves such an opportunity. Rudy's fellow players threaten to stage a walkout if he is not given the chance to suit up and go on the field. In the very last game of his college career, indeed in the final play, Rudy is allowed onto to the field, with the wild cries of "Rudy, Rudy, Rudy" coming from the fans in the stadium, and records a sack on the opposing quarterback. He is carried off the field in triumph.

There are, as in any biographical film, inaccuracies and discrepancies between the real-life events and the story depicted on the screen. For instance, Dan Devine is portrayed in the film as completely unsympathetic to Rudy's desire to play, and is only convinced to allow it when his players dramatically thrown down their jerseys on his desk. This never actually happened, and the real-life Devine is actually credited with the idea of allowing Rudy to play in his final game (Merron, 2002). Also, Rudy actually took part in two plays, not one. Nonetheless, Rudy Ruettinger really did get to play for the Fighting Irish, and really did get a sack on his final play, something that no one—including his own family—would have ever thought possible. The actual Rudy has become a motivational speaker, and the film continues to be one of the most beloved sports films of all time.

Religion and Sport

Like *A League of Their Own* and *Rudy*, the 1981 film *Chariots of Fire* is based on real-life events. It is not surprising that so many sports films are inspired by the lives and achievements of actual people, as so many of these stories are truly remarkable. As the saying goes, if one made up such stories they probably wouldn't be believed. *Chariots of Fire* (which won the Academy Award for Best Picture) is an excellent example. It depicts the friendship and rivalry between a team of British runners who wish to compete in the 1924 Summer Olympics in Paris. The intense preparations, and the grueling realities of the actual race, are vividly depicted. But what gives the movie its heart is the personal story of two of the runners, Eric Liddell (played by Ian Charleston), a devout Christian known as "the Flying Scotsman" because of his athletic abilities, and Harold Abrahams (played by Ben Cross), an English runner who was the brother of the Olympic long jumper Sydney Abrahams. The usual rivalries between the Scots and the English were exacerbated in this case by the fact that Abrahams was Jewish. Anti-Semitism was a powerful reality in 1920s Britain, and Abrahams—who came from a poor family of Lithuanian immigrants—also had to battle against class prejudice as well.

While the lives of other British athletes are also dealt with in the film, it is the relationship between Liddell and Abrahams that predominates. Liddell is convinced that his athletic abilities are a gift from God, and intends to go to China as a missionary. When his sister criticizes him for devoting himself to running rather than religion, he argues with her that that two are synonymous: running is his way of showing the glory of God, and he declares that Jesus Christ is his personal trainer. Needless to say, such beliefs are not agreeable to Abrahams, who is further annoyed when Liddell beats him in a race. Further complications ensue when Liddell learns that the 100 metre race at the Olympics will be held on a Sunday. As a dedicated Christian he refuses to race on the Sabbath. Luckily, his teammate Lord Andrew Lindsey (based on the real Lord Burghley, who was still alive when the film was made and refused to let his name be used in it) agrees to switch places with him, allowing Liddell to run in the 400 metre race the following Thursday instead. Abrahams went on to win the 100 metre, while Liddell—unexpectedly—won the 400 metre, breaking the existing world record of 47.6 seconds.

Chariots of Fire is unusual for a sports film in its depiction of individuals devoted to their religious beliefs. Liddell refuses to compromise his Christian tenets, even at the possible cost of not being able to participate in the Olympics, whereas Abrahams makes it clear that, while not a practicing believer in the Jewish faith, he will not compromise his Jewish identify, even when this causes him to be discriminated against. The athletic talents of both individuals allow them, at least to some extent, to gain the respect of those who otherwise would condemn them for their religious identities, but the film does not whitewash the pervading lack of tolerance of the time period. Ironically, while he was once president of the Jewish Athletic Association, Abrahams later converted to Catholicism (Seddon, 2008). The title "Chariots of Fire" comes from an 1804 poem by William Blake, which had been turned into a famous hymn known as "Jerusalem", and which was inspired by the story that a young Jesus had visited England. The term "chariots of fire" itself comes from 2 Kings 2:11 in the Bible, where the prophet Elijah is taken to heaven: "And it came to pass, as they still went on, and talked, that, behold, there appeared a chariot of fire, and horses of fire, and parted them both asunder, and Elijah went up by a whirlwind into heaven." In Blake's version, the speaker desires to build a new Jerusalem on English soil—a theme central to both the dedicated Christian missionary zeal of Liddell and the desire for religious equality and tolerance of the Jewish Abrahams:

> And did those feet in ancient time,
> Walk upon England's mountains green
> And was the holy Lamb of God,
> On England's pleasant pastures seen
> And did the Countenance Divine,
> Shine forth upon our clouded hills?
> And was Jerusalem builded here,
> Among these dark Satanic Mills?
> Bring me my Bow of burning gold;
> Bring me my Arrows of desire:
> Bring me my Spear: O clouds unfold:
> Bring me my Chariot of fire!
> I will not cease from Mental Fight,
> Nor shall my sword sleep in my hand,
> Till we have built Jerusalem,
> In England's green & pleasant Land.

> —William Blake, Preface to "Milton:
> A Poem"

Chariots of Fire continues to be an inspirational film, in all meanings of that term.

Sports Heroes

When discussing sports films it is impossible to overlook movies dealing with the topic of boxing. There have been dozens of films dealing with this topic, but none is more popular—or beloved—than Sylvester Stallone's 1976 *Rocky*. Not only was it a box-office success, winning the Academy Award for Best Picture and spawning a seemingly-endless number of sequels, it also mirrored the unpredictable success of its writer and star, a journeyman actor who became a superstar thanks to his depiction of the lovable pug Rocky Balboa. Perhaps because the movie came out in America's Bicentennial year, just a few years after the seemingly endless nightmares of Vietnam and Watergate, there was a need for a "feel-good" film to make audiences cheer for a clear-cut good guy, and *Rocky* fit the bill.

While definitely a heroic figure, in the sense of a person who refuses to buckle under to adversity and rises to impressive heights, Rocky Balboa has some rough edges, and the movie itself has a dark undertone. For instance, as it begins, Rocky is a strong-arm collector for a local loan shark, threatening to break the arms of those who don't pay up—hardly an admirable position. He is also a 30-year old former contender whose best days seem long past, and whose future is dim at best. His only friend is the crude and cynical butcher Paulie, who is determined to hook Rocky up with his bespectacled sister Adrian, primarily to get her out of the house so he can have it for himself. But Rocky is offered the chance of salvation when the world heavyweight champion Apollo Creed (played by Carl Weathers and based on the then-reigning champion Muhammad Ali) comes to Philadelphia for a title fight. When the opponent is injured in a training accident, Creed decides it would be good publicity to fight a local boxer, and likes the name he finds in a registry: "The Italian Stallion." In the meantime, Rocky and Adrian, after a rather artless courtship on the former's part, realize that they have much in common, and their love begins to blossom. Rocky—even though he knows it is primarily a publicity stunt and that Creed doesn't really respect him—takes up the challenge, initially training by practicing on carcasses of meat in Paulie's butcher shop. An old-school trainer and gym owner named Mickey Goldmill, who had earlier refused to help the young Rocky, whom he considered a punk, is likewise redeemed when he is able to teach the now-respectful pugilist techniques that stood him in good stead during his own heyday of the 1920s.

What's make *Rocky* such a classic work is that, while obviously dealing with the myth of a hero's rise from obscurity through proper training, personal growth and great courage (a theme that a movie from the following year called *Star Wars* would equally mine), it also is grounded in a great sense of realism. In the early scenes Rocky's dismal apartment, poverty-stricken environment and limited circle of acquaintances is viscerally moving. More to the point, he has a realistic sense of his abilities. He doesn't expect to win the fight, but is determined to go the distance, hanging on for all 15 scheduled rounds. He appreciates Mickey's advice, but also knows that the trainer is living vicariously through him. And, when the nonchalant but cocky Creed enters the ring wearing Bicentennial red-white-and-blue trunks, Rocky— whom one might have thought would be the one decked out in such attire—is amused by the spectacle. He surprises the champion by his dogged persistent and ability to take a punch. The battle between the two boxers, filmed with the then-revolutionary Steadicam camera, remains one of the most famous fight scenes in movie history. Rocky does go the distance, winning Creed's begrudging respect and the adulation of the home-town crowd. While Rocky loses in a split decision, for all intents and purposes he is the champion.

The film, while capturing for posterity a good sense of what life was actually like in 1970s Philadelphia, is still essentially a fairy tale. Regarding the topic of race relationships, critics then and now pointed out that it flirted dangerously with the perennial desire many racists had for "the Great White Hope," a Caucasian heavyweight champion who could overcome the domination of the sport by African Americans. And the growing friendship between Rocky and Apollo Creed (dealt with in greater detail in the following two sequels) is farfetched, to say the least. Still, the exciting action scenes (including Rocky training on the steps of the Philadelphia Museum of Art), the growing relationship between Rocky and Adrian (which reminded many older viewers of the 1950s Academy Awarding winning movie *Marty*), the gritty neighborhood depictions, and most of all the chance for redemption that both Mickey and Rocky undergo, made the movie a surprise hit. Even though the sequels became increasingly preposterous, the fond feelings most people had for the original were untainted. *Rocky* became such a part of the American popular culture that in 2006 it was selected for preservation by the Library of Congress, in the United States National Film Registry, for being "culturally, historically, or aesthetically significant."

Race and Ethnicity

While Tom Hanks might have been correct in saying "there's no crying in baseball," when it comes to one particular sports film, it's at least okay to get choked up. *Brian's Song* (1971) was actually a made-for-television (rather than theatrically released) movie, but it continues to be one of the most popular sports films of all time, and is often mentioned as a personal favorite by individuals who might otherwise not associate themselves with emotionally-charged films. Perhaps this is because *Brian's Song* is based on a true story: the friendship between Chicago Bears running backs Gale Sayers (Bill Dee Williams) and Brian Piccolo (James Caan). Initially rivals, competing for the same spot on the roster, and coming from different economic and racial backgrounds, the two men find much in common. Shattering racial boundaries of the time, the two become roommates, and their wives also become best friends. When Sayers is injured in 1968 in a game against the San Francisco 49ers, tearing ligaments in his right knee, it is Piccolo who aids him in his rehabilitation, even though this is potentially detrimental to his own chance of excelling as a replacement running back.

While Sayers does recuperate, his return to the field is quickly hampered by a second injury, this time to his left knee. Around the same time, Piccolo, at the young age of 26, is stricken with cancer, and it is now Sayers' turn to help his stricken friend, remaining by his side throughout the agonies of his final days.

It is important to note that *Brian's Song* (based on Sayers' 1971 autobiography *I Am Third*) appeared just a year after Piccolo's death, when many football fans still were shaken by his untimely loss, and when racial unrest was still a very real issue, with riots, violent altercations and the rise of black nationalism constant themes on the nation's television broadcasts. By showing that blacks and whites could, at least potentially, work together, and by emphasizing the ways in which friendship can override antagonisms and misunderstandings, *Brian's Song* played an important sociological role. But even more importantly, it is the one movie that many men freely admit makes them cry every time they watch it. While originally made for and shown only on television, the film became such a talked-about sensation that it was eventually released theatrically, and made its stars, Billy Dee Williams and James Caan, two of the most-talked about performers of their generation. It inspired many similar sports buddy films, and was itself remade in 2001, but it is the original production that remains a classic. "Often imitated, never surpassed, *Brian's Song* is an inspiring story of friendship and courage. Going against the grain, this male, sporting equivalent to *Love Story* emphasizes character over winning. *Brian's Song* is one of the seminal movies of all time" (Williams, 2006:332).

These are just a few examples of the countless sports films that have addressed the myriad topics which arise through sports participation and appreciation. When we ask "why do we love sports?" it is difficult to separate the answer from the popular representations that movies have given us over the years.

FINAL THOUGHTS

Sports are not just physical activities and games; they serve as focal points for the formation of social worlds. Social worlds consist of group members who share a subcultural perspective and are held together through interaction and communication. In order to fit into a social world, group members will adjust their behavior and mindsets to revolve around a particular set of activities. People are socialized into sport worlds by the agents of socialization.

Individuals learn to internalize the messages sent to them by their social worlds, which allows them to thereby function more smoothly. Socialization is how we "become" human. This takes place most effectively in primary groups—intimate associates who play a direct role in shaping one's sense of self. Significant others are those who play the most major role in such developments. Such agents of socialization not only foster a sense of self, they also help to sustain it over a lifetime.

Sport is instrumental in creating self identity for many individuals, through their interactions with primary groups involved in sport activities, and through their identification with specific teams and players as well. In team sports, it is critical for all members to play their role and accept the responsibilities, which come with it.

One interesting question is why some people love sports whereas others do not. Even members of the same household often have different attitudes on this subject. For many, this is due to the motivations experienced in childhood. Initial bad experiences can cause a lifetime of aversion to sport, whereas positive experiences and availability of opportunities to play can instill a lifetime of enthusiasm. The influence of family and friends is also crucial in such developments.

One of the most effective and powerful sources of socialization is popular culture. Sport films in particular have introduced most of us to the important themes—such as community, gender roles, religion, the need for role models, race and ethnicity—which shape our very lives.

Think about your own favorite sport films, and ask yourself what it is you love about them. And go ahead—it's okay to cry over them!

Chapter Five

Youth Sports: Growing Up with Sports

Rafael has been playing baseball for as long as he can remember. He has dreamed of playing in the World Series where he could match his skills against the top talent the world has to offer. Does Rafael play for the New York Yankees, Boston Red Sox, St. Louis Cardinals, or the Los Angeles Dodgers of Major League Baseball? Clearly, he does not. Instead, Rafael still plays Little League Baseball. Major League Baseball may claim that its championship is the World Series, but who are they kidding? There are players from many foreign nations that compete in MLB's World Series, but the only representative teams are all from the United States. Well, there is still one team from Canada that plays in MLB, the Toronto Blue Jays, but one team from Canada does not qualify as a *world* series.

Sports fans from around the world mock MLB's claim that the winner of its league's championship has won a world sporting event. MLB officials, and fans alike, discount this criticism because they feel that the best baseball in the world is played in the MLB. And that much is probably true. After all, the Olympics want nothing to do with staging a baseball medal event pitting Americans against the world as the results would, seemingly, be predictable. However, as we have seen with basketball, the United States is not the only game in town.

If you really want to see a *world* series, you will have to settle with watching youths from around the globe compete against one another in Williamsport, Pennsylvania. These youngsters do participate against teams from many nations in a regional qualifying format cumulating with elimination rounds of baseball. That the qualifying format guarantees a team from the United States will reach the finals has not escaped the rest of the world's attention either! Still, for the youngsters who participate in the

LLWS, an opportunity to play against the best teams in the world is an experience they will never forget. And like many other people who once played Little League Baseball, some of the LLWS participants will go on to play baseball professionally, while most players will hang up their spikes and gloves and pursue non-baseball related activities.

CHILDREN AND SPORTS

When you were a child, did you want to play sports? When did you first start playing organized sports? Were your parents supportive of your decision to play sports? Or, did your parents want you to play sports even though you did not want to? If you are a parent now (or if you anticipate being a parent in the future) will you allow, or encourage, your children to play sports? Are there certain sports, especially contact sports, like football and rugby, that you may be more hesitant to allow you children to play? And if you do allow your children to play sports, should they be a certain age? In addition, considering the costs of sport participation, both in terms of time and the money, is sport participation worth it? Wow, there seems to be many questions involved in youth sport participation! Let's see if we can unravel some of these queries and provide specific answers.

Children and Play

The idea that children have always played was established in Chapter 1. Kids seem to naturally want to run, jump and throw things. It is their way of interacting with the world around them. Play helps youths to figure out their physical limitations, but it also encourages them to extend their physical abilities. Successfully jumping over a mud puddle brings with it a sense of accomplishment. Then again, kids being kids, jumping in the middle of the puddle and making a big splash brings joy and happiness. Either way, physical play helps a child develop mentally as well as physically. As the late novelist James A. Michener (1976) states, "I believe that children, like little animals, require play and competition in order to develop. I believe that play is a major agency in civilizing infants. I believe that big-muscle movement helps the infant establish his balance with the space in which he will henceforth operate. I believe that competition, reasonably supervised, is essential to the full maturing of the individual" (Michener, 1976:119).

Parents generally encourage their children's desire to play, starting with such basic activities as peek-a-boo. A baby's imagination runs wild with an-

A young child plays ball at a park. (Courtesy Shannan Delaney)

ticipation during a rousing game of peek-a-boo—where will mommy "appear" next? Parents provide their toddlers with a variety of play things, including balls that can be rolled or thrown. Rolling a ball back and forth with a child helps to form a bond between a parent and child, but it also stimulates a desire to explore other "tricks." As a toddler learns to walk they are encouraged to retrieve thrown balls. Most likely, they will kick the ball! Give a child a plastic bat and they will automatically start to hit the ball.

There is near universal acceptance to the idea that toddlers should be encouraged to play; whether it involves a ball, a doll, or even a stick that serves as an airplane. Play, by all accounts, is a healthy endeavor. Sport, however, especially competitive sport, is different than play.

To Participate in Youth Sports, or to Not Participate in Youth Sports

Parents encourage their children to play, especially with items like bats and balls, because it helps to develop their motor skills and coordination. The active movement involved with physical play also has health benefits. And in light of the growing obesity problem in the United States, even among a large percentage of youth, should be reason enough to encourage playful endeavors.

Organized sports represent an advancement on play. Sport, like play, helps to develop motor skills, coordination, and is a healthy alternative to sedentary activities such as sitting around playing video games or watching television. Youth sport participation offers additional benefits as well. For example, playing a team sport will teach participants teamwork and cooperation. Competitive sports help to prepare youths for life's many challenges. But let's not get ahead of ourselves. Before concentrating on the benefits and pitfalls of youth sport participation, it is advisable that we determine whether or not a child *should* play sports.

A prime factor in determining whether or not a child should participate in sports rests with an individual's desire to play sports. Most parents encourage their children to pursue activities that they find rewarding and enjoyable. A child's desire to play sport should be encouraged in the same manner as any other productive, non-deviant behavior would be. Determining *what* sport a child should play is initially answered by the child's own interests. In other words, if a child expresses a desire to play tennis, tennis should be the first sport introduced. As Micheli and Jenkins (1990) explain: "Perhaps the most important criterion is that the sport should be one the child is interested in and enjoys" (p.2). With the wide variety of sport options, both formal and informal, there are a number of sports available to youths. If children find that they do not like the first sport they try, they should be encouraged to try another. Even children who believe that they are unathletic will learn that they can perform well at some sporting activity. The diversification of sport, "in conjunction with the development of sports such as martial arts as the community and club level, has made it possible for every child to participate in an organized sport or fitness activity" (Micheli and Jenkins, 1990:3).

Not surprisingly, the most motivated youths to play sports are those who receive encouragement from their parents. Peer support is another source of encouragement. Furthermore, as Philips (1993) explains, "Aside from parental and peer encouragement, a rather vague factor, 'tradition' or ethnic influence, appears to play a role in the creation of interest in sports" (p.87). Thus, certain ethnic and groups seem to be "drawn" toward specific sports. "Tradition" is often influenced by geography. This means that kids raised in certain areas of the world, or specific areas within a nation, will be attracted to sports of regional interest. For example, youths in England, Brazil, Argentina, and Mexico have identification with soccer. Youths raised in China and Japan have an interest in the martial arts. In the United States, youths are influenced by the traditional American sports of football, baseball, and basketball. Many kids play soccer because it is such an inexpensive sport to fund;

Box 5.1. You're a Good Sport, Charlie Brown

Probably no other popular culture feature has had more to do with representing children and sports than Charles Schulz's beloved comic strip "Peanuts." Just about every American sport imaginable was represented in the world of Charlie Brown and his friends, and one can think of countless iconic images: Charlie Brown on the pitcher's mount; Lucy holding a football for him to (or so he hopes) kick out of the park; Peppermint Patty and Marcie ice skating; even Snoopy "hanging ten" on a surfboard!

The prevalence of sports images in the strip (which ran for almost 50 years, from 1950 through 2000) is no coincidence, for Schulz himself was an avid sports lover. Toward the end of the strip's run (and toward the end of his own life, for the two basically came to a conclusion at the same time), he reflected on this: "I have always tried to dig beneath the surface in my sports cartoons by drawing upon an intimate knowledge of the games. The challenges to be faced in sports work marvelously as a caricature of the challenges that we face in the more serious aspects of our lives. Anytime I experience a crushing defeat in bowling, or have a bad night at bridge, or fail to qualify in the opening round of a golf tournament, I am able to transfer my frustrations to poor Charlie Brown. And when Charlie Brown has tried to analyze his own difficulties in life, he has always been able to express them best in sports terms" (Schulz, 1999:114).

Much earlier, in a 1973 interview with *Los Angeles Times* reporter Charles Maher, Schulz discussed his love of sports, along with his fears that children were being indoctrinated into a desire to win rather than a love of playing the game for its own sake. He said that "No sooner does the season start than we begin to record how far a team is out of first place. A game between two teams in 7th and 10th place can be just as exciting as any game. But all we're worrying about is who wins. It should be the plays, great goals being scored, great baskets being made, great overhead shots hit. These are the things that count in sports" (Inge, 2000:81). Schulz always maintained a level head when it came to winning—as everyone knows, Charlie Brown's baseball team was "famous" for never winning a game at all!

One of the strengths of "Peanuts" was the way the Schulz was able to time and again return to the same themes, but give them interesting—and often unexpected—variations. This is best demonstrated by the annual tradition, every autumn, of having Charlie Brown rush passionately down the field to kick the football Lucy is holding, only to have it snatched away at the last second. In his 2007 biography *Schulz and Peanuts,* David Michaelis writes about this yearly event: "Schulz originally drew the football-kicking episode to show that Charlie Brown was incapable of combating Lucy's schrewdness. . .From first (1952) to last (1999), each setup of the football encouraged Charlie Brown to one more act of determination and, ultimately, martyrdom" (Michaelis, 2007:510).

(continued)

Box 5.1. (*continued*)

But Schulz, in the very last such example, threw a curve ball at his readers. Lucy is suddenly called into the house by her mother. She asks her baby brother Rerun to hold the ball for her. When he enters the home she asks him anxiously "What happened? Did you pull the ball away? Did he kick it? What happened?", to which Rerun slyly says in return, "You'll never know. . ." And neither will we! Perhaps Good Old Charlie Brown finally did kick one out of the park after all.

---

especially at the youth level. American youths may also be influenced by the specific regional area they are raised in. For example, in the Syracuse, New York area, lacrosse is a dominant sport; in Texas it is football; in the Rocky Mountain region skiing is popular; and in coastal California cities surfing is an attractive option.

Perhaps the most important criterion related to whether a child should play sports or not rests with the realization sport participation for children ought to be *fun*. Too much emphasis on rigorous practices, drudgery and analysis of plays can discourage children and make them no longer wish to take part in games that once gave them pleasure. Scott B. Lancaster, the Senior Director of the NFL Youth Football Development, argues that the overwhelming reason children choose to play sports is to have fun. Competition is one of the least important reasons. A parent that pushes a child to play sport will be met with resistance if the child does not want to participate. Lancaster (2002) has asked numerous kids that he works with what they dislike about sports. Their responses include the following:

> Too much standing around.
> Never get to play as much as others.
> Practices are boring.
> Never improve or learn anything.
> Parents and coaches are too focused on winning (p.36).

Lancaster stresses the need to be sensitive to children's enjoyment factor, as well as their individual styles of play. "For children under eight, skill development should be introduced in the form of fun games, and limited instruction should be applied in short sessions" (Lancaster, 2002:39). Sport participation should be a welcomed event in a child's life, not a dreaded task that must be performed:

> Most parents and coaches don't realize it, but kids approach sports with a viewpoint very different from adults. Adults promote structured programs that in-

clude tryouts, drafts, starting teams (whose players receive the majority of the coach's time at practices and games), and an overemphasis on league standings. From my experience, there are too many parents who encourage and even force their children to participate in sports and then place an inordinate amount of pressure on them to succeed because they believe that somehow it will elevate their family's status. It's as if adults receive recognition in their community based on the achievements of their kids (Lancaster, 2002: 39–40).

Sports Builds Character

It is often argued that sport helps to build character. Although there are many characteristics associated with character building, the more important qualities associated with "good" character include: personal responsibility, persistence, courage, self-discipline, honesty, integrity, a willingness to work hard, compassion for others, generosity, independence, and tolerance (Griffin, 1998). The authors define "character" as the aggregate of individual features, personality and behavioral traits, both good and bad, which define who a person is. Those who abide by a society's cultural expectations are said to have "good" character, while those who stray from the norm are said to have "poor" (or bad) character.

Coaches and parents involved with sports that possess positive character traits will help create an environment wherein youth can develop proper character traits. Furthermore, organized sports are supposed to be a setting that encourages cooperation with others and a willingness to accept society's rules. When children are influenced by positive role models, they are more likely to develop positive character traits. On the other hand, youth sports seem to be a domain with an increasing number of incidents that involve uncivil behavior; coaches attacking players and referees; parents attacking referees, coaches, and players; players fighting with one another; and so on. When children witness violent and deviant acts of behavior within the youth sport community, positive character developed is severely compromised.

When Should Youth Play Sports?

There are a number of factors to consider when determining when a youth is ready to participate in sport. Sports involve physical, motor, perceptual, social, emotional, and intellectual components. "All too often, the physical (size and biological maturity) and motor (skill) components are emphasized in selecting youngsters for sport. A more compressive view of readiness is essential. A youngster might have the size requisites for a sport, but may not have sufficient motor control of sufficient emotional competence to handle stressful situations" (Malina, 1986:46). Readiness for sport is certainly not solely the decision of the child. Parents must also be ready to allow, or tolerate, their child's participation in sport. And coaches and other sport officials need to determine the capabilities and readiness of youth as well.

A youngster is never too young for physical play. That is, infants and toddlers should be encouraged to roll or kick a ball. Playing catch with a toddler is a great way to help develop his or her balance and coordination. Around age seven, most children have experienced a growth spurt, including the size of the brain which increases to 90 percent of its total weight (compared to 25 percent at birth). Physiological growth allows youth the increased ability to handle more challenging physical activities. Children have also developed an understanding of the structure and framework of rules—a critical aspect of organized sport. Furthermore, at age seven (or so) youth have learned to develop reason, and thus they understand the nature of competition. That is, they realize that some times you win, and sometimes you lose. An immature child may not be able to handle possible ridicule associated with defeat and therefore should not play organized competitive sport until he or she has grown older. Some children may have a hard time dealing with the relative amount of stress associated with competitive sports and, therefore, they too should hold off on playing organized sport until they are older.

Because youths at the (approximate) age of seven have learned to develop reason, they are also capable of understanding the difference between winning and losing. It is not as important to them at this age as it will be later, but they are sensitive to ridicule. Too much pressure at this age can lead a child to be turned off from sports. Conversely, success, encouragement, and positive experiences will further cultivate an interest in sport. Lancaster notes that "What many parents don't realize—and are often shocked when I tell them—is research studies have found that 90 percent of young male athletes would rather have an opportunity to play on a losing team than sit on the bench of a winning team" (Lancaster, 2002:75). And Douglas Putnam (1999) further adds that at this age children are particularly sensitive to criticism and harsh treatment by parents and coaches:

> Nothing can put a damper on a soccer game between seven-year-olds like an irate father bounding onto the field to deliver an obscenity-laced tirade in the face of a referee who has made a bad call. The only thing that might be worse is a hyperventilating coach heaping abuse on a nine-year-old who hasn't put on his "game face." About 25 million boys and girls participate in team or individual sports in the United States each year. By the time they reach age fifteen, nearly three-quarters of them have quit, according to a survey of 26,000 kids by the Institute for the Study of Youth Sports at Michigan State University (Putnam, 1999: 49).

In brief, by age 7 or 8, children are ready for organized physical activities, including sport. Participation in organized sport before this age should correspond with a child's needs and abilities. Age 8, or so, also seems to be the "magic" age of distinction between when a child is ready for contact sports. Most children are not ready for contact sports before age 8; by contrast, most youth are ready for contact sports around age eight. Again, it is advisable that parents and coaches keep in mind individual differences of preparedness of each child. Youth sports should be a fun experience for all involved. If it is not fun for kids, they will be turned off from future organized sport involvement. And this helps to explain the appeal of unorganized, alternative sports.

Bill of Rights for Young Athletes

To protect young athletes from overbearing adults who wish to control their sports participation a number of lists of guidelines have been proposed. Perhaps the best known is the "Bill of Rights for Young Athletes" written by Martens and Seefeldt (1979:15):

1. Right to participate in sports.
2. Right to participate at a level commensurate with each child's maturity and ability.
3. Right to have qualified adult leadership.
4. Right to play as a child and not as an adult.
5. Right of children to share in the leadership and decision-making of their sport participation.
6. Right to participate in safe and healthy environments.
7. Right to proper preparation for participation in sports.
8. Right to an equal opportunity to strive for success.
9. Right to be treated with dignity.
10. Right to have fun in sports.

This particular example of a "Bill of Rights" is 30 years old. But perhaps it is time for all those involved with youth sports to adopt some version of the character code. After all, sports are supposed to build positive character traits, aren't they?

ORIGINS AND DEVELOPMENT OF YOUTH SPORT

Throughout most of human history, children were looked upon as "little adults" without special needs connected to their level of mental and physical development. As a rule, children were not pampered the way most are today. In the past, children were expected to work (often long hours on farms, guilds, or factories) as early as age 5 or 6. There were no child labor laws to protect children in the workforce, just as there were no laws to protect them at home.

> The treatment of children as a distinct group with special needs and behavior is, in historical terms, a relatively new concept. It is only for the past 350 years or so that any mechanisms existed to care for even the neediest children, including those left orphaned and destitute . . . In Europe, during the Middle Ages (A.D. 700 to A.D. 1500), the concept of childhood as we know it today did not exist. In the paternalistic family of the time, the father was the final authority on all matters and exercised complete control over the social, economic, and physical well-being of his wife and children. Children who did not obey were subject to severe punishment, even death (Siegel, Welsh, and Senna, 2003:11).

Young children were expected to blindly obey the rules of the family and seldom did the law step in to protect abused youth. There was no "childhood" status and certainly no distinction of "life as a teenager." Education and leisure pursuits were luxuries reserved for children of the privileged class (Delaney, 2006B).

During the past 200 years the role and status of youngsters in society has changed dramatically. In the eighteenth and nineteenth centuries a separate stage of human development became recognized — childhood. Childhood was now viewed as a unique phase of life, where children were supposed to be protected and educated (Thornton and Voigt, 1992). From this point on, young people's identification changed from that of a "small adult" to that of a *child*. The designation of a childhood status also brought about different role expectations. Children were now free from full-time work obligations resulting in free time. Children who go unsupervised often engage in acts of delinquency. In an attempt to reduce the free time of children, and yet protect them from work obligations, mandatory education and truancy laws would be passed and sports activities developed and encouraged.

In the early 1800s, British educators, unlike other European faculty, frowned upon school sports but allowed students to participate in order to avoid student dissension. English college students (and youth) played cricket, soccer, an early version of rugby, and rowing. "The British Amateur Sport Ideal of playing the game for the game's sake, rather than for remuneration, prevailed in these sports competitions" (Lumpkin, 1994:190). Thomas Hughes' 1857 publication of *Tom Brown's School Days* embellished the sporting life of English football (soccer) and eventually had a significant influence on popularizing sports in American schools (Rader, 2004; Figler and

Whitaker, 1991). A figure who played a major influence in this development was the famous English educator Thomas Arnold.

The headmaster of Rugby School from 1828 to 1842, Dr. Thomas Arnold unintentionally encouraged the distinctive Rugby game. Intent on reforming the old lax and aristocratic nature of the public school, Arnold welcomed sons of professional and business families. He forbade traditional aristocratic field sports such as hunting, shooting, and fishing (which in fact meant poaching from fields and streams of farmers in the Rugby area), replacing them with team sports. A contemporary headmaster of Shrewsbury School, Samuel Butler, denounced football as a game "more fit for farm boys and labourers than young gentlemen," but at Dr. Arnold's Rugby School football was encouraged as a means of instilling manly virtues (Baker, 1982:120–121).

English politicians jumped on the bandwagon of the popularity of sport in schools. In 1861, the English Parliament's Clarendon Commission proclaimed that playing cricket and football promoted such social values as team spirit and group loyalty. Furthermore, it has often been reported that the Duke of Wellington stated that "The Battle of Waterloo was won on the playing fields of Eton;" implying that sports helped to prepare soldiers for battle. Furthermore, since Napoleon met his Waterloo at the hands of Wellington in 1815, it can be assumed that sports played an important role in English schools long before they received official recognition by the government (Figler and Whitaker, 1991).

Many modern sports have their origins in England. These sports were spread throughout the world during the English centuries of colonization. "Most American sports were introduced by and popularized by British colonists" (Lumpkin, 1994:191). The origins of sports in the United States can be traced to other European nations as well. The Greek glorification of sports and the overall aesthetic appeal of sports have made a lasting impact. Roman sport revealed how sporting venues could be used as spectator spectacles. European athletics in general, laid the foundation for sport programs in the United States.

Near the end of the nineteenth century, youth sports were equated with morality via an ideology known as "Muscular Christianity." Muscular Christianity, as the name implies, refers to a religious philosophy of teaching values via sport. Muscular Christianity had a grand impact on the development of sport in the United States and the United Kingdom.

> Most Protestants, and especially the Puritans, had viewed participation in sports and games as sinful. However, when people refused to conform to rigid prohibitions, attitudes gradually softened to permit sporting diversions as long as moral values could be taught and reinforced. Religion and sport peacefully

coexisted whenever ethical virtues remained foremost. Fair play, honorable victories, respect for the opponent, and sports for fun, not for winning at all costs,
characterized British upper-class and schoolboy sports (Lumpkin, 1994:190).

Organized youth sports were also being organized outside of the influence
of schools and religion through a "play movement." The continued massive
immigration occurring in the United States throughout the 1800s led to over-
crowded cities and youth with no place to play. As a result, a number of playgrounds were developed in Boston and New York City. The famous Hull
House in Chicago, established by Jane Addams, was also equipped with a
playground. By the turn of the century, numerous communities across the
U.S. created parks, playgrounds, and/or indoor facilities for youth sports.

As sports programs sprung up in and out of school it became increasingly
necessary to train people to teach physical education courses and to coach
sports. As a result of the National Education Association's recognition of
physical education as a subject of study in 1891, many colleges began to offer degrees in physical education.

Physical education programs flourished throughout the twentieth century.
Schools became involved in interscholastic athletic competitions. Organized
youth sport programs were developed for the summer months in an attempt
to keep children physical and athletically active year-round. The post-World
War II baby boom and increased leisure time led to the development of an extensive number of athletic programs. Sports received funding from a variety
of sources including public, private, and commercial sponsors. Parents were
actively involved as well. Generally, fathers served as coaches, managers, referees, and league administrators and mothers were responsible for driving
their kids to practice and games. Family dinner hour all but disappeared during summer months as kids had to eat on the run.

By the end of the 1970s, girls were beginning to participate in sports as
well. This development led to the creation of new sports programs. Today, a
number of organized youth sports programs remain hugely popular, including
Little League Baseball, Pop Warner Football, and the American Youth Soccer
Organization. Informal sport participation also remains very popular.

ORGANIZED YOUTH SPORTS

Compared to the past (as well as present-day less-developed nations), American youth (and youth of any Western society for that matter) of today have
much easier lives. They are expected to go to school and earn good grades
and many have household responsibilities such as doing the dishes, cleaning

the home, mowing the lawn, and so forth; but beyond that, they enjoy a great amount of leisure time. Just think of how many hours a day numerous youth spend on cell phones or playing video games instead of being required to do something productive, like working to earn their keep.

In an attempt to keep their children busy and away from the temptation of delinquency that comes with idleness, a number of parents enroll their kids in organized youth sports.

Formal Youth Baseball

The first step in many youngsters' indoctrination into organized baseball begins with T-ball. T-ball is a game designed to indoctrinate young children (starting around age 5) into the game of baseball. T-ball is geared to provide an outlet of healthy activity and training under the leadership of parents and to a lesser extent, coaches. The primary goals of T-ball involve establishing the values of teamwork, sportsmanship and fair play. As the name of this sport may imply, children swing a bat at a stationary ball placed on top of a batting "T." Because the ball is not moving, it is relatively easy to hit (similar to hitting a golf ball). After hitting the ball, the child is allowed to run the bases. Anyone who has watched a "T-ball" game knows how amusing this can be, as the child, responding to parents and coaches yelling "Run! Run!" often heads toward third base. Children barely understand the game of baseball at this age, but their desire to play the game spirits them onward. There is an "in-between" level of development in youth baseball after T-Ball and before Little League that involves a pitcher lobbing a soccer ball directly at the child's bat. In this case, the child merely needs to stick the bat out and he or she will hit it, and again, be afforded an opportunity to run the bases. The sense of achievement demonstrated by these youngsters is gratifying even to a cynical adult.

After T-Ball, many youth will play "pony league" baseball. At this level, children are playing "real" baseball, but in a relatively non-competitive manner. Little League baseball follows pony league ball. It is played by 11 and 12-year-olds. There are more than three million youths world-wide that play Little League baseball; making it the world's largest formal youth sports program. At the local level, Little League provides youths an opportunity to play competitive baseball against other youth with the same skills level. However, through regional tournaments, teams, including Tournament Teams of All Stars, can qualify for the Little League World Series (LLWS). Teams from all 50 U.S. states and more than 70 countries around the world compete against one another for the chance to meet in Williamsport (PA) for the annual LLWS held each August. The formal nature of the LLWS is revealed in a number of ways. For one, all 16 teams that qualify to play in Williamsport have their expenses paid (travel, meals, and housing) by Little League Baseball. Secondly, the game is televised live in the United States and in many other countries. And third, Little League Baseball has its own Hall of Fame Museum located in Williamsport.

Youngsters who wish to continue playing baseball formally (outside of school) can play in the Babe Ruth League. The BRL was formed over 50 years ago in honor of Babe Ruth. There are nearly 1 million 13–15 year-old participants in this league. There is also a Babe Ruth division for 16–18 year olds that has been growing in size over the years. It should also be noted that there exists a Cal Ripken division of organized baseball that parallels T-ball, Pony, and Little League Baseball.

Formal Youth Football

Many youth enjoy playing football with friends and family members. However, anyone with a desire to play professional football is likely to start their journey at the "Pop Warner" level of organized ball. Pop Warner Football precedes junior varsity, high school varsity, and college football. At the Pop Warner level of play, youth are taught the basics of football. The origins of Pop Warner Football can be traced to Philadelphia in the late 1920s when a group of factory owners—who were tired of having youth throw rocks through their factory's windows—decided to organize a youth football league. The factory owners believed that Philadelphia youth were turning to delinquency because they had too much free time on their hands. Playing football, they reasoned, would help to keep idle kids occupied and out of mischief.

The Philadelphia youth football league would eventually be named Pop Warner Football in honor of Glen Scobey "Pop" Warner, the legendary football coach at the Carlisle Indian School. Warner also coached at Cornell, Pittsburgh (where he won two national championships), Stanford (winning 3 Rose Bowls) and Temple. In 44 years as a coach, Warner compiled an incredible record of 312 wins, 104 loses, and 32 ties. Warner is credited with introducing a number of innovations to college football, including the spiral punt, the screen play, single- and double-wing formations, the naked reverse, the three-point stance, numbering players' jerseys, and the use of shoulder and thigh pads (*Pop Warner*, 2008).

By 1938, there were 157 teams in the league and most of the players were at least 15 years old and few were over 30 years old. With the onset of World War II, the Pop Warner Conference lost most of its older players to the war effort. Many squads folded, while others merged. After the war, the Pop

Warner league teams were composed mostly of kids 15 years old or younger. From the 1950s, the Pop Warner football league became a league strictly for youths to play. During this time, Pop Warner grew in popularity (in part because of the "Baby Boom") and became a national youth sports league. By the 1960s, Pop Warner Football was found in small towns, suburbs and cities. By the end of the decade there were over 3,000 teams.

Today, there are over 360,000 boys and girls, ages 5–16, mostly in the United States (there are teams in Japan and Mexico), playing in eight different age categories of Pop Warner Football (*Pop Warner*, 2008). In some areas of the country Pop Warner football is taken as seriously as high school or college football.

Pop Warner also sponsors the Pop Warner Little Scholars, a non-profit organization that provides youth football, cheer, and dance programs for youth ages 5 – 16. Pop Warner maintains a commitment to provide youth with opportunities to play football, cheerlead, and dance. It is the only national youth sports organization that requires scholastic aptitude to participate. Thus, if a youth's grades are not high enough, they cannot participate in Pop Warner (*Pop Warner*, 2008). As stated in the Pop Warner Rule book, The Pop Warner Football program stresses "lessons of value far beyond the playing days of boys and girls involved, such as: self-discipline, teamwork, concentration, friendship, leadership, and good sportsmanship."

Football is a very physical game and full body contact scares off many youth from participation. In addition, it is quite costly to equip a football team. These two factors help to explain why many parents and youth sought an alternative to football. This inexpensive and safer alternative is soccer.

Formal Youth Soccer

Soccer has grown tremendously in terms of popularity in the United States over the past two decades. As stated above, soccer represents a relatively inexpensive formal sport option as a ball and empty field are the only two real requirements. Soccer is an appealing sport for youth and parents because it is an easy sport to learn; especially when compared to baseball and football. Furthermore, there is little physical contact in soccer and youth are less likely to injured playing this sport than they are playing football and rugby.

According to the American Youth Soccer Organization (2008) there are approximately 13 million Americans under the age of eighteen who play soccer. Perhaps the most popular of all formal youth soccer associations is the American Youth Soccer Organization (AYSO). The AYSO was established in the Los Angeles area in 1964 with nine teams. Today, it sponsors more than 50,000 teams and more than 650,000 players. Nearly 40 percent of AYSO's players are girls (The American Youth Soccer Organization, 2008). The AYSO is a "nationwide non-profit organization that delivers quality youth soccer programs in a fun, family environment based on AYSO's Five Philosophies: everyone plays; balanced teams; open registration; positive coaching; and good sportsmanship" (The American Youth Soccer Organization, 2008).

With the great success of U.S. women's international soccer competition and the relative success of the men's national team, the popularity of soccer in the United States has not reached its peak. It is highly likely that youth will continue to play soccer in an organized (as well as informal) manner and in increasing numbers for some time to come.

Soap Box Derbies

Another popular form of organized youth sports is the well-known Soap Box Derby. The original derby started in 1933 in Dayton, Ohio and later moved to Akron. Derbies are now held throughout the United States. Myron E. Scott, a photographer for the Dayton *Daily News,* saw three young boys racing home-made engine-less cars down an inclined brick street. He came up with the idea of sponsoring a contest based upon this. Nineteen boys took part in the first event. There was no cash prize (this was during the heart of the Depression, when money was hard to come by for most Americans), and Scott was amazed by the enthusiasm of the participants, who competed just for fun. He was able to get the *Daily News* to sponsor a more formal race, with the then-princely prize of $200.00 for the winner, on August 19, 1933. Over 300 contestants took part, in vehicles made from orange crates, old wagon parts, baby buggies, and other scraps, although no actual soap box was apparently so utilized. Soon national competitions began, and a "soap box derby" craze swept the United States. It was felt that such events were good bonding experiences for fathers and sons, who worked together to create the various self-powered vehicles, and corporate sponsors soon began to make this a major event in most big cities.

Unfortunately, such sponsorship, by creating larger cash prizes, along with the danger of competitiveness, has sometimes led to cheating scandals. In 1973, for instance, the annual National Derby in Akron was won by fourteen-year old Jimmy Gronen, who hid a powerful magnet in his vehicle. It was later determined that his uncle, Robert Lange, Senior (whose son Robert Lange, Junior had, significantly, won the Derby the previous year) had helped his nephew develop the sophisticated gravitational system which illegally allowed him to win. Lange was unrepentant upon being discovered, and was quoted as saying: "It is common knowledge that eleven year olds cannot build winning racers . . . After seeing my nephew work hundreds of hours to build his own car, knowing that he would be competing in Akron against professionally built cars, and against cars that would be in violation of the official rules, and having heard that some fast cars in Akron would be equipped with a magnetic nose, I determined that he should build and install a magnetic nose so as to be in competitive" (Michener, 1976:117).

Since this scandal, the Derby administrators have been more vigilant about watching out for cheaters, and have made it a greater point to stress the fun aspects of the contest. In addition, the Derby itself has become much more of an international event, with participants now coming from throughout the world, and it has also welcomed the participation of female racers for many

---

Narrative 5.1.   An Interview with Mark Scuderi, Soap Box Derby Enthusiast

Rochester, New York native Mark Scuderi can attest to the positive aspects of Soap Box Derby participation. In 1968, as a young fatherless boy, Scuderi was befriended by a neighborhood postal deliverer who encouraged him to get involved in the local racing scene. Another of his mentors was Dr. Richard Rohrer, a dentist who had won the 1955 Soap Box Derby World Championship. Mark managed to raise enough money to buy the materials to build his own car, and the experience changed his life. In 1994, when his own daughter Julie, then aged 12, wanted to race, he helped to revitalize the Rochester association, which had disbanded after the national scandal mentioned above, with the withdrawal of sponsors who didn't want to be associated with it. Julie ended by going to Akron and placed 10th in the World Championships. Her brother Mark, Jr. would later win the European Championship in 2001. Their proud father has seen the annual Rochester event draw a larger audience each year, with growing sponsorship and increased media attention. "I've never said no to any kid who's called me and wanted to race", Scuderi said. Many of the children are handicapped, or live in foster homes. "All those guys who helped me race in 1968", he added, "made such a difference in my life, but I didn't know it at the time. Now I'm trying to do the same for those kids" (Giles, 2005). Scuderi also accompanied Richard Rohrer to Akron in 2005 for the 50th anniversary celebration of his championship there. Rohrer died a few weeks later, but was happy to know that his legacy has lived on.

In an interview with the authors of this text, Scuderi adds: "It's important to remember that a true national scandal would involve the All-American Soap Box Derby somehow being involved in one car having an unfair advantage. In the 1973 case, an individual was involved in their own unfair advantage and the All-American eventually uncovered the plot and disqualified the perpetrator. The Soap Box Derby could easily have hushed up the incident and suffered no negative publicity or sponsor backlash. However, that's not what the Soap Box Derby is about. 1973 was a simpler time. We actually disqualified another champion about 5 years ago and no one even heard about it."

years. Its colorful history has been chronicled in Melanie Payne's 2003 book *Champions, Cheaters, and Childhood Dreams: Memories of the All-American Soap Box Derby.*

The popularity of soap box derbies rests with the realization that parents and youth can work together on this sporting activity. And any opportunity for family bonding would reflect why so many people love sports.

There are numerous other examples of formal youth sports that we have not reviewed. (This is not meant to diminish their importance to the participants.) Gymnastics, for example is another type of organized youth sport and it is open to both boys and girls. Heather Gibson, a former competitive gymnast and coach, explains that gymnastics helps to keep participants in shape while teaching them valuable life lessons in discipline and dedication. (See Narrative #5.2 for Gibson's take on the value of gymnastics.)

**Narrative 5.2.   An Interview with Heather Gibson, a level
9 competitive gymnast and coach of the level 4 & 5 team
at Wimbleton Gymnastics in Memphis, TN.**

1. At what age did you first become involved in gymnastics?

    I was 12 when I started gymnastics. There wasn't a gym in our area, but I had taken dance/tumbling and was much more interested in the tumbling. My mom took me to all the gyms in Memphis, all of them about 30 miles away, and I fell in love with Wimbleton Gymnastics.

2. What do you consider the positive aspects of gymnastics to be?

    Of course gymnastics keeps you healthy and physically fit, and it also teaches you discipline and dedication.

3. What is the best age for children to first start gymnastic training?

    I think children should be at least 4 or 5. Children younger than this don't have the attention span or physical ability.

4. What were some of the highlights of you own gymnastic career?

    Some of the highlights are: getting my first 9.0, winning 3 events and the AA at level 8 State meet, winning 10 State titles, qualifying to Regionals 3 times, winning 2 bronze medals at Regionals, becoming a head coach at my gym, having 3 of my girls win State titles my first year coaching them.

5. Who are your sports heroes, male and female, and why?

    My favorite gymnast is Shannon Miller. She was always a great role model in and out of the gym. I admire John Roethlisberger for staying in the sport for so long. Another sports hero of mine is Michele Kwan. All 3 of these athletes have been so successful because of their dedication and love for their sport. As for the current Olympic gymnasts, I absolutely love Nastia Liukin and Shawn Johnson. Regarding the sport itself, I was very disappointed in a lot of the judging that

I saw in Beijing. I also do not like the new scoring system—gymnastics is not gymnastics without the perfect 10!

6. Is gymnastics something that young girls in particular should consider, and if so, why?

Most girls like to stay in shape and gymnastics is the perfect way to do so!

7. How important are coaches? How does your own experience of being a coach differ from your experiences as a gymnast?

Coaches are extremely important, especially for younger gymnasts. It has been easy for me to switch my attention from myself to my gymnasts and their routines at meets. It's just as exciting when they hit their routines as it is when I do well.

Most, but certainly not all, youth find great benefit from their organized youth sport participation. Formal youth sports prepare participants for the dominant features of society, including: adult-controlled activity; activity that is often repetitious and boring; elitism, the better performers play more often; organization via a playbook/work manual; an emphasis on specialization; rule enforcement; and people who evaluate performance, coaches/bosses; and personal and family schedules that need to be adjusted to meet the needs of sport/work.

However, youth are not adults. And the current structure of society allows young people to act like young people free from adult responsibilities, such as work. Thus, it should come as no surprise that many youth are turned off by organized sports and all the rules and structure associated with organized sports. As a result, many youth turn to informal sports because they are less structured and offer greater freedom and creativity.

INFORMAL SPORTS

There are alternatives to organized youth sport. In fact, most kids who participate in organized youth sports still participate in less formal sporting activities such skateboarding, BMX biking, and snowboarding. Consider the elements in these activities that appeal to kids more than traditional sports programs:

- No need to register to participate
- No required practices
- No adults telling them what to do or not to do
- No scoreboard
- No sitting on the bench watching while others deemed worthier participate

Informal sports also allow youths the freedom to be creative in developing their own individual styles of play while using the fundamentals of the sport as their foundation. Kids who participate in these informal sports seem to have a more widespread dedication to learning the basics and perfecting them alone or with the help of friends. Most importantly, these youth find ways to make the entire process fun.

It is not completely accurate to say that informal sports are the opposite of organized or formal sports, because in many cases the two overlap. In other words, youth football can be played in an organized fashion as part of Pop Warner, but it can also be played by a group of friends in someone's yard. But informal sports are quite different in that the game is player-controlled, free from governing bodies and adult supervision and allows for flexible rule changes such as three older kids against five younger ones. The allure of flexible rule changes reinforces a number of general characteristics of informal sports that include, activity that is player-controlled; activity that leads to action, especially scoring; action that maximizes personal involvement; spontaneity, such as the allowance of "do-overs;" no adult interference in the form of referees; a close score and relatively even teams; and, no time limits or minimum time requirements, kids can quit whenever they want.

Informal sports include such sports as skateboarding, bike riding, running, fishing, hunting, and all the other traditional sports that are free from league supervision. According to 2001 statistics complied by the American Sports Data (SGMA International "Superstudy"), many of the most popular sports for youngsters are informal sports (Connors, 2002):

Activity—Participants (in millions):
 1. Basketball—11.287
 2. Soccer—7.692
 3. Inline Skating—7.482
 4. Baseball—4.719
 5. Scooter riding—4.469
 6. Freshwater fishing—3.712
 7. Running/jogging—3.340
 8. Calisthenics—3.327
 9. Stretching—3.169
10. Skateboarding—3.144

Sports such as inline skating and skateboarding continue to gain in popularity due in part to increased media exposure. However, as we have seen with the introduction of ESPN's "X Games" (which reached its fourteenth year in

2008), many informal sports have become organized and supervised by governing entities and covered by the mass media.

FINAL THOUGHTS

Most youth enjoy playing sports; some prefer organized versions and others prefer informal sporting activities. Some children experience injuries, burnout, or frustration with organized youth sports and turn to informal sports. Experiences with sports during childhood can affect one's outlook on sport as he or she ages.

Organized formal youth sports are viewed by some as a means of social mobility. They believe that if the child hones his or her skills while young, that he or she may some day find fame and fortune at the professional level. With that idea in mind, there will always be those who favor organized youth sports.

An important factor in whether children should participate in sports is their own desires to do so. There are a wide variety of sport options, both formal and informal, that should be made available to youths so that they can try them out and decide for themselves which, if any, they enjoy playing.

Organized youth sports have arisen throughout the Western World since the middle of the nineteenth century, and have been linked with physical education. Such formal youth sports, including Little League Baseball, Pop Warner Football, and Youth Soccer Leagues, have become an integral part of American culture.

Generally, the love of sports that millions of Americans share was likely to have been cultivated in their youth.

Chapter Six

High School and College Sports: The Passion Continues

During the summer of 2008, ESPN aired a story on Mixed Martial Arts (MMA) during one of its "Outside the Lines" programs. A number of participants were interviewed and asked about MMA. One girl said that she enjoyed MMA but would most likely quit this controversial sport when she reached high school. She noted that she wanted to play "regular" sports, like cheerleading.

Mmm . . . cheerleading a sport? Undoubtedly there are people who would disagree with the notion that cheerleading is a sport. On the other hand, there is an argument to be made that some forms of cheerleading should qualify as a sport. As discussed in chapter 1, labeling particular activities as a "sport" is a matter of definition. Because cheerleading has long been an aspect of high school and college sports we will take a closer look at this popular sporting activity later in this chapter.

HIGH SCHOOL SPORTS

By the time formal youth sport athletes reach high school they have three primary courses of action with regard to sports: they may continue to play sports; stop playing sports and transform their sports identity to that of a fan; or give up on sports entirely. Non-youth sport athletes have roughly the same three options: start playing formal sports; become/remain a sports fan; or have little or nothing to do with sports. Because sports are a very important aspect of the social life of high schools across the United States, most students are either participants or fans.

Students who opt to ignore their high school sports teams are often the social outcasts. Some may think they are too cool for sports while others may have different priorities such as helping out with family matters. In some school districts, many high school aged students are already members of a street gang and have no time or desire to support their schools' sports teams. Students who attend games and befriend the athletes are almost always involved with social events like school dances and house parties. It is the athletes, however, that benefit the most from high school sports participation. Being a star athlete all but assures one a certain level of popularity in high school. It surely draws a great deal of attention to oneself.

And this has been the case for multiple generations. Consider that research dating back to Abraham J. Tannenbaum's classic 1960 study has consistently revealed that high school aged youngsters admire athletes more than nonathletes. Tannenbaum presented 615 high school juniors with written descriptions of stereotyped, fictitious students. On the basis of the traits ascribed for each of these fictitious students, respondents were asked to rank them in order of most to least acceptable. The results are shown below:

1. Brilliant nonstudious athlete
2. Average nonstudious athlete
3. Average studious athlete
4. Brilliant studious athlete
5. Brilliant nonstudious nonathlete
6. Average nonstudious nonathletes
7. Average studious nonathletes
8. Brilliant studious nonathletes (Eitzen and Sage, 1989)

The results indicate that the "dumb jock" (brilliant nonstudious athlete) was rated the most acceptable, while the brilliant studious nonathlete was ranked the lowest. Even when athletes were equal in athletic "brilliance" the nonstudious one was more popular than the studious one. Coleman (1961) argued that the reason the brilliant athlete was so admired was because he (or she) brought glory to the whole school, while the brilliant scholar brought glory only to him or herself. Consequently, high school students would rather be known as great athletes than great scholars. In other words, it is uncool to be smart, but very cool to score touchdowns, hit homeruns, or score a winning basket.

This attitude changes in college, of course, as the vast majority of college students have no delusion about playing professional sports and therefore realize the importance of earning good grades and acquiring knowledge that will help them find a well-paying job. Furthermore, as the authors can attest (and other college professors have also noted), freshmen and sophomores are unlikely to visit professors during their office hours, whereas juniors and seniors are far more likely to do so. Upper-level students recognize that they will soon be in "the real world" and that good grades are important to their success after college. Lower division students tend to keep with them the carry-over affect learned in high school—that talking to teachers is uncool. Juniors and especially college seniors realize, too, that they may need help from their professors finding a job (e.g., the need for a letter of recommendation).

The Consequences of Interscholastic Sport Participation

Since athletes are often the most highly valued individuals in their schools, and the social life (e.g., school dances, pep rallies, homecoming) of most high schools center around sports, successful athletes generally enjoy an inflated sense of self and social life. High school athletes receive a great deal of attention, cheers, relative fame, write-ups in the local or school newspaper, and if the program is big-time, radio and television coverage. In smaller towns and cities the local merchants are likely to proudly proclaim that they are "Panthers supporters" and will place posters and banners in sport of the hometown team. And when small towns when big championships the school colors will dominate the local landscape.

The fame that comes with being a high school star athlete was a male reserve until fairly recently. Before the passage of Title IX in 1972 girls had far fewer opportunities to play sports. And even with the passage of this landmark legislation it still took a couple of decades before girls were playing high school sports in significant numbers. Overcoming sexist resistance further hampered the acceptance of female athletes as "true" stars. Things began to change in earnest by the mid-1990s. For example, Madeleine Blais, author of *In These Girls, Hope is a Muscle,* writes about a girls' high school team in Amherst, Massachusetts which becomes state champion in the early 1990s. Donald Poe, father of key player Kathleen Poe, saw the significance of the attention the team received during its championship season:

> To him, what was important was not that Amherst had this great lead, but that the spirit of girls' sports endured. Next year, it wouldn't have to be Amherst; it might be West Side in Springfield. Its junior varsity was undefeated. When he'd been a student at W. T. Woodson High School in Fairfax, Virginia, the girls were not allowed to use the boys' gym, which was fancy and varnished with the logo in the middle of the floor; the girls had a little back gym, without any bleachers. Now, after a game, whenever he saw the little kids asking his daughter for autographs, he was glad to see the girls, pleased that they had models. But he was just as pleased to see the boys asking; to him their respect for the girls' team was just as important (Blais, 1995: 254).

Success draws attention to high school athletes whether they are boys or girls. However, because boys' sports are still viewed more favorably than girls' sports, it is most likely that the male stars will enjoy the greatest accolades.

The awareness that sport participation brings to high school athletes places them in a potentially advantageous social position. They seem to receive special treatment from teachers, administrators and community members. In short, top jocks often "rule" the schools. However, all teenagers are not the same and some have a hard time dealing with attention and stress that accompanies heightened expectations. While youth sports present the pretense that participation is all about fun, high school sports do not hide the fact that winning is the primary goal. Egalitarianism is replaced by elitism, meaning that the stars play more often than the role players. And those less-talented may not play at all. Star players may seem like they *have* it all, but in actuality, they have to *do* it all. That is, athletes must balance educational, social, and family duties and responsibilities like non-athletes, but they must also find a way to incorporate hours of practice with the pressure of performing in front of others on game day. When expectations are high, performance anxiety may occur. Some athletes may find all these demands to be a bit overwhelming. On the positive side, athletes that find the proper balance between all these social expectations may be better prepared for the work-world that demands multi-tasking abilities.

High School Sport Participation on the Rise

According to the National Federation of State High School Associations (NFHS) (2007), the number of high school athletes increased for the eighteenth consecutive year. Based on figures from the 50 state high school athletic/activity associations, plus the District of Columbia, there were over 7.3 million boys and girls playing high school sports during the 2006–07 academic year (NFHS, 2007). And, for the first time, girls' participation exceeded three million with 3,021,807 females participating in 2006–07 (NFHS, 2007). The 4,321,103 million boys playing high school sports is the second highest number ever, trailing only the "Baby-boom" produced 4,367,442 figure recorded in 1977–78. Texas has the highest total number of high school athletes (763,967), followed by California (735,497), and New York (350,349).

The most popular sport by gender remains as football (11-player) for boys and basketball for girls. According to data complied by the NFHS (2007) the breakdown is represented in Table 6.1.

Table 6.1.   High School Sport Participation

Boys Sports	Girls Sports
Football—1,104,548	Basketball—456,967
Basketball—556,269	Outdoor track and field—444,181
Outdoor track and field—544,180	Volleyball—405,832
Baseball—477,430	Fast-pitch softball—373,448
Soccer—377,999	Soccer—337,632
Wrestling—257,246	Cross country—183,376
Cross country—216,085	Tennis—176,696
Golf—159,747	Swimming and diving—143,639
Tennis—156,944	Competitive spirit squads—95,177
Swimming and diving—106,738	Golf—66,283

More than 7.3 million athletes would seem to indicate that the love of sport is alive and well in high schools across the United States. It should also be noted that many students this age play organized sports outside of school. For example, there are elite high school aged soccer players who play on club teams; competitive spirit squads (cheerleaders) that also have club associations; baseball players that play in leagues such as the American Legion; and hockey players who play in Junior hockey leagues.

Whether high school aged athletes play on high school teams or private club teams, they both possess many critical elements of formal sports: an emphasis on rules, rule enforcement, referees, and governing bodies, just to mention a few. The existence of governing bodies is important when the emphasis of sport participation shifts from having fun to winning.

Athletic Training

Another important aspect of formal sports is athletic training. With informal sports, participants are more or less on their own to develop new and enhance existing skills. Club teams and high school sport programs provide coaches and trainers. The activities of high school athletic trainers are guided by the National Athletic Trainers Association (NATA). As the governing body of athletic training, NATA sponsors certification through its Board of Certification (NATABOC). "Historically the practice of athletic training was confined to the collegiate sports setting with an emphasis on caring for injuries in tackle football. It was not until the 1970s that this situation changed significantly, as the services of athletic trainers began to be recognized as extremely valuable in the high school sport setting" (Pfeiffer and Mangus, 2002:23).

Because of the costs involved with hiring a certified athletic trainer, less than half of all high schools in the U.S. have access to a NATABOC-certified

Narrative 6.1.   An Interview with Jim Thompson, founder of the Positive Coaching Alliance, a national nonprofit organization based at the Stanford University Department of Athletics.

1. What do you mean by the concept of "double-goal coach"?

    A Double-Goal Coach wants to win (goal #1) and has the even more important goal of using sports to teach life lessons. There is a unending procession of "teachable moments" that youth sports provides but often those moments are lost because coaches and parents are under the spell of a win-at-all-cost mentality. A Double-Goal Coach is always looking for the opportunity to teach life lessons and reinforce positive character traits, no matter what happens on the scoreboard.

2. How do you try to overcome the "win-at-all-costs" mentality?

    Many youth coaches operate from a mistaken model of coaching—they act as if winning is the only goal of youth sports. This "mental model" of win-at-all-cost is often subconscious because if it were raised to the conscious level people would realize how crazy it is. Because the win-at-all-cost model is subconscious, it can control how coaches (and parents) behave. PCA changes that model by psychologically "unfreezing" coaches and parents, and replacing the win-at-all-cost model with the model of the Double-Goal Coach. This is why we think live workshops are so crucial—it is hard to unfreeze a win-at-all-cost coach with a book or video. When you get coaches in a room with a dynamic trainer with deep coaching experience who engages them in an interactive workshop with practical tools that will make them better coaches both on the scoreboard and in terms of life lessons, you see them unfreeze and open them up to this new model. Then when these coaches start to use the tools we teach them, they find that they work! And so the movement grows. It has been a challenge but we have developed a network of more than 100 trainers around the U.S. who deliver our workshops.

3. How can youth coaches work with parents and other adults to have a more positive impact on athletes?

    Coaches set the tone for their team and the parents of their players. Coaches who embrace the Double-Goal Coach model coach in a way that calls forth the best from their athletes. They also set a standard for parents of being "Second-Goal Parents" who let athletes and coaches worry about winning. Second-Goal Parents have a much more important job—to ensure that their children take away from sports the life lessons that will allow them to be successful after their playing days are over.

4. What do you consider to be the major problems facing youth coaches today?

    The biggest challenge facing youth coaches is to coach in a way that recognizes the potential for youth sports to be a virtual classroom for teaching life lessons and positive character traits. Keeping their eyes on the ball regarding

(*continued*)

Narrative 6.1. (*continued*)

the second goal of teaching life lessons through sports in the face of a larger sports culture that promotes win-at-all-cost coaching and competing can be difficult. The win-at-all-cost model promoted by the sports media and professional sports is incredibly powerful and can erupt in a moment to undo the great work of Double-Goal Coaching.

5. You've used the expression "The Battle for the Soul of Youth Sports"—can you explain what you mean by this?

Professional sports is an entertainment business with a huge marketing reach. Youth sports should be about the education of youth. However, many adults involved with youth sports are confused about the difference. Because the rules, equipment and playing surfaces are similar, people tend to think that the experience of professional sports and youth sports should also be the same, which leads to dreadful outcomes!

Adults come to youth sports events with the same mindset as those of professional sports—almost anything goes if it helps our team win. This leads to the kind of horrific actions by coaches, athletes, parents and fans that Positive Coaching Alliance has publicized with our "Bottom 10 Moments in Sports," available at www.positivecoach.org.

The battle for the soul of youth sports is fundamentally a cultural struggle. Professional sports has an entertainment culture in which entertaining fans and corporate sponsors is the goal because that leads to a profitable business. Virtually every decision is made with an eye to making money which results from a winning team. Therefore at the professional level of sports, a win-at-all-cost mentality has some rationality—people don't want to buy tickets or season box suites for teams that are losers. At the youth sports level this mentality is a tragedy, which is why it is so critical that youth sports not be allowed to continue becoming a subsidiary of the professional sports entertainment business.

PCA defines culture as "the way WE do things HERE." At the youth sports level, every decision should be made with an eye to what is best for the educational development of the youth participating in sports. The culture of youth sports—the way we do things in youth sports—needs to be focused on the development of self-confident, capable, empathetic, contributing members of society.

---

athletic trainer (Pfeiffer and Mangus, 2002). Most parents of high school athletes, especially of those who play football, lacrosse and hockey, want their high school to have a full time athletic trainer. The trainer can help athletes prevent injuries, recover from injuries, maintain strength and provide tips on how to eat right. Each state maintains their own guidelines regarding athletic trainers at high schools. In New York, for example, the state Education Department does not require schools to have athletic trainers. However, the New York State Athletic Trainers Association recommends that all schools have them. Only about one-third of the approximate 950 high schools in New York have athletic trainers (Groom, 2004). Athletic trainers are taught to recognize and treat specific injuries which can reduce the number of referrals to doctors and specialists. Schools without trainers often look to the coach to address injuries of players. Unfortunately, most coaches are not trained as athletic trainers (though they are all trained in CPR—cardiopulmonary resuscitation—and first aid) and they must concentrate on *coaching* players. Athletic trainers are a wise investment. They help to prolong the playing careers of many athletes and in some cases help to save lives.

Socialization and School Support

Sports serve as social worlds by providing an environment where students can rally and show school spirit. As for the former, sports provide individuals with opportunities to bond with others (especially in team sports). It also offers sport participants a chance to stand out above others; in other words, sport provides a social arena for individuals to be noticed and perhaps star. Both success and failure are far more visible in athletics than in academics. Most students are unaware of the test scores of other students (especially today with privacy concerns and where grades are no longer posted by a student's name or social security number), but the entire community (and in some cases the entire nation) is aware of the results of high school sports. Sport participation provides a high school athlete with an enhanced social status both in school and in the community. For obvious reasons, athletes that play on a winning team benefit the most. In addition, some sports (e.g., football and basketball) are valued far more than others (e.g., tennis and golf) are and, as a result, mere participation on such teams provides a social status benefit.

As mentioned earlier, high school sports are often the center of school spirit activities. Dances, pep rallies and homecomings, are routinely scheduled around sporting events; especially the elite sports of football and basketball. At pep rallies and sporting events, students wear the school colors and proudly proclaim that their school is "Number One!" Team songs are often sung by the entire student body. Such occasions provide school administrators with an opportunity to address the students on fundamental issues (such as proper behavior) while rallying the community to get behind the home team and cheer them onto victory (or console the players in defeat). Success on the playing field brings increased school spirit and a general willingness to support other school programs. (And, as we shall see later, success in college sports increases enrollment.) Further, sport participation, and the corresponding school spirit that comes with it, encourages younger children to pursue athletic and physical activity so that they too may one day bask in the glory of being an interscholastic athlete.

High school sports are generally a positive experience for athletes. Periodically, high school sports provide us with stories of inspiration. Bobby Martin, a former high school football player at Dayton's (Ohio) Colonel White High School, who was born with no legs, serves as such an inspiration. He moved on the field by using his hands and arms and generally played on defense and special teams (kicking teams). In a September 16 (2005) game referees barred Martin from playing in the second half because he did not wear the proper equipment specified by the National Federation of State High School Associations handbook. He wasn't wearing shoes, knee pads or thigh pads. Days later, Martin was ruled eligible for the remaining season. The 3-foot-1, 17 year-old was also on the high school wrestling team (Valade, 2005). Martin serves as an inspiration to anyone who questions his or her own ability to overcome great odds and achieve.

COLLEGE SPORTS

Many people perceive that graduating from college will provide them with a better chance for economic stability. For the most part, this is true, as college graduates earn more money, on average, than non-college graduates. However, many potential college students are not quite sure which college is "best" for them. If earning lots of money is a top priority, a recent Forbes (2008) report indicates that graduates from Dartmouth College finish on top of the list of earnings of alumni at colleges around the country with a median compensation of $134,000. Princeton University graduates came in at second place with a median income of $131,000. Of course, it is rather difficult to gain entry into Dartmouth and Princeton, as well as any Ivy League school for that matter, so these colleges may not be an option for all would-be collegians. Furthermore, the only public college to break the top 20 list of earnings for its graduates was the University of California at Berkeley (it ranked twelfth with a median salary of $112,000).

Perhaps the prestigious colleges and universities are not an option. There are still lots of other factors to consider. For example, maybe you want to play sports, but you realize you are only good enough to play intramural sports. According to the 2008 Princeton Review (not affiliated with Princeton University), an organization that conducts extensive (more than 120,000 students are interviewed) nationwide research (368 colleges in 2008) on a variety of topics, the University of Notre Dame ranks #1 in the nation in intramural sport participation. As reported in the *Niles Daily Star* (2008), more than 91 percent of Notre Dame's student body participated in at least one program during the 2007–08 year. Notre Dame also ranked third nationally in "filling the stands for games" and fifth in the "jock schools" category. The University of Florida ranked number one in "filling the stands for the games."

The ability of the Gator faithful to fill sports stadiums is a concern for administrators at the University of Florida. No, they don't mind the economic windfall attached to the popularity of their sports teams. Instead, it is all the parties, before and after games, that has officials concerned in Gainesville. The success of Gator sports is the major contributor to Florida's number one ranking as the "best party school" in the country. Although Gator bureaucrats are not seeking Brigham Young University's number one ranking (for the eleventh consecutive year) as the top "stone-cold sober" school in the nation, they do not care for the negative publicity that comes with being associated as the top party school in the land. Although there are certainly many brilliant students at Florida, a large number of students are there primarily to party.

Officials at any college will state that their number one goal is to educate students. However, savvy administrators realize that with the costs of a "party reputation" that winning college sports team may bring to some campuses, there are also potential rewards; specifically, increased enrollment. Based on recent research, winning in sports does bring universities more students. This relationship is known as the "Flutie Effect."

The Flutie Effect

The "Flutie Effect" refers to Boston College's 30 percent enrollment increase in the two years after quarterback Doug Flutie's "Hail Mary" pass that beat Miami in 1984. Although Boston College did not go on to win the mythical national championship in college football in 1984, the media's positive portrayal of the seemingly over-achiever Flutie's accomplishments was enough to entice a number of people to enroll at BC. (Flutie won the Heisman trophy that year, an honor bestowed upon college football's best player based on voting from a panel of sports writers across the nation.) Indiana University professor Murray Sperber (author of several books on college big-time sports) receives credit for coining the term "Flutie Effect."

Motivated by the enrollment statistics that led to the naming of the "Flutie Effect" at Boston College, brothers Jaren Pope (an assistant professor in applied economics at Virginia Tech) and Devin Pope (an assistant professor at the University of Pennsylvania's Wharton School) conducted their own research to see whether or not the Flutie Effect is applicable at other schools.

The brothers compared information on freshman classes at 330 NCAA Division I schools with how the school's teams fared from 1983 through 2002 (Potter, 2008). Among their conclusions:

- Any college that makes it to the field of 65 for the Men's Basketball Tournament will see an average increase in enrollment of 1 percent. Schools that make it to the "Sweet 16" in the tournament see an average 3 percent boost in applications the following year. While the college that wins the championship is likely to see a 7 to 8 percent increase in enrollment the following year.
- George Mason University (outside Washington, D.C.) enjoyed a whopping 22 percent increase in freshmen applications following its magical run in the men's tournament in 2006—they reached the Final Four.
- Applications go up 7 to 8 percent at all schools that win a national championship in football.
- Schools that finish in the Top 20 rankings in football have a 2.5 percent gain.

As these statistics indicate, Americans do not simply love sports, they love sports *winners*. And the University of Florida has enjoyed national championships in both basketball and football in recent years. No wonder there is a great deal of partying going on in Gainesville: they have lots to celebrate.

Community Support

Of course, it is not just the students who support college athletics. Students, as the cliché states, come and go. Every year, graduating students are replaced by incoming students. But there is a constant. And that constant is the community, alumni, and general fan-base that cheers for certain college sports teams year after year. In many cases, people have cheered for a particular college an entire lifetime and long before a freshmen class joins the bandwagon. However, it's not just college-aged students that join the bandwagon. Community members also like to support a winning team. And when a team wins, it is more likely to draw fans from the community. In economic terms, when demand is high and supply is low, prices go up. Colleges and universities raise ticket prices for winning teams and because of our desire to be identified with a winner, sports fans will pay any "reasonable" price. Colleges have an additional way of making money on sports teams beyond the sale of tickets. Season ticket holders must make a donation to the school just for the privilege of being able to pay for season tickets. (One of the authors has been making regular "donations" for years to watch his favorite college basketball team play winning hoops!)

In our earlier discussion of the most popular sports in the United States, it was revealed that professional football ranks as number one among Americans; but recall that college football ranks number two. Many fans find college sports to be more fun and entertaining. The simple fact that there are far more college sports teams than professional teams helps to explain, in part, the huge legions of supporters. In addition, and importantly, there is little, or no, chance of a college relocating, as many professional sports franchises do. In this regard, an emotional attachment to a favorite college sports team will not be ripped apart by a greedy owner that wishes to make more money and as a result, moves the team to a new market. The United States is unique in its passion for college sports. And American colleges and universities field multiple teams for us to cheer.

The passion Americans have for college sports did not begin with Doug Flutie. It not only predates his playing days and his birth, it predates the birth of his great-great-grandparents.

The Early Development of Collegiate Sport

Collegiate sports have their roots in England with the primary rivals of Oxford, formed in 1167, and Cambridge, founded forty years later, dominating sport competition. The sports played at these two universities reflected the

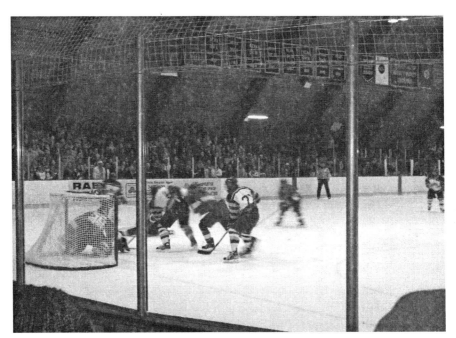

Fans pack an ice hockey rink to watch a college men's hockey game. (Courtesy Tim Delaney)

elite socio-economic status of the students. During the sixteenth, seventeenth and eighteenth centuries the primary sports were boating, cricket, horse racing, hunting, lawn bowling, boxing, cock-fighting and tennis (Smith, 1988). The first official intercollegiate sport in England is the Oxford-Cambridge cricket match at Lord's Ground in London in 1827. Rowing was added to the competition between these two universities a couple of years later. In June 10, 1829, Charles Wordsworth and Charles Merivale, "two former Harrovians studying at Oxford and at Cambridge, organized a boat race on the Thames" (Guttmann, 2004:95). By the late 1820s, most colleges at Cambridge had assembled their own rowing crews.

As found in England, a number of U.S. colleges fielded sports teams before the origin of official intercollegiate sporting events. In 1839, Harvard freshmen played versions of both baseball and football; while at Dartmouth students played football. The first American intercollegiate sporting event took place in 1852 on Lake Winnipesauke, New Hampshire, in a regatta between Harvard and Yale. The eight-day event, won by Harvard, was paid (all expenses) by industrialist James Elkins and organized by Yale's James Whiton. (Note, in 1861, Whiton became the first recipient of a Ph.D. in the United States. His dissertation was a mere 6 pages—in Latin.) The Yale and Harvard athletes were provided with "lavish prizes" and "unlimited alcohol". There were nearly one thousand spectators for this event, indicating to Elkins that collegiate sports possessed a commercial appeal.

> Intercollegiate sport, after that first meet, grew up with the emerging industrial America. Colleges and their sports took on many of the features of the larger America and its capitalistic rush for wealth, power, recognition, and influence. In the years between 1852 and the initial meeting of the National Collegiate Athletic Association in 1905, the basis for the highly commercial and professional sports in colleges was established. Huge crowds in enormous stadiums with large gate receipts, highly paid coaches in control of recruited athletes receiving handsome financial rewards, and the media telling the story and promoting the events were all in evidence (Smith, 1988: 4).

As Andrew Zimbalist (1999) points out, this regatta, and first intercollegiate sports event in the US, is also the first known eligibility abuse case. "The Harvard coxswain was not a student, but an alumnus" (Zimbalist, 1999:7). Thus, scandal in collegiate sports can be traced back to day one.

The number of sports played by colleges in intercollegiate athletics would increase slowly at first and then increase dramatically by the end of the nineteenth century. "In 1859 Williams lost to Amherst in the first intercollegiate baseball contest (by a score of 73-32!), and in 1869 Princeton lost to Rutgers in the first football game" (Shulman and Bowen, 2001:6). Football was the sport that developed the quickest. The football played on college campuses in the late 1800s was far different than the football played today, but with the absorption of many rugby rules, the game would transform itself to a more familiar modern version. Richard Goldstein (1996) writes that:

> In November 1872, Yale issued a challenge to Columbia and came away with a 3-goals-to-0 victory at the Hamilton Park racetrack oval in New Haven. Columbia played Rutgers twice, a scoreless tie and then a 7-5 defeat. In October 1873, things began to get organized. A convention was held at New York City's Fifth Avenue Hotel out of which sprang the Intercollegiate Football Association, comprising Yale, Columbia, Princeton, and Rutgers. Harvard has also been invited but stayed away (Goldstein, 1996:6).

By the 1890s, 40,000 fans were attending football games. "By 1905, football was living up to the 'larger than life' legend that was building around it. Because passions ran so high and rules were still being improvised and ingeniously manipulated, the game took on a brutal tone . . . People were dying—literally—for their schools; eighteen players died playing football in 1905 alone" (Shulman and Bowen, 2001:7). The introduction of the "forward pass" is credited with changing the game of football. The forward pass was designed to eliminate a lot of the scrum activities characteristic of rugby. By "opening" up the game, and allowing players to use their hands, American football had distanced itself from rugby and soccer.

Michael Oriard (1993) argues that the growth of football as a national sport was directly connected with the rise of the popular press: the two immediately took to each other.

> Football's formative years were also a golden age of print, an era when more newspapers and periodicals reached more people and a wider range of readers than in any time before, and when the print media had greater power than in any time after. Books and magazines, even newspapers, had been largely restricted to the privileged economic classes until the 1830s, when the first "penny papers" issued in the age of cheap print. The expansion of literacy, new technologies in printing and in the manufacture of paper from inexpensive and abundant wood pulp, and new possibilities for distribution and marketing contributed to a revolution in reading of incalculable importance. By the second half of the nineteenth century, virtually every American was a reader of newspapers and magazines . . . In the 1890s, football was discovered by most Americans in the newspaper (Oriand, 1993:xix-xx).

By the turn of the twentieth century, sport had become an official function of most post-secondary schools. There are a number of reasons why sports became so intertwined with colleges:

> The lack of a clear, accepted definition of the purposes and programs of the American college; unabated pressure on administrators to secure students and

funds for their institutions; the relative weakness of the faculty vis-à-vis the administration; industrialization, which had promoted urbanization, leisure, and expendable capital; technological advances in transportation and communications that promoted the possibilities of extraregional student recruiting; the development of a psychology that legitimized adolescence and supervised play; the business orientation of a new breed of college presidents and trustees who replaced the religiously and academically grounded administrators of an earlier time; and the effects of the newly rediscovered Olympic Games and the English sporting tradition (Chu, 1989: 49).

In short, there were a number of factors that assured the primary role of sport in colleges and universities throughout the United States—they grew together. The commercialization of athletics combined with the growth of the entertainment industry would assure that college sports would remain important throughout the twentieth century and entering the twenty-first century.

Student-Athlete

Time management skills are important for all college students, but they are especially critical for student-athletes. The ability to learn to handle schoolwork, sports practices and games are invaluable for success at college. Ideally, these lessons were learned in high school. Interestingly, many athletes have more difficulty with their grades and schoolwork during their "off-season." The primary reason for this is the relaxed feeling athletes have while their sport is not in season. The need to relax and rebuild muscles and strength (and perhaps recover from an injury) sometimes leads to slacking off at school work. Getting off an academic-based schedule is easier during the off-season because of the additional spare time. Thus, student-athletes must learn to balance their busy schedules during their playing season; but also, they must learn to keep focused on their schoolwork during the off-season.

Scholarships, Eligibility, and Academic Requirements

Many students earn full or partial academic scholarships to attend college. Athletes are also eligible for scholarships, both academic and athletic. Most college athletes on scholarship were awarded athletic ones. Athletic scholarships usually include "room and board" (tuition, textbooks, lab supplies, food allowance, and housing). Athletes who are not awarded a scholarship but wish to play collegiate sports have a few options: try out for the team as a walk-on; play Division I AA, Division II, or Division III sports; or play at a community college.

As the governing body of college sports, the NCAA (to be discussed in greater detail later in this chapter) oversees eligibility requirements. In Division I, for example, an athlete is eligible for college sports if he or she is a high school graduate and has taken the following courses: English (4 years); Math (2 years); Natural or physical science (including at least one lab course if offered by the high school) (2 years); additional courses in English, mathematics, or natural or physical science (1 year); Social science (2 years); and additional academic courses in any of the previously mentioned areas or foreign language, computer science, philosophy, or nondoctrinal religions (e.g., comparative religion) (2 years) (Sponholz, 1997). The NCAA also recognizes a "partial qualifier" as someone who has not met all the requirements of eligibility but has graduated from high school, successfully completed a core curriculum of at least 13 academic courses in appropriate core areas, and has either a minimal acceptable GPA average or SAT (or ACT) score (NCAA Manual, 2008). A nonqualifier is someone who has not met any of the NCAA requirements needed to participate in either Division I or Division II athletics. Nonqualifiers cannot compete or participate in practices during their freshman year (Sponholz, 1997).

Once an athlete has been accepted to college, he or she must remain and/or maintain good academic standing in order to continue playing sports. Athletic departments at all colleges and universities keep a close eye on the academic progress of their athletes. As any college faculty member can attest, the athletic department routinely sends out academic progress reports to professors of athletes (especially those "at risk") in order to keep abreast of the academic standing of athletes. Although the demands placed on student-athletes are often quite extreme, graduation reports routinely reveal that college athletes graduate at, or above, the rate of nonstudent-athletes (Duderstadt, 2003). The NCAA also requires that all athletes are progressing at a "normal" rate toward graduation. In this regard, athletes must maintain at least a 2.0 GPA and take a full course load that leads toward a degree. In other words, athletes cannot take one course per semester and fail. They must be a full time student working toward graduation.

THE NATIONAL COLLEGIATE ATHLETIC ASSOCIATION (NCAA)

As previously mentioned, the NCAA is the governing body of college sports (that is, for all schools that voluntarily belong). The NCAA was not the first organization designed to oversee the activities of athletes and colleges that offer competitive sports teams but it has been the ruling body for the past century. The guiding principles and primary functions of the NCAA include: providing institutional control, especially in the form of intercollegiate sports conformity, accountability, and standardization of the rules; enforce the rule through the implementation sanctions; provide a safe playing environment; and preservation of intercollegiate athletic records.

The Formation of the NCAA

Football games were so brutal in the early 1900s that players, who wore little or no equipment and used undisciplined formations that encouraged collisions (e.g. the "flying wedge"), routinely had their limbs and noses broken. During the 1904 season, 21 players were killed and over 200 injured while playing college football (Sack and Staurowsky, 1998). Theodore Roosevelt, President of the United States at that time, urged the creation of a national association to help regulate games and prevent injuries on the field. The Intercollegiate Athletic Association of America (IAAA) was established on March 31, 1906 to set rules for amateur sports throughout the United States. In 1910 it changed its name to the National Collegiate Athletic Association (NCAA). "The NCAA was formed in 1906 in response to problems in college football . . . As a result, colleges, fans and players alike, asked for some regulation of college football. President Theodore Roosevelt responded by summoning the leaders of college athletics to the White House to discuss reforms in collegiate athletics. Hence, the NCAA was born" (Sponholz, 1997:1). The NCAA was actually formed as a result of the American Football Rules Committee's (made of representatives of the various football playing colleges of the early 1900s) formation of the Intercollegiate Athletic Association of the United States (IAAUS). IAAUS was renamed the NCAA in 1912 (Sack and Staurowsky, 1998). The NCAA began as an institution designed to make rules that ensured fair competition and safety of athletes. As the number of college teams and collegiate athletes increased, so too did the NCAA's responsibility.

In its first 50 years of existence, the NCAA attempted to clean up corruption by steadfastly maintaining a commitment to the amateur ideal. That is, athletes who played college sports were to be amateurs in the truest sense of the word—they would not receive monetary compensation (e.g., scholarships, appearance fees) for playing sports. The NCAA's 1906 bylaws made it very clear that every member institution was to ensure amateur principles. It was clearly forbidden for any college or university to offer inducements (scholarships, special admissions) to individuals because of their athletic ability. Thus, financial aid and athletic scholarships were strictly forbidden. College athletes who received such compensation were not viewed as amateur athletes. The NCAA was formed to stop corruption in sport, but it had little power to actually enforce the rules. As a result, many abuses occurred throughout the early years of the NCAA.

Although violations of the principles of amateurism were often ignored by college officials, there were risks if such activities became public. In 1929 the Big Ten handed out its first suspension when the University of Iowa violated a number of conference rules. The violations included the operation of a businessmen's slush fund for the subsidization of athletes, tuition refunds, and the improper use of scholarships for athletes . . . The decade of the 1930s saw a continued rash of charges and countercharges concerning illegal payments (Sack and Staurowsky, 1998:39).

In an attempt to control the illegal payments, tuition waivers and other violations of amateurism that were becoming commonplace in college athletics, the NCAA legalized athletic scholarships in 1956. "By legalizing them (in the hope of controlling abuses), the NCAA also encouraged their proliferation and, in effect, raised the bar determining what participation at the highest competitive level would require of institutions . . . Before 1956, paying for an athlete's tuition on the basis of the student's athletic ability rather than financial need was considered breaking the rules" (Shulman and Bowen, 2001:12–13).

The NCAA still considers scholarship athletes as amateurs even though they receive financial compensation because of their athletic ability. The NCAA Manual (2008) states, "Only an amateur student-athlete is eligible for intercollegiate athletics participation in a particular sport" (p.51). The Manual describes how an athlete may lose his or her amateur status, but does not actually define the term amateur. Rather, the NCAA defines a professional athlete: "one who receives any kind of payment, directly or indirectly, for athletics participation except as permitted by the governing legislation of the Association" (p.51).

The NCAA President

The NCAA is headed by a President. The role of the President is to act as Chief Executive Officer, promote its educational mission, and resolve conflicts within and without the vast membership infrastructure. The fourth and current President is Myles Brand, former President of Indiana University (where he achieved notoriety for firing controversial men's basketball coach Bob Knight). Hired in October, 2002 Brand announced at his first State of the Association address at the 2003 Convention that reform and advocacy were the guideposts that would shape his presidency. He described five principles to support advocacy and reform:

- Intercollegiate athletics must be integrated into the academic mission of colleges and universities.
- Presidential control of intercollegiate athletics is essential.
- The positive value of intercollegiate athletics should be stressed and reinforced.
- fThe integrity of intercollegiate athletics is and must remain paramount.
- The norms of ethical behavior and fairness must guide all of intercollegiate athletics.

As president of such a powerful organization as the NCAA, Brand has his critics. But he has taken a strong leadership role as a spokesperson for academic integrity and as an advocate of personal responsibility for student-athletes. He has stated that ". . . student-athletes are entitled to the full opportunity for an excellent education. Every coach and athletics administration and every university president has a duty to take steps necessary to make that the case" (Madigan, 2003: 12).

Division III Collegiate Sports

Many colleges and universities have opted not to join the competitive world of big-time athletics (Division I, Division I-AA, and in some cases Division II); they play sports but at the Division III level. "Beginning in the 1970s with the partitioning of the NCAA into divisions, selective colleges and universities had another option. Liberal arts colleges and some universities found refuge in Division III, where no athletic scholarships were allowed" (Shulman and Bowen, 2001:17). In the 1990s, the presidents of Division III schools decided to allow teams to compete in postseason competition. Originally, only the first place team from each conference was allowed to participate in postseason Division III play. Currently, a few at-large bids are offered to schools that perform well enough to qualify for postseason play but did not win their conference. With the advent of postseason play, the stakes were raised at the D-3 level. "Even in a conference praised by the national press as 'pure and simple,' arms races accelerate when the competitive gates are opened" (Shulman and Bowen, 2001:18).

With the introduction of postseason play and the long-time existing desire of many athletes to continue their athletic careers after high school, Division III is an attractive option for many. Recruitment at Division III schools is also quite different than at Division I or II. The rules of recruitment are generally less restrictive at the D-3 level. "Coaches in Division III do not have to wait until July 1 to contact a prospective player; in fact, contact by mail or telephone is permitted any time after the student enters ninth grade. Also, there is no limit in Division III on the number of contacts that coaches and others are permitted to make" (Bowen and Levin, 2003:50). Recruiting at the Division III level is often very competitive, especially in select sports that any give D-3 school attempt to excel at.

In 2005, an unusual event took place at the Division III level that would never be allowed, let alone considered, at the Division I level. Northwestern College of St. Paul played a day-night, home-road, football doubleheader on October 8. Football is such a rough and demanding sport that it is nearly unheard of to play more than game a week. Northwestern hosted Trinity Bible College at noon and then played five miles away at Macalester College at 7 P.M. Among the concerns surrounding this rare doubleheader was whether or not it was even legal to play two games in one day. "Northwestern athletic director Matt Hill called the NCAA, where a woman told him after an hourlong consultation of the rule book, 'There isn't a rule against it. *Yet*'" (Rushin, 2005:19). First-year Trinity coach Jim Dotson said of Northwestern College's double-header ambition, "To me, it's kind of a put-down of both our program and Macalester's" (Rushin, 2005:18). As a Division III school, Northwestern had to work with certain fiscal realities (which was the main reason for playing two games in one day); among them was the fact that D-3 football teams only have one set of pants. There was not enough time to wash the uniforms from the first game so the players had to wear the same equipment for both games. They did switch from their home jerseys to their road jerseys. For the record, the nearly 80-strong Northwestern College Eagles beat the undermanned Trinity Bible College (22 players suited up) 59-0 and the Eagles defeated Macalester 47-14. Do not expect Division I schools to be playing two games in one day any time soon.

Community Colleges

Community colleges were originally established to benefit low-income students who use them as a stepping stone to better jobs and higher income (Santibanez, Gonzalez, Morrison, and Carroll, 2007). Because community colleges are so important for the economically poor, some states (e.g., California) have an open admissions policy. There is a debate among academics as to whether an open door policy should be offered at the collegiate level. An open admissions policy dramatically decreases the value of the diploma for one thing and it creates a classroom with students that possess vastly different levels of preparedness for college-level work for another. On the other hand, without an open door policy, many people would never have the chance to attend college, and ideally, eventually improve their standard of living.

With the rising costs associated with attending a four-year college, many students enroll at junior colleges as a cost-saving measure. They plan to earn their degree in two years and then transfer to a four-year school. Community colleges also benefit students who want to stay close to home their first two years of school. In short, there are nearly 1,200 community colleges in the United States and they are responsible for educating about half of all the nation's undergraduates (Santibanez, et al, 2007).

Athletes take advantage of the junior college (JUCO) option as well. For example, athletes who were not talented enough to participate at the higher level sports programs (Division I, II, or III) but want to continue playing sports view the JUCO option as appealing. Athletes who were ruled academically ineligible for Division I sports often play at JUCO schools with the hope that they will raise their grades and become eligible for transfer. As with Division I, II, and III schools, community college sports programs are also supervised by a governing body, the National Junior College Athletic Association (NJCAA). The NJCAA has over 500 member institutions and is committed to providing quality opportunities to enhance the entire collegiate learning experience of its students (NJCAA, 2008).

CHEERLEADING: FLUFF OR SPORT?

Few aspects about sports are truly American in origin. Cheerleading, however, is a pure American phenomenon both in its inception and in its development. "Cheerleading, an American invention with roots in the institutions of sport and education, has become a staple in American culture. The cheerleader is a nationally recognized symbol invested with positive as well as negative cultural values" (Hanson, 1995: 1). Through years of development, cheerleading has become a highly structured activity. Some people view cheerleading as wholesome extracurricular activity, while others view it as an exploitative form of entertainment. Hanson (1995) explains, "The cheerleader is an icon, an instantly recognized symbol of youthful prestige, wholesome attractiveness, peer leadership, and popularity. Equally recognized is the cheerleader as symbol of mindless enthusiasm, shallow Boosterism, objectified sexuality, and promiscuous availability" (p.2).

In essence, cheerleaders exist because of school sports programs; without sports there is no need for cheerleaders (Chappell, 1997). A cheerleader is defined as a person who leads, calls for, and directs organized cheering at sporting events from the sidelines of the field or court. Cheerleaders verbally exhort the crowd during athletic events, promote school spirit, and provide dance and acrobatic entertainment. Interestingly, cheerleaders have little or no influence on the outcome of the game. Players have rarely, if ever, been quoted saying, "We won the game today because of the inspiration and cheering provided by our cheerleaders." Players will, occasionally, give credit to the fans in the stands, but not the cheerleaders. The cheerleaders seldom even face the game. They usually face the crowd in an attempt to stimulate and increase their cheering. Do cheerleaders help the team indirectly because they inspire the fans? Seldom do we hear spectators giving credit to cheerleaders for inspiring them to cheer. (Family members of youth sport cheerleaders would be a possible exception.) However, we all have heard of fans discussing cheerleaders in their scantily clad outfits.

If cheerleaders have little impact on the sport they cheer, what exactly is their function? Are they useless American iconic figures? The more than 4 million people who participate in cheerleading in the United States would

---

Box 6.1. Go Tell the Spartans

One of the most popular representations of cheerleaders in modern times was the recurring "Saturday Night Live" routine of "The Spartan Cheerleaders", two clueless students at East Lake High School named Arianna (played by Cheri Oteri) and Craig (played by Will Ferrell). After being spurned by the real cheerleading squad, the Spartan Spirits, the two somehow purloined some uniforms. In their first appearance on the show, in November of 1995, guest host Quentin Tarantino plays a genuine Spartan, who is on to their charade and chases them away.

In subsequent appearances, Arianna and Craig—whose enthusiasm is only rivaled by their awkwardness and cluelessness—arrive at increasingly less appropriate settings to lead their cheers, including a math competition, bowling game, ping-pong match, and chess tournament. Their unbridled goofiness made the Spartan Cheerleaders two of the most famous "SNL" characters, and, while Oteri and Ferrell stopped performing as the Spartans in 1999, their "routines" live on today on countless YouTube sites and webpages, where one can relive their encounters with exasperated students played by such celebrities as Teri Hatcher, Paula Abdul, Jim Carrey, and Jennifer Love Hewitt (as Arianna's nemesis Alexis). In fact, the Spartan Cheerleaders have inspired many high school and college students to emulate them in performing at unlikely sporting events. And why not? Who says that chess tournaments don't deserve cheerleaders? Remember Craig and Arianna's spirited chant: "Well you want a victory/Well that makes you a wisher/Cause one thing's for sure/You ain't no Bobby Fischer/Bobby Fischer, where is he?/I don't know/I don't know." Only Boris Spassky knows for sure!

disagree that cheerleading is a useless, mindless activity. In addition, Greg Webb, vice president of the Universal Cheerleading Association (UCA) argues that cheerleading in small towns is a sign of patriotism and nationalism at a local level (Adams and Bettis, 2003). Small towns across the United States build an identity around high school sports and cheerleading is a big part of that identity. Thus, cheerleading is a part of American cultural identity.

Teamwork and Dedication

A cheerleader is a part of a team and spends many hours a week practicing with teammates. The cheerleader must demonstrate dedication and commitment to the squad. Working as a team helps the individual cheerleader build group cohesion with others while maintaining a commitment to common goals. Participating in cheerleading can provide individuals with valuable experiences that will impact them in later years. In order for cheerleading to be an overall positive experience for individuals and teammates a number of objectives must be met. Chappell (1997) believes that the five most important cheerleader objectives are:

1. To develop physical skills and to learn about personal conditioning, good health habits, and safety.
2. To develop psychologically through increased self-confidence, self-esteem, and emotional maturity.
3. To develop socially through cooperation, competition, and appropriate standards of behavior.
4. To make a serious commitment to academics.
5. To develop effective time management strategies.

These objectives must be evaluated by the cheerleading coach. It is important that cheerleaders, like sports athletes, have good coaches to develop and improve the potential skills of the participants. "Because cheerleading offers a myriad of experiences, a good coach realizes that 'building people through cheerleading' entails emphasizing positive values, responsibility, and dedication" (Chappell, 1997:5).

At small schools, a cheerleading squad may be chosen for all of the sports. Larger schools often have cheerleaders for specific sports (e.g., football, basketball, and wrestling) and may have a varsity and junior varsity squad. Junior high schools may also have cheerleading squads. Club sports outside of the direct influence from schools (e.g., Pop Warner Football) may also have cheerleaders. There is also a distinction between cheerleaders and competi-

With their backs facing the game, cheerleaders lead fans at a college basketball game. (Courtesy Tim Delaney)

tive spirit, or cheer, squads. Competitive spirit squads compete against other cheer squads in front of judges rather than cheering for a sports team. Competitive cheer squads do not lead a crowd in cheering; instead, they spend time perfecting such skills as jumps, pyramids, and tumbling to be evaluated by judges.

Chappell (1997) acknowledges many changes in cheerleading over the years but states that the "soul" of cheerleading has remained the same:

- The excitement of winning a spot on the squad
- The determination to prepare for the season
- The exhilaration of the first game's performance
- The celebration of friendship and love

Regardless of the type of cheer squad, cheerleaders always remain upbeat and maintain a positive attitude. They complement the game and help fans and players celebrate the moment. Ideally, cheerleaders always display behaviors that demonstrate good sportsmanship and spirit building.

History of Cheerleading

Even though today, cheerleading is perceived almost exclusively as a feminized role, cheerleading began as a masculine activity (Hanson, 1995; Adams and Bettis, 2003). The first documented organized cheers at a sporting event took place in 1869 during the Princeton-Rutgers football game. Some student members of Nassau Hall used the "Siss, boom, Ahhh! . . . rocket cheer" to try and inspire other spectators to cheer and/or toss various objects (e.g., ladies' handkerchiefs, toppers) onto the field (Hanson, 1995). During the late 1800s a number of colleges had volunteer cheerleaders stand at ground level with their backs to the field, waving to the crowd and exhorting the crowd. By the early twentieth century many colleges had organized cheer squads and "yell leaders." The position of cheerleader in this time was very prestigious and honorable—he was the "Big Man on Campus." Colleges held strenuous competitions and examinations to select cheerleaders. "Just as elite athletes were singled out to compete for the college, cheerleaders representing the college were now selected for their tumbling skills and extroverted personalities. Cheerleaders were chosen by various groups, including faculty committees, physical education departments, or the student body" (Hanson, 1995:13).

The cheerleaders of the late 1800s and early 1900s were men. In fact, many elite men took part in cheerleading during their college days in this epoch. For example, former President Franklin D. Roosevelt, class of 1903, was a Harvard cheerleader. While future President George W. Bush was a cheerleader at Yale University in the 1960s, the image of the cheerleader has changed quite a bit over the years. "The heroic, idealized image of the male cheerleader stressed aesthetics as well as skill. This image was replaced by a trivialized image of the female cheerleaders which emphasized isolated body parts and minimal ability" (Hanson, 1995:3). How did this transformation from a male-dominated activity to a female-dominated activity take place? There are a number of specific socio-historical explanations.

First, prior to the 1920s, most colleges were reserved for the social elite and an overwhelming percentage of these students were male. Since cheering was a collegiate activity performed by males, it was originally idolized as a masculine ideal. Indeed, as late as 1939, women were barred from being chosen for the All-American Cheerleading squad that was selected by sportswriters. Even as a masculine ideal, cheerleading had its critics as far back as the early 1900s. "In 1911, when all cheer leaders or yell leaders were males, the president of Harvard University attacked 'organized cheering' as a deplorable avenue for college men to express emotion, and contended that this new college tradition offered nothing of value to respectable educated men" (Adams and Bettis, 2003 :2). This attack on cheerleading did not stop its growth.

Second, during the 1920s more women started attending college. Attractive women were being used to promote the early movies; they were in advertisement and beauty pageants during this era. On college campuses, sororities were becoming increasingly popular and a source of social life for women. Women also began trying out for cheerleading squads. Women continued to slowly enter the domain of cheerleading for the next couple of decades. Girls were participating as cheerleaders in high school in increasing numbers during the 1930s. Although some educators were concerned that cheering might adversely affect a girl's behavior or character, the popular sentiment of cheerleading was that it was prestigious to be a cheerleader. Boys and girls both continued as cheerleaders in a coeducation setting throughout the 1940s. Because cheerleading was still considered a masculine activity, it was okay for girls to dance while cheering; but there was great concern as to whether or not the girls should be allowed to perform acrobatics. The implication was that girls were not physically capable of doing such routines. The sex appeal of female cheerleaders would override the more cautious concerns.

The changing role of women in cheerleading was mirroring that of the greater society. Adams and Bettis (2003) explain:

> Women becoming cheerleaders also closely parallels the story of women becoming workers during World War II. In both cases, men left their jobs to become soldiers and inadvertently opened doors that previously had been closed to women. When men returned from the war, they fought to regain their 'rightful' place in the worksite and on the cheerleading squads. In fact, the University of Tennessee banned female cheerleading squads in the early 1950s. However, women prevailed, and following World War II, cheerleading squads became predominantly female, especially in elementary and secondary schools (p.4).

During World War II, women had shown that they could perform the same tasks as men. However, the 1950s was a period designed to "refeminize" American women. The media (movies, radio and television) featured women in terms of being good housewives and homemakers, full figured, wearing skirts, carefully prepared hair and plenty of makeup so that they would look attractive for men. Young women were encouraged to participate in beauty contests and become majorettes and cheerleaders. By the 1950s, cheerleading camps became popular and were increasingly attended by girls in greater numbers than boys.

Cheer camps continue to be popular today. Millions of girls cheerlead. At the high school level it is now rare for boys to be cheerleaders. At most colleges, males are on cheerleading squads but are expected to assist women in their stunts and cheering routines. The promotion of health and fitness has

also benefited the cheerleading industry as many parents see the health benefits of an active child who cheerleads. Many people view cheerleading as a
positive way for girls and young women to develop confidence, maintain fitness, look athletic, but also pretty and feminine. "Cheerleading in the twenty-
first century captures this new vision of ideal femininity. Cheerleading still
remains one of the highest-status activities for girls. It is the most visible
space for them to inhabit, and being known and liked by everyone continues
to be a priority of school life. Cheerleading provides that public visibility"
(Adams and Bettis, 2003: 4–5).

Not all cheerleading is about health and fitness and popularity in school.
Professional sport team cheerleaders fuel the criticism of cheerleading as little more than soft porn performed by scantily dressed women who shake their
pom poms. In 1972, the Dallas Cowboys formed a dance squad known as the
Dallas Cowboy Cheerleaders. Their hot pants, midriff revealing tops, and go-
go boots outfit came to symbolize the essence of professional cheerleading:
glamour, sex appeal, celebrity, and merchandising success (Hanson, 1995).
The contradiction of cheerleader types fuels the debate, is cheerleading a
sporting activity, or is it fluff?

Cheerleading is Fluff

Critics of cheerleading are especially upset with professional sport team
cheerleaders, like the Dallas Cowboy Cheerleaders—who are today considered a social institution in the sports world. Dallas' introduction of cheerleaders fueled the demand for "go-go dancers on the sidelines" among nearly
all National Football League franchises. High school cheerleaders, who were
commonly used at professional football games, were replaced by slightly
older, but legal-aged, sexier and scantily-dressed women. These cheerleaders
do not perform routines. In fact, their primary job on the sidelines is usually
restricted to shaking pom poms, kicking their legs in the air, and smiling
pretty when the television camera is on them. Professional basketball teams
hire the same type of cheerleader—a sexy young woman who does little more
than shake her body while wearing a tiny outfit. Hoch (1972) refers to cheerleaders as the modern day equivalent of the vestal virgins that the Romans
used to bless their mass gladiatorial spectacles. Professional cheerleaders are
a prime example of the "fluff" of cheerleaders and represent eroticized femininity.

The professional cheerleader benefits marketers who still rely on the "sex
sells" attitude. Professional sport team cheerleaders benefit the franchise
through merchandising and the league as part of the mass entertainment package it presents viewers. As Hanson (1995) states, "The development of pro-

fessional cheerleading was shaped by the mass entertainment and promotional demands of professional sport. These demands created a paradox for team management—how to exploit a consciously sexual sell while avoiding the appearance of sexual impropriety. The resulting tension between 'good' and 'bad' publicity continues to be reflected in the image of the professional cheerleader" (p. 49). Professional sport teams usually have their cheerleaders pose for calendars and sell them at a huge profit. The teams also have cheerleaders make public appearances. One of the authors used to work for a chain of convenience stores in Los Angeles—while the Raiders resided there—that was a corporate sponsor of the Raiders. As a field supervisor in the new store development department, he routinely had Raiderettes (the Raiders' cheerleaders) at his disposal for such promotions as "Grand Openings" for new stores. He can attest to their appeal to the typical convenient store customer!

Criticism of overly-sexy cheerleaders is not restricted to the professional cheerleader. In 2005, Al Edwards, a member of the Texas House of Representatives introduced a bill to prohibit overtly sexually suggestive cheerleading routines in Texas high schools. The bill, which passed the House, languished sponsorless in the Senate (Sefton, 2005). Edwards argues that some school districts, including elementary and junior high schools, allow cheerleaders to wear bare midriffs, very short skirts, and perform routines to bump and grind music with vulgar lyrics. He wants an end to these types of routines and styles of dress among the cheerleaders. Karen Halterman, vice president of the National Cheerleading Association in Dallas, the original American cheerleading organization, is very disappointed with the negative way the bill attempts to portray cheerleading (Sefton, 2005). While there is concern in Texas over cheerleaders wearing very short skirts at sporting events, a high school in Elma, Washington wants an end to the game-day tradition of cheerleaders wearing their uniforms to classes. Elma school officials believe that the short skirts expose too much bare thigh causing a distraction to adolescent boys. One of the mothers of the Elma cheerleaders, and a former cheerleader herself, thinks the ruling is terrible and argued that "Boys are going to be horn-toads, anyway, whether (the girls) are wearing a short skirt or not" (*Seattle Post-Intelligencer*, 2005). The cheerleaders commented that they felt like they were being unfairly stereotyped because they wore short cheerleader skirts.

The cheerleading as fluff perspective incorporates all the negative stereotypes of cheerleaders. "Negative traits assigned to the female cheerleader include the following: she is dumb, conceited, and a 'bimbo,' a sexually promiscuous trophy for victories males. Such qualities mirror cultural anxieties about appropriate female roles. Women who are beautiful, independent, intelligent, or sexually active threaten social expectations based on the subordinate Good Girl" (Hanson, 1995:103). In November of 2005, for instance, two Carolina Panther cheerleaders received national attention when they were arrested in Tampa for starting a barroom fight, after which bar patrons complained they were having sexual relations with each other in a bathroom stall. Both cheerleaders were fired by the Panthers after the incident, but it was widely reported and did little to enhance the reputation of National Football cheerleaders overall.

Another negative stereotype of the cheerleaders is that of the "airhead." The "airhead cheerleader" is synonymous with the "dumb jock" stereotype. Anyone guilty of using negative stereotypes of cheerleaders is just as guilty as anyone else who uses stereotypes to judge any other group of people. Some critics of professional cheerleaders may be surprised to learn that some of them are graduate students, young professionals, and wives and mothers. Some professional cheerleaders do fit the promiscuous profile, but that does not make them any different than some members of the greater society, or the athletes they cheer, for that matter.

Cheerleading is a Sport

Most cheerleaders are not professional. They are found at the midget level of sports, junior high schools, high schools, colleges, and on cheerleading squad teams. Most of these cheerleaders go to practice, just like the athletes do. The spend hours on routines. They risk injury. They must be mentally prepared to perform stunts. Cheerleading requires coordination, conditioning, teamwork, physical endurance, dedication and the daring to perform relatively dangerous moves. Cheerleaders must persevere just as other athletes, but they must also do so with a positive attitude (e.g., smiling throughout the routine). In general, most people seem to have a positive image of cheerleaders—especially the nonprofessional cheerleader. Hanson (1995) explains, "Contemporary images of the cheerleader often invoke positive connotations: a young female who is physically attractive (cute), socially popular and influential—a wholesome, extroverted, enthusiastic Good Girl. These qualities mirror cultural definitions of appropriate female roles. Women are valued for youth and beauty, which convey status, and for their social role as behavioral gatekeepers and providers of emotional support" (p.100). A cheerleader who is also capable of performing relatively complex and physically demanding sporting routines is sure to be highly valued in contemporary society.

Many cheerleading squads (the competitive spirit teams) are involved in intense competitions requiring physical skills and attributes. Competitions last for two-minutes and 30 seconds jammed packed within a well choreographed routine. Cheerleading competitions generally involve five main com-

---

**Narrative 6.2.   An interview with cheerleader Patricia Millet,
formerly of Pittsford Sutherland High School and now a
cheerleader at Buffalo State College**

1. How long have you been involved in cheerleading, and what got you started in it?

    Well, I have been cheerleading for about 8 years. I had just moved to Pittsford in the 5th grade and I wanted to do something where I could get more involved and make new friends, so I joined the Pittsford's cheerleading program.

2. Do you think that cheerleading is a sport?

    Of course, I think cheerleading is a sport. We practice just as much (or more — we have practice 6 days a week) as any other sports team, we condition every day, it's very easy to get hurt because of how demanding it is, and you have to tryout to be on the team because we only take girls with drive, determination and skill.

3. What do you consider to be the benefits that you've gotten out of being a cheerleader?

    I have become friends with the best of girls, it gives me encouragement to push myself. I have learned time management, and that has given me the capabilities to work well with others in whole and in stressful situations, and I have learned how to listen to others and incorporate everyone equally.

4. What do you think about the negative stereotypes often associated with being a cheerleader?

    I think they are horrible. My whole team is made up of smart, classy, respectable girls and it's a shame that we are thought of any other way.

5. How often do you have to practice?

    When the season starts we practice every day for 2½ to 3 hours, and sometimes on Saturday when we don't have a competition.

6. What awards have you won?

    I have won 3 leadership awards myself and my team Pittsford Sutherland has won many more. We placed 1st at the greater Rochester competition last year and last season we placed 3rd at nationals.

7. What are your future plans?

    I plan to go to Buffalo State and take up cheerleading again second semester so I can concentrate on my school work when I start college.

---

ponents: jumps (which require extreme flexibility and stamina); tumbling (where agility and endurance are needed); dance (requiring hours of practice, rhythm and grace); cheers (based on memorization); and stunts (a wide variety, including pyramids).

Stunts may be the most challenging and dangerous. The "flyers" need to have skill, balance, elegance and, of course, be daring and fearless. Flyers are the cheerleaders that literally fly in the air performing seemingly gravity-defying stunts with the faith that their "bases" (teammates on the floor) will catch them, no matter what. Sometimes, however, accidents do occur and cheerleaders may be seriously injured and in rare cases, their injuries are catastrophic. Consider, of the 104 catastrophic injuries (defined as head and spinal traumas that may lead to death) suffered by female athletes from 1982 to 2005 more than half resulted from cheerleading (Pennington, 2007).

Furthermore, cheerleading represents the number one sporting activity involving women to end with catastrophic injuries. Between 1982 and 2000, 25 high school cheerleaders died. The next closest sport was gymnastics with 9 fatalities and softball with 3 deaths (Brady, 2002). In college, 17 cheerleaders died during this same time period, compared to 2 deaths in women's gymnastics and 2 in field hockey (Brady, 2002). According to a 2006 study published in the journal of *Pediatrics*, cheerleading injuries in general have more than doubled from 1990 to 2002 while participation grew just 18 percent over the same time. The high-risk stunts account for most of this increase. More than 208,000 cheerleaders were treated at U.S. hospitals during that same 13 year period. More than half (52%) of the injuries were strains or sprains; 18% were soft tissue injuries; 16% were fractures/dislocations; 4% concussions/closed head injuries; 4% cuts and tears; and 6% of other (Burton, 2006).

Why do girls participate in competitive cheerleading if it is so dangerous? Mirroring the changing dynamics of what it means to be a woman in contemporary society, perhaps females are attracted to this sport for the same reason that males are attracted to risk activities—it provides a rush! That's right, competitive cheerleading provides girls and young women with an adrenaline-thrilled type of excitement that those outside of cheerleading might find hard to believe. Before competitive cheerleaders take part in highly synchronized and gravity-defying stunts, they practice for months. They become obsessed with the routine. And just like any other sport, a single point can make the difference between winning and losing. And winning may mean advancement to a state championship, and that may lead to a national competition. As with other sports, every time a team advances, the stress level increases and the importance of near-perfect performances escalates. Couple all this with the possibility of catastrophic injury, and well, it sounds a rush-situation to us.

In short, cheerleading presents a paradoxical image. On the one hand, we have competitive spirit cheering participants who we believe qualify as athletes and as a result they clearly play a sport. On the other hand, we have girls and young women who shake pom poms and stand on the sidelines cheering for a team. We do not believe that such activity qualifies as a sport. However, these cheerleaders represent an American institution and are as much a part of sports as, well . . . American pie.

FINAL THOUGHTS

Most young athletes have positive experiences with high school and college sport participation. Nearly all secondary schools offer some sort of inter-scholastic athletics. In addition, most colleges and universities have sports teams, and encourage both intra and intermural competition.

Studies consistently show that the stereotype of the "dumb jock" does not correspond with the actual academic performances of student-athletes. Such individuals, on average, perform better than student-nonathletes, at both the high school and college levels. While most student-athletes participate in interscholastic sports, there are many alternatives unconnected with school systems.

Sport participation can allow a student to bond with others, as well as stand out above the rest. School sporting events can provide an opportunity for school spirit activities, which can rally the entire academic community. Cheerleaders are an ever-present part of the school spirit phenomenon. Whether cheerleading constitutes a proper sport will continue to be debated, but there is no doubt that cheerleaders play an important role in encouraging participation by both athletes and fans. In the next chapter, we will focus specifically on the role of the latter. Three cheers for the fans!

Chapter Seven

Sports Fans

Have you ever sat on your favorite chair all day long watching sports on television? Many people have, especially during football season. Like millions of others, one of the authors regularly watches college football coverage for up to 15 hours on Saturdays—and he rarely misses a college bowl game. If they air it, he will watch it!

But what about this: could you watch sports nonstop, without sleep, for two or three consecutive days? If you answered "yes" to this question you should enter the "Ultimate Couch Potato Contest" sponsored by ESPN. The "Ultimate Couch Potato Contest" is an annual event that began in 2003 (in Chicago) and now takes place simultaneously at the New York and Chicago ESPN Zone restaurants. The contest begins on January 1st, a day filled with college football bowl games. As with any formal event, there are rules to this contest. First, all interested couch potatoes must submit a 200 word essay to ESPN detailing why they should be selected. Entries are judged on passion for sports, competitive spirit, and overall creativity. Just four contestants are selected for each of the two locations.

Once selected, the four contestants sit in the front row of the ESPN Zone's "Screening Room" facing a wall of HD TVs, all showing non-stop sports programming. Oddly, the contestants sit on recliners, rather than on couches— perhaps the contest should be called the "Ultimate Couch Recliner Contest". Contestants are served an unlimited amount of food and beverages, which is really nice. However, as anyone who has consumed beverages all day long can attest, it becomes necessary to use the bathroom. This leads to, perhaps, the most challenging rule of all—restroom breaks are permitted only once every eight hours. The other critical rule of this contest is a little less challenging for a true sports fan—that is, sleeping is not allowed. Contestants who leave their seats for an unscheduled restroom break or fall asleep are disqualified.

The "Ultimate Couch Potato Contest" is also a part of the Guinness Book of World Records and as a result contestants are competing for a chance for inclusion into the record books. As of 2009, the world record for watching the most continuous hours of televised sports was 69 hours and 48 minutes, set by Suresh Joachim in a separate 2005 event. ESPN's aspiring couch potatoes have fallen way short of the Guinness record. In 2007, Jason Pisarik successfully defended his Chicago title of top potato with a fairly respectable time of 39 hours and 44 minutes. Pisarik's time still fell way short of the world record. In 2008, Stan Friedman—a Manhattan librarian—emerged as the New York champion despite lasting only for an embarrassing 29 hours. Please, ESPN, get some real competitor in this contest! Friedman won when the last of his three rivals ran to heed nature's call.

For their efforts, winners of the "Ultimate Couch Potato Contest" are rewarded with nearly $7,000 worth of prizes, including a 42-inch LCD HD TV, a DreamSeat recliner, and a number of ESPN-related gift cards and certificates. Friedman was happy to win his prizes but admitted that he would have difficulty finding room for them in his 350 square-foot apartment.

Speaking of couch potatoes, modern medical science has developed a drug that provides some of the same benefits of exercise without the hassle of actually working out! However, before getting your hopes up too much, the drug has only been applied to date to sedentary mice. Nonetheless, recent research conducted by scientists at the Salk Institute for Biological Studies and the Howard Hughes Medical Institute have created a drug that actually burns off calories and fat from mice. Furthermore, when tested on a treadmill, the treated mice could run significantly faster and farther than untreated mice (Ritter, 2008). The scientists hope that some day this "exercise in a pill" will be available for humans. The researchers believe that the drug will help treat obesity, diabetes, and people with medical conditions that keep them from exercising.

THE EMERGENCE OF SPORTS FANS

Sports fans come in all shapes, sizes, colors, ages, socio-economic background, and sexes. Some are couch potatoes who literally sit around all day watching sports while others are not. Sports fans are united in their love for sports competition even if they are divided by favorite teams, athletes, and specific sports. Some are fans of baseball, others of softball. Many fans cheer for football, both professional and college, while others cheer auto racing, basketball, or tennis and golf.

But a number of questions have to be asked, including: "Where do all these sports fans come from?" and "Why *are* people fans of sports?" Let's begin with the first question. Socially, sports fans come from all socio-economic levels, that is, rich and poor, and all those in between. Often, people from different socio-economic classes prefer one sport over another. The rich, for example, enjoy yachting and horse racing—the sport of kings—while the middle class prefers football and baseball. But sports have a way of transcending social class, so it is common for people all social classes to enjoy the same sport(s). American sports fans come from the east coast and the west coast, from the northern states to the southern states, and throughout the Midwest and mountain regions. They come from big cities like New York and Los Angeles and small towns. They come from our families and yours. Most sports adherents have been fans since childhood. Life-long sports fans who were not athletes developed an identity based on their sports enthusiasm. Former youth, high school, and college athletes transform their identities from athlete to sport fan. And, when professional athletes retire, they become sports fans as well. In short, sports fans come from everywhere.

The answer to the second question—"Why are people fans of sport?"—is a little more difficult to answer because the explanations are so varied. So, let's start with what we know for sure, that there have been sports fans throughout history. That is, whenever sporting events have been staged, people have been there to cheer the athletes. The ancient Greeks began the tradition of idolizing athletic victories in monetary, literary, and bronze and marble (statues) form. And while the Greeks thought about sport and leisure a great deal, the ancient Romans sought to drown themselves in sports. Roman leaders used sport activities to train soldiers but also as a means to provide the masses with entertainment spectacles. For the Romans sports became a show, a dramatic event for the purpose of diversion. As mentioned in Chapter 2, by 300 C.E., one-half of the days on the Roman calendar were public holidays. Their overindulgence in sports and leisure would lead to the demise of the Empire.

After the collapse of the Roman Empire and throughout the Middle Ages, sporting events took a back seat in priority to the masses' simple pursuit of survival. However, as French sociologist Emile Durkheim (1858–1917) explained, the French Revolution would revitalize the Roman tradition of celebrating secular holidays, as France established a cycle of holidays that were designed as mass leisure ceremonies to celebrate the secular values of liberty, equality, and fraternity. Sports and leisure provided a means for the masses to uphold and re-affirm collective sentiments based on rites and ceremonies. Modern sports provide the same type of secular collective sentiments.

Sigmund Freud (1856–1939), a contemporary of Durkheim, also took note of the fact that culture was changing quite dramatically during the age of industrialization. Because many people in society were now able to satisfy their basic needs/necessities (food, clothing, and shelter), they sought other avenues in their quest of reaching personal fulfillment. Freud believed that the pursuit of leisure was a fundamental aspect of the "pleasure principle." The pleasure principle is a psychoanalytic notion centered on the idea that people seek pleasure in their everyday lives and attempt to avoid anything that brings pain. It is a hedonistic concept. Thus, humans seek pleasurable experiences, such as attending or watching a sporting event, rather than participating in less enjoyable behaviors like visiting a sick friend or relative in a hospital or nursing home. With this notion in mind, people would rather consume their time with sports than with dealing with more serious problems like the economy, politics, or the environment.

Decades earlier, Karl Marx (1818–1883) provided a similar analysis in his condemnation of religion when he referred to it as "the opiate of the masses." What Marx meant by this statement was that, as long as people have religion in their lives—which provides the promise of salvation and happiness in the afterlife—they become passive recipients of the socio-political system that controls their daily lives. Today, many conflict theorists argue that sport is the opiate of the masses because it serves as a diversion from real, serious problems. Thus, the ruling class encourages a mass consumption of sport because it distracts people from more important issues.

Just as spiritual believers never took Marx seriously, sports fans are not very likely to accept the "sport as an opiate" view. Sports fans generally take sports at face value. That is, they know they like sports and they know they like to cheer for sports. Sure, sports fans are upset with intrusions from reality such as a referee fixing NBA games so that gamblers can win a bet; but most fans want the story to disappear and prefer to think of such acts of deviancy as isolated events. To think otherwise would distract from the pleasure that sports are supposed to bring. Furthermore, sports fans do not feel the need to apologize for the fact that they often turn to sports—purposely—because it does provide a diversion from the more serious concerns of life.

Sports as a Diversion

During the contemporary era, people turn to sports for a number of reasons: athletes often present us with marvelous feats of accomplishments; athletes and sports teams create history in front of our very eyes; and while sports bring us continuity via a variety of traditions, they also present us with something new. And yes, sports provide us with a *necessary* diversion. Consider just a few occurrences in 2008 that people desired a temporary escape from: gas prices that topped the $5 mark in some areas of the country, before falling back to a national average below $4; two wars that continued to rage in Iraq and Afghanistan, costing thousands of American (and other) lives; a presidential election year filled with general, and specific negativity; the collapse of banks; people losing their homes to foreclosure; and so on. Most of these social problems are beyond the control of the average person. Is it any wonder people like to watch a ballgame or the Olympics?

Major college and professional sports are a business. We know it, we don't like it, but we deal with it. Make the games and sporting events entertaining and we are happily diverted from the everyday life. We want to be entertained. We want all kinds of entertainment. We want to see the *Dark Knight* at the movies and, like the ancient Romans, we want our athletes to put on a show. Enter sports. There is no mistaking the reality that sports are a form of entertainment. Sports are so entertainment-driven that many of the commercials aired during sporting events are also entertaining. The Super Bowl receives a great deal of attention from non-die-hard sports fans because they want to watch the commercials!

In brief, there are millions of sports fans in the United States alone. They come from all parts of the country and from all social groups. Sports fans exist for a lot of reasons, some of which were described above. Every individual sports fan will have his or her own unique explanation as to why they are sports fans. They were raised in a family that consumed sports, they played sports, or simply, they find sports to be an entertaining diversion from the more serious problems of everyday life.

SPORTS AND THE COMMUNITY

There are fans who cheer for their favorite team or athlete in the privacy of their own home. They do this for a number of reasons. For instance, after working all day, the sports fan comes home, has dinner, and turns on the TV. Bam! A ball game. Some people are shut-in and watch sports by themselves not so much because they want to, but rather, because circumstances have created the situation. Someone who is traveling and away from home may end up watching a game in a hotel room or hotel bar. There are also times when people prefer to watch a game at home, alone (or with a very select few others) because of the game's importance. That is, they do not want any interruptions from others who do not share the commitment and passion for a particular game. Undoubtedly, there are other reasons people may watch a sporting event alone. However, most people like to watch sports *with* others because such an occasion affords an opportunity for bonding. Furthermore, entire groups, neighborhoods, cities, or even nations can unite as a community of sports fans.

The Community

What is a community? Is it a physical locale, or is it a "state of mind?" The traditional way to view a community is presented by Turner (2006), who defines a community as "social structures organizing residence and activities of people in physical space" (p. 106). The organizational aspect refers to such things as roads, schools, churches, government, work place, and other structures. This interpretation of community was adapted from Hawley's (1981) view of communities as social structures that organize people's residence as well as their activities within physical boundaries or geographic space. The physical boundaries of communities vary in size, of course, from a small rural community to a large megalopolis. The view of a community as that which is found within certain physical boundaries has been prevalent since the agrarian era when humans settled in one area and learned to "work the land" rather than constantly moving as the hunters and gatherers had.

However, one would assume that the hunters and gatherers had a *sense* of community. They lived and traveled together. And, they found safety in the numbers that the "community" provided. In other words, a community need not be restricted to a physical location. Due to a number of complicated socio-economic factors (e.g., "capital flight," geographic relocation, long commute times, and so forth), there are a number of physical communities throughout the nation where neighbors do not know each other and do not socialize with one another. This may be the case because neighbors may not share the same social characteristics as one another; they may not even speak the same language. Thus, there are people who do not experience, or feel, a "sense of community" in the geographic area where they reside. As a result, many people seek alternatives to the "traditional" concept of community. They seek a community based on shared ideas and values, rather than one based on physical proximity.

Alternative views include the idea that a community may best be defined as a network of social relations marked by mutuality and emotional bonds. A community characterized by shared interests and associations is known as a "community of interest" (Foster, 1990). Nisbet (1969) describes community as a fusion of feeling, tradition, commitment, membership, and psychological strength. Athletes in a particular sport share a community. Teammates share a sense of community. Fans of sport have formed leisure-based communities, or booster groups to support their favorite team. Fans of auto racing will often camp out near the racetrack for days leading up to a race. They bond over their love for the sport and argue over who is the number one driver.

The traditional idea that a community is a physical location with boundaries is, of course, still relevant today. Additionally, sports are as important to local communities today as any other time in history. "Big League" cities must have professional sports and the requisite corresponding stadium to show off to other cities—no one wants their home team playing in a deteriorating stadium, as it is a negative reflection on the entire community. College communities have the same idea as Major League cities; they want a winning team and a huge stadium filled to capacity. In fact, the largest stadiums in the United States are on college campuses. As of 2004, the University of Michigan in Ann Arbor has the largest stadium in the nation. Known as the "Big House," this stadium has a capacity of 107,501. The second largest is Beaver Stadium at Penn State (106,537), followed by Neyland Stadium, on the campus of the University of Tennessee at Knoxville (104,079), Ohio Stadium at Ohio State University at Columbus (101,568) and the Rose Bowl, home to UCLA, holds 95,000 people. The importance of sport in the community continues all the way down to high schools and little league baseball.

Every community values athletic excellence. They honor and glorify sport heroes with statues (e.g., Michael Jordan's statue outside the United Center in Chicago), books, publicity photo opportunities, stretches of highways renamed in honor of athletes, and an endless array of print and visual media that glorify their pursuits. Athletic coaches are often important figures in any community. Many coaches have buildings and streets named after them to show appreciation and honor for their successes in the sports world. If college coaches can bring home a national championship it is often said that they could successfully run for political office. Communities like to post signs declaring their hometown athletic achievements. This is true whether a high school sport wins a state championship or an individual athlete accomplishes some noteworthy achievement. And, what community wouldn't want to post a sign proclaiming: "Welcome to <BLANK>, Home of the Little League Champions?"

Sport plays a vital role in many communities. Sport is often the focal point that brings a community together. Generally, sport serves to unite a community; but occasionally, sport can divide a community.

Sports Unite a Community

Sport unites a community in many ways. For example, most people within a community believe that youth sport participation has positive consequences. In simplest terms, it is better to have children playing organized sports than running around the neighborhood without guidance and structure. Individuals not engaged in socially-approved activities are more likely to become involved in social deviance. This idea reflects the Social Bond/Control Theory tenet that emphasizes individuals must form a bond with society in order to fully accept society. Travis Hirschi (1969), a social bond theorist, specified four elements of the social bond:

1. Attachment—A tight connection to significant others; especially parents, peers and school.
2. Commitment—Involves the amount of time that individuals spend with conventional behavior and their dedication to long-term goals (delayed satisfaction). The more time that individuals spend with conventional activities the less time they have for deviant ones.
3. Involvement—Actual participation in conventional activities, such as doing homework and athletic training and practicing.
4. Belief—Believing in the legitimacy of the community, society, and law.

Sports incorporate all these elements. Typically, becoming an athlete, whether on a team sport or an individual sport, involves attachment and great commitment. Sports are consumed by rules and regulations. Participants learn the value of following the rules, and thus, become good citizens. Involvement in sport leads to a belief in the legitimacy of the system. Harry Edwards (1973) argued that sport participation reflects seven specific value orientations found in society: character building; discipline; competition; physical fitness; mental fitness; religiosity; and nationalism. For example, there are numerous occasions where athletes give freely back to the community with their time and/or financial generosity. Athletes routinely visit sick people in hospitals; take part in the "Make a Wish" foundation; hand out turkeys at Thanksgiving and toys at Christmas; and so on.

Sports help to bond a community in many other ways as well. Consider, many communities host a variety of sporting events such as 10K/5K (kilometer) walks or races—often for charity. These events provide wonderful opportunities for people in the community to gather together, centered on a healthy, physical endeavor. It is a "can't miss," "feel good" type of activity guaranteed to unite people through a sense of community spirit. Of course, there are those who complain because they are temporarily inconvenienced by the traffic restraints of a small number of street closings. (Note: this serves as an example of how sports can sometimes divide a community.)

Often after local or national tragedies, sporting events provide a sense of continuity, and serve as ways of bringing communities back together. In other words, sports provide normalcy. For instance, after the September 11, 2001 terrorist attacks on the United States, the National Football League postponed its games for one week. Many fans noted that, when games resumed the following week, they appreciated the sense of normality this brought back to their world. After the devastation caused by Hurricane Katrina in 2005, numerous athletes, sport teams, and sports leagues donated huge sums of money to help the victims of this tragedy. When the I-35 west-bound bridge collapsed in Minnesota in 2007, sports helped to put things in perspective. Some of the people that were on the bridge (or died because of the calamity) were on their way to the Metrodome to watch the Twins play baseball. Fans, players, coaches, and other personnel already at the game were concerned about their loved ones — were they on the bridge? The Twins front office decided to keep playing the game, fearing that people leaving the Dome would cause greater traffic problems. Everyone in the Minnesota community, and throughout the nation for that matter, understood the magnitude of the bridge collapse and the relative unimportance of playing a game. And yet, baseball and other sports would be played in Minnesota because life must go on. *Star Tribune* (Minneapolis) columnist Jim Souhan (2007) sums the role of sport in a community:

> What in Minnesota, other than our local sports teams, can command the attention of millions of people hundreds of days a year? What else can persuade thousands of unaffiliated people to flock to the same venue wearing the same colors? What, other than the weather, provides easier entry into a conversation with an acquaintance? Yes, sports and sportswriters and sports debates can be shallow or overwrought. These silly ballgames, though, can stand as symbols of normalcy and community in a splintered world (p.C-2).

Sports not only stand as symbols of normalcy and community, they provide people with a diversion, a temporary escape from the mundane, everyday life. We marvel at athletic accomplishments and cheer for the spectator. When a local team (at any level) is enjoying a successful season the intensity of every remaining game/event increases and builds into a fever pitch within the community. A high school state championship, especially in such sports as football and basketball, will generally energize members of the community to organize a parade honoring the athletes and coaches. The school colors appear in various forms throughout the community as well. In addition, winning major sporting events such as the World Cup in soccer can unite an entire nation, and bring a sense of joy to a country that few, if any, other events can match.

Sports Divide a Community

Sports can also divide communities in many ways. For example, citizens like the idea of youth playing sports; it keeps them off the streets where they may be tempted into delinquency. Schools need funds to run sports, and it keeps getting costlier to fund sports. Often, the local schools will propose school budgets that will lead to a tax increase. Most people do not readily agree to a tax hike. Typically, sports are among the first items to be trimmed (the arts are often victimized as well) when school budgets do not pass. Consequently, athletes are sent out into the community in an attempt to generate support for the school budget—usually with signs and posters that read "save our sports!" This often causes a division within the community. People don't like feeling coerced, or made to feel guilty, to do things like vote for a budget that will cost them more money. The people who voice opposition (to supporting sports) are made to feel like they are not "good" citizens and may be ostracized by the community. Conversely, those who promote increasing taxes in order to support sports at school risk being ostracized by the community if they are clearly in the minority.

Players' disputes with management often divide fan loyalties, especially when the disputes involve money. Many fans believe that players are overpaid already and consequently are often unsympathetic to their demands for higher pay. The average person will be lucky to earn two million dollars over the course of an entire life-work span, while marginal professional athletes in the major sports will earn millions of dollars in a year or two. Then again, frustrated fans are not sympathetic to billionaire owners. Fans have the right to demand that ownership provide the best team possible. We want a trade to be made if it will help our team. In short, the fans do not care about money disputes between players and owners; they want to see the athletes play. Period.

TAILGATING

Among the most joyous aspects of attending certain sporting events is the tailgate party. This is especially true if the fans involved are cheering for a team with a losing record and/or little chance of winning. At least there is fun to be had at the tailgate party, many fans reason.

And yet, despite the fun atmosphere associated with tailgating, very few sports actually involve fan tailgate parties. The sport most closely associated with tailgating is football. This is true both at the professional and collegiate levels. (Tailgate parties are a feature at a number of high school football games as well.) The one game a week format of football is a major contributing aspect of this association. Further, professional football teams are only guaranteed eight regular season home games that are spread out over a four month period. This adds to the critical nature of the home team defending its turf. The two-game per month average is not lost on the fans either. They see every home game as a social event, and certainly not *just* a game. College football is very similar. Most colleges have anywhere from five to eight home games a year spread over an approximate three-month period. And because college football has existed longer than professional football, the tailgate party has been a feature of college games long before professional ones.

Tailgate parties seem as natural at football games as cheerleaders and opening kickoffs. So why don't other sports feature tailgate parties? Tailgating at wrestling and track and field meets seems a bit out of place. Professional baseball teams have 81 home games, and although some games are clearly more important that others, it is tough to get motivated to tailgate before each one. Additionally, most MLB stadiums do not allow tailgate parties. The owners want fans purchasing food and beverage products inside the stadium. Basketball and hockey, which are played mainly during the winter months, are not conducive to outdoor parties in cold-weather cities. (Although cold and snowy weather will not stop football fans from tailgating!) As with MLB, NHL and NBA franchises have a lot more home games than the NFL. It would seem, then, that there is a correlation between tailgating and the number of home games in each sport.

This is not to suggest that other sports, including baseball, basketball and hockey, do not have fans that tailgate; it's simply not as prevalent as it is in football. Auto racing, especially NASCAR, is one big weekend-long party and is therefore tough to include as simply a pregame tailgate party. And those folks certainly know how to party! One of the authors regularly attends Syracuse University lacrosse games where tailgating *after* the game is the norm. What is unique about this experience is that the players and their families join together with the fans in the tailgate celebrations. In this regard, the SU lacrosse program is a true community that bonds players, families, and fans together.

The Secular Sentiment of Tailgating

Tailgating at sporting events represents a type of secular sentiment (in the tradition of Durkheim) that helps to bond fans together in collective action where ritualistic behaviors are the norm. As with staging any gala, there is a relative amount of planning involved for the host of a tailgate party. At the top of the list: bring the grill and food for the grill! Guests of the tailgate host simply have to show up with a dish or beverages to share with the rest of party. Often, any nearby fan is welcomed to join in the feasting, as an abundance of food is a mandate at tailgate parties.

Let's take a look at some of the many features of a tailgate party. As stated above, a tailgate party begins with the host packing a grill and food into his or her vehicle. Generally, a number of chairs—in a variety of forms—are also packed. Upon arrival at the stadium, many tailgaters have a "usual" spot where they like to park. A number of factors are involved with the choice of parking as well, including: an area with easy in and out access, an area where all the party-goers know how to find, an area with plenty of space to set up tables full of food, and/or a spot close to the portable bathrooms.

The most important facet of any tailgate party is food and beverage. A wide assortment of beverages is recommended, but, of course, alcohol is the primary liquid refreshment. It is a good idea to also pack soda, juices and water. As for food, some sort of meat (e.g., steak, pork chops, chicken, sausages, or bratwurst) is mandatory. Sorry vegetarians, but this is a football tailgate party and there must be meat on a grill. Like Pavlov's dogs, nothing causes such a primal reaction for humans as seeing meat and fire. However, a good tailgate host wants to appease all guests, so keep some sort of veggie option available (but never place veggies on a tailgater's grill!). Beyond the meat, all types of food are acceptable. Nachos, potato chips and dip, and other snacks to munch on should be available as the grill fires up. Submarine sandwiches are always

These tailgaters have plenty of room to set up tables and they are close to the portable bathrooms. (Courtesy of Wayne Quatrochi)

Cleveland Browns fans gather outside the stadium for early morning tailgating. (Courtesy of Wayne Quatrochi)

Rival fans share a "beer bong" during pregame tailgating. (Courtesy Wayne Quatrochi)

a hit with partygoers. Salads, baked beans, and other appetizers, such as chicken wings, served as side dishes. And of course, desserts.

Obviously, before the food is served the tables need to be set up. Some people like to place a tablecloth atop the table. If you do this, make sure the tablecloth is in the team's colors and not something fancy or frilly. In fact, the team colors should be highly visible everywhere. You can never place too many team-related items in the tailgate area. Let everyone know what team you are cheering for; but beware, if you are on the road, the home team fans will not take too kindly to your open display of support for the "enemy." Tailgaters should all be wearing their colors. Face painters and fans who dress with a gimmick are especially revered. For example fans of the Cleveland Browns have long taken on the persona of the unofficial "Dawgs" nickname. In this manner, Browns fans can dress and act like dogs and incorporate such items as dog-bone helmets.

Tailgating at football games will last hours. Most people arrive four or five hours before kickoff (depending on when parking lots open). Tailgaters need something more to do than eat and drink. Music or radio pregame shows blare across stadium parking lots. A number of fans bring televisions with them,

---

Box 7.1.   Tailgating with *The Simpsons*

Take a car, a game, food, friends, and a parking lot, and mix. What do you have? A tailgate party. And nothing seems more American than bonding with friends, family, and fellow fans at a football tailgate party. Even America's favorite (cartoon) family, the Simpsons, enjoy tailgating at football games.

In the "Any Given Sundance" episode, Homer Simpson is driving his family to Springfield Stadium where arch-rivals Springfield University and Springfield A&M will meet on the gridiron. It is early in the morning and most of the family members are quite sleepy, but not Homer. He is wide awake and quite excited about the prospect of tailgating. Reflecting the sentiments of all but his father's, Bart complains aloud, "Why are we arriving so early? The game does not start for hours." Homer laughs at his son's complaining and decrees, "We're not here for the game. The game is nothing…The real reason we Americans put up with sports is for this. Behold, the tailgate party! The pinnacle of human achievement. Since the dawn of parking lots man has sought to stuff his guts with food and alcohol in anticipation of watching others exercise." Homer goes on to explain that eating "trunk meat" is a glorious thing, especially for men.

Perhaps summing up the sentiment that all we tailgaters share, Homer proudly proclaims, "What could be greater than eating and drinking for hours in a drizzly parking lot?!" Indeed, Homer, indeed.

usually to watch pregame shows or highlights from games played earlier in the day. Many fans bring a football with them and friends toss the ball back and forth. Other people bring tailgating games with them like ladder ball, corn toss (or bean bag toss), washer pitching, and, of course, a drinking game favorite, beer pong.

And then there are the accessories, like plates and silverware; napkins; condiments; plenty of ice; and of course, trash bags. The more items that are disposable, the easier it is to pack up when the time comes to leave. Oh yeah, one other thing you might not want to forget, the game tickets!

EMOTIONAL COMMITMENT AND LOYALTY AMONG SPORTS FANS

As we described in chapter 1, all sports fans are not created equally, as some are far more passionate than others. The most passionate are the "highly identified" fans. These sports fans outwardly display their allegiance to a favorite team or player by wearing team apparel and/or in other visible manners. Because the highly identified fan has his or her character connected to the team, loyalty is uncompromised. The highly identified fan also possesses a very strong emotional commitment to the team. In contrast, the lowly identified, or marginal fans, are less loyal and emotionally committed.

Fan Enthusiasm

Emotional commitment and loyalty to a team (or a loved one for that matter) is a process. And this process begins with shared activities among friends and significant others. Activity allows for ritual behavior and celebrations. Ritualistic behaviors and celebrations are instances of intense involvement which allow members an opportunity to express emotional unity. Group participation, such as tailgating, or simply attending a sporting event with friends, provides occasions for members to join together in collective behavior and sentiment (e.g., cheering collectively when the preferred team scores a touchdown). The tailgate party, the sports bar, a buddy's home, or the arena itself provides a site location for friends and family members to bond. The shared activity becomes an example of sociability, or interaction. After a period time, the sociability aspect of the collective action becomes rewarding. Thus, social interaction creates opportunities for emotional commitment and loyalty.

Harry Edwards (1973), the creator of sport sociology, argued that the chief factor determining fan enthusiasm for sports is to be found within the function of sport as an institution. As an institution, having primary socialization and value training functions, sport affords the fan an opportunity to reaffirm the established values and beliefs that define acceptable means and solutions to central problems in the secular realm of everyday social life. Leisure groups (e.g., sports booster groups) and sports in general, provide for identity enhancement, and allow for expression of loyalty, commitment and emotional expression. Typically, a highly identified fan will enjoy the fruits of victory more intensely than moderate or marginal fans. Additionally, the highly identified fan will experience a stronger feeling of personal defeat when his or her team loses, compared to moderate or marginal fans. Hence, the highly identified fan will more likely experience an emotional letdown following a defeat than will the moderate or marginal fan.

There are many fans who believe that they play an active, rather than passive, role in sport outcomes. They believe that through their support, cheering and intensity, that they play some small part in the final outcome. This belief is constantly reinforced by the fact that athletes attribute home field advantage to their passionate fans; crowd noise can intimidate opponents (in Football this is called "The 12th Man" effect); and by observing the instances of athletes trying to pump the crowd to frenzy—which athletes do as much to psyche themselves. Passionate fans show an increase in heart rate before and during the game (Corbin, 1973), exhibit emotional pregame stress (Roberts, 1976), and feel emotionally exhausted at the conclusion of a viewing a game (Delaney, 1999).

Group Cohesiveness

Loyalty, commitment and bonding among group members contribute to group cohesiveness. Cohesiveness is the liking, the sense of belonging, and the bond that creates the sense of being a unit, which in turn, has powerful effects on the group itself (Douglas, 1983). Johnson and Johnson (2002) state that the most frequently used term to describe a member's commitment to a group is "cohesiveness". Group cohesion, sometimes referred to as group solidarity, is the extent to which the influences on members to remain in the group are greater than the influence on members to leave the group. Individuals become members of a group because they believe that the rewards of their membership outweigh the costs (Mowday, Porter and Stegas, 1982). As cohesiveness increases, so does the capacity of a group to keep its members. A high level of loyalty and commitment to the group will, in turn, increase an individual's sense of self. Loyalty, by definition, involves interest, partiality and identification with the object of one's loyalty (e.g., lover, sports team, employer, country). Loyalty involves unconditional devotion and maintenance of the relationship in the face of challenges and contradictory information. Loyalty and commitment, then, are closely associated with one another. They serve as effective components to behavior.

Fans will generally stay loyal and committed to their favorite teams for a lifetime. As Gregory Stone (1955) said over a half-century ago, sport helps to provide continuality to life. Team loyalties formed in adolescence and maintained through adulthood serve to remind one that there are some areas of stability in life. As described earlier in this chapter, one of the biggest threats to stability and continuality for the professional sports fan is franchise relocation. If the team moves away from the community, how does stability remain? What will happen to the emotional well-being of a community and individual sport fans when the loyalty and commitment by professional sports franchises to their community ceases to exist? After all, trust, once broken, can never be regained. When a sports franchise abandons a community, they destroy the emotional well-being of fans. Cleveland Browns fans will tell you, it's just not the same. Once your heart has been ripped open, even a new team does not completely heal the scar.

The emotional component of being a highly identified sports fan can not be minimized. Some fans are very passionate in their support of their favorite team. For some, sport provides a socially acceptable way to engage in a varying array of emotions. For others, sport and the accompanying emotional attachment and commitment it brings borders on fanaticism ("fan", after all, is a shortened version of the word "fanatic").

Sport fans are not alone in feeling deep emotion in sport. The athletes themselves experience emotional highs and lows. Feelings of elation accompany creative athletic moves and plays, while agony goes along with defeat. Athletes experience intense self-feelings while competing in crucial sport situations. This is true whether an athlete is sprinting for gold in the Olympics or is about to attempt a game-winning field goal, as time expires, in the Super Bowl. Such situations are known as "moments in time" that underscore an athlete's career and/or legacy. Leonard (1988) explains the significance "of the moment" as an intense emotionality that appears to stop time. As an example, one of the most dramatic moments in World Series history occurred when an ailing Kirk Gibson came off the bench in the bottom of the 9th inning to hit a dramatic game-winning homerun. It turned out to be his only at-bat in the entire 1988 World Series but it was enough to emotionally charge his Los Angeles Dodgers to an underdog championship. This moment in time has been replayed repeatedly in the media and it has as much to do with the emotionality of the moment as anything else. Athletes, coaches and fans all live for the "moment of time." The elation that accompanies "the moment" is why people invest so much of their time and passion in sport.

**Narrative 7.1. An interview with Wayne Quatrochi,
a longtime Cleveland Browns fan**

1. How long have you been a Browns' fan?

   I have been a Browns fan my whole life. I was born in Hoboken, NJ in 1950. I grew up there in the 1950s and 1960s. Everyone was a Giants or Browns fan. Some people were Eagles fans. When I was a kid, the Browns and Giants were the best rivalry in professional football. I remember watching Jim Brown on television—he is still the greatest player I have ever seen.

2. When did you attend your first game in Cleveland? What do you remember from that experience?

   I moved to Auburn, New York in time for high school. Most of the kids in upstate New York at this time were Browns and Giants just as in Hoboken. But now I met people who had gone to Browns games. They all spoke so highly about going to the Stadium, like it was a shrine or something. In 1981, I finally attended my first game, and it was not just any game; it was a game against the hated Steelers. I was excited about the game all week. I can remember walking into the Stadium for that first time and it was like all the Christmas mornings I had experienced all rolled into one! I could feel the electricity in the air. I thought to myself, I am finally at a Browns game in Cleveland. I have been going to Cleveland every season since 1981.

3. What was your most memorable trip to Cleveland?

   I have so many great memories of games in Cleveland but the wildest one was the January 6, 1989 playoff game against the Bills. It was the year before the Buffalo Bills first of four consecutive trips to the Super Bowl, so they were a good team. My friends and I rented an R/V and headed off to Cleveland. We got to the parking lot at 6:00am. The gates were not opened but people were already tailgating and partying. We partied all day long and the Browns won a shootout. We stayed in the parking lot for another day!

4. Which game is your all-time favorite and why?

   That would have to be the Browns—Steelers game in December, 1983. This was the first time I had tickets in the infamous "Dawg Pound"—although it was not called that back then. The Dawg Pound section of Cleveland Stadium is insane. These used to be the cheap seats and a lot of working class, die-hard, local Browns fans bought these tickets. However, this is where the out-of-town fans sat as well. And to enter into Cleveland Stadium (Cleveland Municipal Stadium at the time) and cheer against the Browns in those days was dangerous. On this particular day, there was a downpour of rain all day. Stadium concessions sold garbage bags for rain coats. It didn't matter that it rained; I was in the Dawg Pound. And, we beat the Steelers 30-17. This was also Brian Sipe's last home game before he went to the USFL.

(*continued*)

Narrative 7.1. (*continued*)

5. When Cleveland lost its football franchise, how did you react?

   At first I was in shock. How could the city of Cleveland not have a football team? I felt very betrayed by Art Modell. He sold us fans out. And I am still upset with the NFL for letting it happen. I did not watch any NFL games for the three years that the Browns did not exist.

6. Did you attend the first game of the Browns' franchise return to Cleveland? What was it like in the Stadium that day?

   Yes, I felt like I came out of a football-less coma. Finally, the Browns were back and I could enjoy a Fall day of football. The Stadium and city was electric that day, like a playoff game. I am a proud season ticket holder and still attend games every year.

Differences between "Real" Sports Fans and Sports Gamblers in Loyalty, Commitment and Identity

What's the difference between a "real" sports fan and a fan of sports gambling? The primary answers center on issues of loyalty, commitment, and identity. As described previously, loyalty generates interest, partiality, and identification with the object of a fan's loyalty, rather than with a team's competitors. A minimal requirement of loyalty is the maintenance of the relationship, which requires the rejection of alternatives that undermine the principle bond. Thus, a loyal lover will not be seduced by another, and a loyal sports fan (a "real" fan) will continue his or her allegiance to the team even when the team is not successful. Sport gamblers do not enjoy this feeling of loyalty; they will abandon a team as soon as they start losing money for them.

Loyalty is a type of committed behavior that is manifested by the tendency to participate in a particular recreational community. Sports fans accomplish this through cheering for a team, or favorite athlete, with fellow fans. Team loyalties developed over a period of time provides fans with a sense of belonging and stability, elements that are often missing in a modern society. The game itself offers fans a feeling of continuity, resolution and closure. This can even be multi-generational, with children continuing to root for teams they first learned about from their parents. Sports gamblers miss out on all of this. They move from sporting event to sporting event without any sense of continuity beyond gambling for a team or athlete until it no longer becomes profitable.

The term "commitment" often is used as a synonym for the term "loyalty." Commitment involves an emotional attachment to the object of loyalty (the team or athlete). Committed sports fans remain loyal to a team, whereas sports gamblers are quick to abandon a team that loses them money. Since sports gamblers do not have a team that they can remain loyal to, they also do not identify with teams like real fans do. Identity involves those aspects of one's life that are deemed as essential to the character and maintenance of self. Without identification to a team, sports gamblers do not experience the effects of "basking-in-reflected-glory" (BIRG) because of their low level of identification, loyalty, commitment, and allegiance to a team. Seldom do they have the opportunity to use the phrase "We Won!" This is something reserved for real fans. One could argue, however, that sports gamblers may BIRG in a financial manner. The opposite phenomenon of BIRG is cutting-off-reflected-failure (CORF). Real sports fans, because of loyalty, will maintain an allegiance to a team; even if they continuously lose, they do not CORF. However, sports gamblers will abandon teams (CORF) that lose money for them.

The manner in which sport gamblers and real fans watch a game is also different. Sport gamblers are cheering merely for a final score that covers their bet. That is, they cheer for/against a point spread. Sports fans are primarily concerned with whether or not their team wins. The margin of victory is a secondary concern—at best. Real sport fans cheer with genuine passion and a sense of identity with the team. Real fans also experience much more of a "rush" when their favorite team wins than gamblers do when they pick the right team to cover the spread. Real fans do not like being around sports gamblers. Real fans especially dislike a sports gambler who is cheering against a team that they are loyal to. Real fans do not care about a gambler's bet on a game and they certainly do not care how much money they have on the game. Real sport fans endure far more pain when their team loses than someone who merely lost a bet. Conversely, a real sports fan will always enjoy the fruits of victory more than a sport gambler who simply collects on a bet.

In short, real sports fans are loyal to their team, win or lose. Sports gamblers are loyal only to a team that "covers" the point spread. Real fans do not care about "point spreads" they only care about "W's" (wins) and "L's" (loses). Sports gamblers abandon a team as soon as they start losing money because of them. Real fans stick with their teams through thick and through thin.

SPORT RIVALRIES

The role of "rivals" in sport is significant. A rival, in a sporting sense, is a person, or team that competes for the same desired goals as the preferred person, or team. The philosopher Friedrich Nietzsche, in his work *Thus Spake Zarathustra,* extolled the virtue of having a good enemy rather than a good friend, for enemies bring out one's competitive spirit and encourage one to always be at one's best in order to challenge them. "You may have only enemies whom you can hate", he wrote, "not enemies you despise. You must be proud of your enemy: then the successes of your enemy are your successes too" (Nietzsche, 1979:160). Nietzsche provides us with food for thought, indeed. But Nietzsche never met modern-day sports fans! Passionate sports fans not only hate their enemies, they *despise* them. And the very idea of a heated-rival winning a championship brings pain to sports fans, not thoughts of associated success.

Every athlete and sports team has a rival. The athletes and fans alike will freely admit to this. Sports rivalries are far more important to highly identified fans than they are the athletes themselves. There are many reasons for this. First, older fans that have an allegiance to a team have identified rivals before today's athletes were even born. Present-day athletes identify rivals based on uniforms realizing full well that some time in the career they may play for the rival of their current team-day team. For example, in 2004, MLB player Johnny Damon was leading his Boston Red Sox to their first World Series championship in 86 years. As a member of the Red Sox, he fully understood the hatred that Boston and New York Yankees fans have for one another and clearly he was on the side of the Red Sox. However, a couple of seasons later he is now playing for the Yankees. As a Yankee, he now views the Red Sox as the enemy. And this scenario is true for every player that changes uniforms. Thus, a player's perspective on rivalries can change. But Red Sox and Yankees fans, like all passionate fans, never changed their viewpoints. Furthermore, for retired players, the hatred toward rival teams diminishes over time. For fans, the feelings toward rivals never weaken.

The "Best" Sports Rivalries

Sports fans display their loyalty and commitment toward a preferred team, or athlete, in a number of ways, including those previously discussed. Showing animosity toward a rival is another way of demonstrating team allegiance. Highly identified fans are often as passionate about their dislike, or hatred, toward a rival as they are with showing love to their favorite team. Thus, it should come as no surprise that sports fans are also passionate about their declaration that their favorite team's rivalry with an adversary is the "best" of all rivalries. Sports talks show sure know this. "Let's open the phone lines now, Delaney and Madigan declare X and Y as the best rivalry in sports. Callers, do you agree?" Mayhem will ensue, passions will become heated. After all, if you disagree with another sports fan's preference, you are an idiot!

Delaney and Madigan will freely engage sports fans with talk about the "best" sports rivalries. But we want to declare a few ground rules first. Someone cannot simply say that team "A" and team "B" are the best rivalry just because they think so; there must be some sort of established parameters. So give it up, ESPN—just because you say that the Boston Red Sox and New York Yankees are the number rivalry in sports doesn't necessarily mean it is so. You must establish criteria for such a designation. Among the components for making a "great rivalry" are: geographic proximity; regular meetings between the two teams; a long history that includes significant past events; fans of both teams must have strong feelings of dislike for one another; the cities involved should also be rivals; each team has won approximately the same number of titles; and each team has knocked the other out of playoff contention a significant number of times.

With the above criteria, apply two rival teams and determine whether or not they are mild, moderate, or strong rivals based on the number of factors that apply to them. The Yankees and Red Sox, for example, have nearly all the criteria, but one. Only recently has the rivalry been fairly equal. Boston having gone 86 years in-between World Series Championships, provides a tough obstacle to overcome when stating the Sox and Yanks are the greatest rivalry. No one would debate that it is among the best that professional sports has to offer.

College rivalries (not to mention a number of high school rivalries) are also huge. And there are many reasons for this, beginning with the realization that college sports have been in existence longer than professional sports. College rivalries, with the most noted being based on football, are very emotional and passionate for two primary reasons. One, many fans actually attended the college they cheer for and therefore *do* have a sense of identification and attachment to the school. And second, the majority of college sports fans are from the community in which they reside. So once again, fans have a sense of attachment and identity to the school and its sports teams. College sports come equipped with school colors, past successes, and fight songs that give chills to fans when they hear the band proudly belting out the tunes. Among the great college rivalries are: Texas and Texas A&M; USC and UCLA; Florida and Georgia; Kansas and Missouri; Ohio State and Michigan; Pittsburgh and West Virginia; Cal and Stanford: Army and Navy; and Harvard and Yale. And yes, there are many others deserving of mention here.

At the heart of heated rivalries is the matter of identity. That is, we all identify with some sort of group. The need to identify with a group dates to ancient tribalism. And it was tribalism (group formation) that helped early humans to survive the many challenges from nature. The authors do not intend on attempting to solve the "mystery" of the best rivalries in sports here, but again, we are happy to join in the debate.

The Rival Index

Although we have side-stepped the immediate determination of the best rivalry in sports, years ago Delaney created a "Rival Index" while conducting original research on a sports booster group—the Southern California Browns Backers Association (SCBBA). At the time that the research was conducted (1993), the SCBBA was the largest sports booster group outside of its home state. The "rival index" is a device used to determine one team's best rivalries based on fan voting.

Although Delaney's research was centered on the Cleveland Browns, the "rival index" is designed to be utilized in research conducted on any sports team. The rival index utilizes a point system. Respondents are asked to list the top three teams that they believe are the biggest arch-rivals (of the team under study). The rival index involves the following formula: The team listed first (the number one rival) receives three points; the team listed second receives two points; and the team listed third receives one point. Consequently, the highest score possible in the Rival Index would be "N" times 3, with "N" equaling the number of responses. A measure of association is also utilized as a means of demonstrating the degree to which fans dislike a rival team. In Delaney's (1999) research, there were 506 respondents (N=506), indicating that the highest possible score would be 1,518. As Table 7.1 reveals, the Pittsburgh Steelers are clearly the number one rival of the Browns (based on survey results conducted on the SCBBA) garnering the greatest number of points and with a very strong level of association (.85). A level of association above .7 is considered strong; levels between .4 and .7 are considered moderate; and a level below .4 is a weak measure of association.

It is interesting to note that the Houston Oilers no longer exist. The franchise relocated to Tennessee and became the Titans. Houston was later awarded a franchise and plays under the nickname of Texans.

Table 7.1.   Top Five Rivals of the Cleveland Browns*
The Rival Index
N = 506

Rival Team	Points	Association
Pittsburgh Steelers	1,291	.85
Denver Broncos	778	.51
Cincinnati Bengals	587	.39
Houston Oilers	257	.17
Los Angeles/Oakland Raiders	62	.04

*As determined by 1993 data collected on the SCBBA.

Another significance of discussing rivals rests with the realization that fans are socialized into disliking a team. Significant others (the agents of socialization) influence the young, or novice, fan into accepting the fact that if you cheer for one team (e.g. the Cleveland Browns) you cannot cheer for their rival team (e.g., the Pittsburgh Steelers). The significance of rival socialization is especially evident in high school. Schools host pep rallies in an attempt to generate support for the home school and simultaneously put down the rival school and its team. This tradition continues on in college and extends to professional sports. Fanatical fans that raise their children to cheer for one team at the same time socialize their children to despise the rival team.

SEEKING DIVINE AND SECULAR INTERVENTION

Although there are times when athletes give the fans an "assist" in their efforts to cheer the team onto victory, and many fans think that they can influence a game by cheering or booing loudly, most fans realize they are powerless over the final outcome. Players, on the other hand, have a direct influence on the game, even though there are, at times, events that occur that are beyond their control. As a result of their inability to control specific events such as ballgames and races, many fans and athletes seek divine and secular intervention in their pursuit of victory.

Divine Intervention through Prayer

How many times have you prayed for a favorable sports outcome? Did it work? How many times have you seen athletes pray? Did it work for them? Who are fans and athletes praying to anyway? God, presumably; but not necessarily so. And what makes sports fans and athletes believe that God cares who wins a sporting event?! (Note: We will ignore the argument over whether God or some other holy representations other than God even exists, as this is not the proper forum for such a debate.)

Suffice it to say, many people inside and outside of sports pray. But why do people pray? They pray because they have lost "faith" in human ability. They search for unearthly intervention. That sports fans pray is relatively understandable; after all, they do not have any direct influence over the outcome of a game. Athletes, on the other hand, do have direct control over who wins and loses.

We all realize that sports fans, especially highly identified ones, have an emotional (and sometimes financial — games are not free!) investment with their favorite team or athlete. Defeats are costly to one's psyche and cause emotional distress and may even contribute to depression. The reality that sports fans face in their realization that they cannot control what occurs on the playing surface leaves them feeling powerless. The cheer and boo, but still the opponent is prevailing. What else can they do? They can pray. "Please God, let the <BLANK> win." Sports fans may even bargain with God, "If you let <BLANK> win, I promise to be a better person, I will attend religious services more often, I will . . . " You get the point.

In a sense, turning to God is a "rational" last-ditch effort of sports fans when seeking a desired end. After all, if God is all-powerful, as adherents believe, than certainly "He" is capable of bestowing victory to my team. In this regard, praying to God almost seems logical for some fans. And besides, what else can a fan do? Unfortunately, there is no correlation between prayer and outcome. Yes, a favorite team or athlete may when after a fan(s) prays, but chances are, fans of the other team also prayed and their prayers were not answered. Interestingly, fans and athletes alike will give credit to divine intervention when things turn out favorably, but they will not blame God when things do not. Imagine a sports fan, or an athlete for that matter saying to a reporter, "Well, the reason we lost today was God was against us." We will hear the opposite; however, "I have to give praise to God for our victory today."

That athletes resort to prayer seems quite odd, at least on the surface. Athletes have direct influence on the outcome of the game and yet prayer often serves a functional role for them. Consider the pregame prayer in team sports. When teammates gather together in the locker room before the start of the game, the pregame prayer can help to unify players into one collectivity. Furthermore, athletes also realize that there is always a chance of injury, so they may turn to prayer for safety and protection during competition. Athletes are also known to pray for divine intervention, again, even though they control the end result. In reality, however, athletes are not always that confident on the playing field, and because they doubt themselves and their ability to perform up to their capabilities, they may turn to prayer. Prayer has certainly been shown as an effective coping mechanism for stress. In addition, prayer may actually give athletes a boost in self confidence and as a result, they do perform better.

Athletes seem to be increasingly incorporating religious gestures on the playing field/court. For example, some baseball players make the sign of the Cross before they go to bat; assumingly hoping that such a religious gesture will help them to get a hit, maybe even a homerun. After making a good play, some athletes will look skyward as if to thank God for helping them to perform well. At the conclusion of certain sporting events, such as a football game, teammates and opponents may gather in the middle of the field, join hands, and pray together.

The comedian Lewis Black puts all this into a nice perspective:

There is nothing more obnoxious to an avid sports fan—okay, to me—than an athlete telling the audience after a big victory that God was the reason for it. As Jeff Stillson puts it so well in his act: "I like football games, but I hate the interviews after the games, because the winning players always give credit to God while the losers blame themselves. Just once I'd like to hear a player say, 'Yeah, we were in the game . . . until Jesus made me fumble. He hates our team. Jesus hates us.'" It implies that the losers on the other team just didn't love God enough to have enough faith in the Supreme Being (Black, 2008:36).

The authors of this book advocate a strict wall of separation between church and sport.

Secular Intervention through Rituals and Superstitions

Prayer is not the answer for all sports fans and athletes. But even fans and athletes that do not turn to prayer still seek some sort of intervention. Among the secular forms of intervention are rituals and superstitions. Ritualistic behaviors are very common in sport because they help to relieve anxiety and stress and help to prepare athletes face the competition with self-assurance. Womack (1992) argues that rituals are important in sport for the following reasons:

1. Ritual helps the player focus his attention on the task at hand. It can be used by the player to prevent anxiety or excessive environmental stimuli—such as the chanting of fans—from interrupting his concentration.
2. Ritual can signal intent to the other team. Specially, ritual can be used to "threaten" the other team.
3. Ritual provides a means of coping with a high-risk, high stress situation.
4. Ritual helps establish a rank order among team members and promotes intra-group communication.
5. Ritual helps in dealing with ambiguity in interpersonal relationships, with other team members, and with people on the periphery of the team, such as management and the public.
6. Ritual is a "harmless" means of self-expression. It can be used to reinforce a sense of individual worth under pressure for group conformity, without endangering the unity of the group.
7. Ritual directs individual motivations and needs toward achieving group goals (p.200).

Sports fans also engage in ritualistic behaviors because they think such activity influences the outcome of a sporting event. Sports fans may, for example, wear specific clothing (e.g., a "lucky cap") while viewing or attending a game; eat certain foods; take specific routes to the game or a friend's house to watch the game; pay strict adherence to pregame tailgate rituals; schedule restroom breaks after certain on-field events occur; celebrate significant on-field events in a specific manner (e.g., some combination of "high-fives" or fist bumps with fellow fans); turn their ball caps backwards as a type of "rally call;" and so on. Highly identified fans are likely to hold fast to specific ritualistic behaviors than marginal or moderate fans.

Often, the ritualistic behaviors of sports fans are tied to superstitions. How else would we explain why fans believe a certain ball cap or t-shirt is "lucky" and therefore must be worn on gameday? There are people who believe certain objects, like a rabbit's foot or a lucky coin (or that certain ball cap or t-shirt), possess magical qualities that can somehow be summoned to bring forth a sports victory. Like religious persons who rely on prayer for favorable sporting outcomes, superstitious persons find causal relations between certain behaviors and outcomes where they do not really exist. Sports fans and athletes generally turn to superstitious behaviors as a way to reduce their level of anxiety before and during the game. In this regard, they are controlling, or doing, *something* to influence the result of the game. And, gaining any type of "edge" in sports is the goal of all athletes and fans.

FINAL THOUGHTS

Whether one plays a sport or not, anyone can be a fan. People identify strongly with their favorite teams and players, often basking in reflected glory when a victory occurs. In addition, fans usually form a community—they organize together for the common purpose of supporting their team, and thereby form a network of social relationships which give purpose and excitement to their lives.

Traditionally, communities had the same physical location, but this has changed in recent times. Every community values athletic excellence, and sports plays a vital role in many communities. There are many ways in which sport can unite a community—through both active participation and passive support. Such identification with a team can provide a healthy diversion from mundane reality and a sense of identification with the larger group. Sport can also divide communities, particularly when athletes and owners do not seem to have the interests of the community itself as their primary concern.

Sports fans generally have a strong emotional attachment toward their team. This can help them to feel as though they are a part of a group or community. One way to do this is through participation in a sport booster group.

Friendships are often formed through such activities of people interacting with each other for sheer enjoyment. Such identification with a sport can reaffirm the fan's established values and beliefs, and provide for identity enhancement. It can also allow individuals to express loyalty, commitment and emotional ties, which leads to group cohesiveness.

Perhaps nothing is more exciting than the rivalry that often occurs between teams. Think of your own favorite sport team—is it even possible to also *not* think of their most hated rival? Perhaps paradoxically, one thing we love about sports is the hated rival. There's nothing wrong with that—so long as we don't take such hatred too far!

Chapter Eight

Sportsmanship

A cherished ideal of sport participation is the development of positive character traits that collectively can be referred to as "sportsmanship". An athlete that displays culturally acceptable sports-related behavior is said to be a "good sport." In volleyball, for example, athletes have periodically been known to make an "honor call" wherein they will admit to a referee that a call that went in their favor was actually inaccurate. Consider this scenario for example: A referee awards the ball to Team "A" because Team "B" was ruled to have illegally struck the ball four times before sending it over the net. But a member of Team "A" admits to the referee that the ball hit his wrist during the alleged four tries of Team "B."

We don't often hear about "honor calls" in sports; and the higher the level of competitiveness, the less likely such admissions will be forthcoming. Think about it. Can you imagine an NBA playoff game where a player turns to a referee and states, "I just committed a foul and you did not see it. Please award my opponent free throws." His teammates, coaches, owner and fans would react in stunned amazement and then anger. How about a soccer player such as Diego Maradona admitting, *during* a World Cup match that his hand touched the ball (a "hand ball") even though the referees do not call the violation. The goal in question dates back to the 1986 World Cup quarterfinal match between Argentina and England. Maradona was given credit for scoring a goal even though it appeared he had punched the ball into the goal. At the time, Maradona insisted that his hand never touched the ball and that God willed it into the net. This explains why Maradona's famous goal is known as the "Hand of God" goal. Nearly twenty years later, Maradona admitted that he did indeed punch the ball with his hand. But there is little honor in this late admission. (See chapter 3 for more details.)

The Maradona story provides us with a glimpse at the bipolar nature of sportsmanship. Parents of youth athletes, coaches, school and league administrators, and even most sports fans will profess that athletes should act as good sports and display good sportsmanship. And yet, in most cases, displaying good sportsmanship should not come at the expense of victory, especially team victory. But where do we draw the line? There are high school districts that have banned the tradition of post-game handshakes because in the past this ultimate gesture of sportsmanship has been marred with physical confrontations and brawls.

Shouldn't winning come *with* sportsmanship and not in spite of it? Don't get us wrong, we are not preaching here. The authors themselves may "blow a fuse" if suddenly a favorite professional, or college, team's victory was stripped away because an athlete decided to do the "right" thing and admit to an infraction that was not seen by the referees and thus changed the outcome of the game. But then again, when athletes charge into the stands to fight fans, or fans throw objects at athletes, isn't there something wrong? This is why we feel strongly about the ideal of promoting good sportsmanship, at all levels of sports.

Sportsmanship

Sportsmanship involves fair play, decency, and respect—for oneself, the competitor, and for the sport itself. Ideals of sportsmanship, such as competitiveness, hard work, fair play, obedience to authority, and dedication, are tied to a society's cultural morality. Sportsmanship is tied to morality because it represents an ideal form of behavior—to be a good sport and play fairly. As Keating (2001) explains:

> Sportsmanship is not merely an aggregate of moral qualities comprising a code of specialized behavior; it is also an attitude, a posture, a manner of interpreting what would otherwise be only a legal code. Yet the moral qualities believed to comprise the code have almost monopolized consideration and have proliferated to the point of depriving sportsmanship of nay distinctiveness. Truthfulness, courage, Spartan endurance, self-control, self-respect, scorn of luxury, consideration for another's opinions and rights, courtesy, fairness, magnanimity, a high sense of honor, co-operation, generosity. The list seems interminable (p.12).

Sportsmanship, then, is an expression of morality and provides a code of acceptable behavior for athletes to abide by in their pursuit of fair play. Good sportsmanship involves conduct and attitudes considered befitting to participants, especially in regards to a sense of fair play, courtesy toward teammates and opponents, game officials, and others involved in sporting contests, as well as grace in losing. Good sportsmanship generally implies that participants play sports for the joy of playing. However, it should be noted that because sportsmanship is tied to cultural standards of morality, norms, and values, ideal types may vary from one society to the next.

Often, it seems, athletes are driven by other intentions beyond fair play and morality. The pressure to win may compromise the fair play ethos. Athletes may desire fame and recognition, material benefits and self-realization through victory even if it comes at the cost of sportsmanship. The desire to win, sometimes at-any-costs, causes some athletes to circumvent ideals of good sportsmanship. As the philosopher Friedrich Nietzsche told us long ago, the values of the past are dead, and new values replace them. Yet Nietzsche himself valued the ancient Greek concept of sportsmanship (see chapter 2 for a discussion of the ancient Greek ideals). To him, the struggle to be one's best necessarily involves respect for one's opponent—it is the genuine struggle with a worthy adversary that allows a person to truly understand his or her own abilities. As the old saying goes, when you cheat you're only cheating yourself.

One can ask, have the ideals of sportsmanship really disappeared? Or are they often merely overshadowed by incidents of narcissism and a "me first" philosophy? The authors contend that sportsmanship in sport is not dead. Sportsmanship does, however, at times, take a back seat to other sport priorities; specifically winning and making a profit. Thus, there are times when sportsmanship seems to be in contradiction with the primary goal of sport—winning. This is because sportsmanship, "insofar as it connotes the behavior proper to the athlete, seeks to place certain basic limitations on the rigors of competition" (Keating, 2001:15). At times it seems more important in sport to win than to be a good sport.

What happens when an athlete places honesty and sportsmanship over winning? Is he or she supported or condemned? The story of the volleyball player in the chapter's introductory story was based on a real-life case that took place a few years back in Buffalo, New York. In 2000, a Clarence High School volleyball player, Jeffrey Glick, chose being honest and fair—good sportsmanship—over winning. During a tied (15-15) volleyball match, the referee awarded Clarence a point, ruling that opposing Williamsville players illegally struck the ball four times before volleying the ball over the net. However, Glick knew the ball hit his wrist between the four Williamsville strikes and told the referee that his team did not deserve the point. The referee ordered the point played over and Williamsville won the replay and, shortly afterwards, won the game 18-16 to clinch the match. Glick, who was also the president of the National Honor Society, had no regrets about his decision, reasoning that it would not have been right to say nothing about the incorrect call. Glick's coach, Kevin Starr, supported his player's decision, affirming that he teaches character and good sportsmanship as much as skills development (Simon, 2000).

It is refreshing that this student did the "right thing." However, Glick's honest behavior may actually be viewed as deviant among his peers and sports fans. Perhaps sadly, it is unlikely that such a display of sportsmanship would be rewarded at the collegiate or professional level of sports, where winning generally takes precedence over admitting to a referee about an infraction committed.

The NCAA and Sportsmanship

Often times, the concept of sportsmanship is a little vague. It is one of those concepts, like the word "sport" itself, that we all feel as though we know and understand, and yet, when pressed for a proper definition, the parameters are a little cloudy. There are, however, entities that have precise meanings for the term "sportsmanship." The NCAA is one example.

The NCAA Manual clearly states its policy on sportsmanship in Article 10.01.1 (Standards of Honesty and Sportsmanship). "Individuals employed by (or associated with) a member institution to administer, conduct or coach intercollegiate athletics and all participating student-athletes shall act with honesty and sportsmanship at all times so that intercollegiate athletics as a whole, their institutions and they, as individuals, shall represent the honor and dignity of fair play and the generally recognized high standards associated with the wholesome competitive sports" (*NCAA Division III Manual*, 2008:47). A number of unethical behaviors are articulated by the NCAA as well. Examples include the use of illegal drugs, cheating, and fraud. In recent years, due to the dramatic increase in gaming in many states and the proliferation of online wagering, gambling on games has become an increasing challenge. NCAA President Myles Brand makes it very clear that sports wagering will not be tolerated: "The NCAA is unambiguous about requiring student-athletes, as well as everyone engaged in intercollegiate athletics, from coaches to officials, to abstain totally from any form of sports wagering. Intercollegiate sports wagering is illegal in almost every state, illegal on the Internet (according to the 1961 Wire Communications Act), and the use of credit cards for sports wagering is illegal" (Madigan, 2003:12). Yet he ruefully admits that student sports bookies can be found on every major campus, necessitating constant vigilance from NCAA and other officials.

National Sportsmanship Day

Did you know that there is such a thing as "National Sportsmanship Day?" March 3, 2009 marked the 19th annual National Sportsmanship Day. It was celebrated in more than 14,000 schools throughout the United States, as well as in countries such as Ghana, Nigeria, India, Australia, and Bermuda. Jackie Joyner-Kersee, former Olympic Gold Medalist, served as the 2009 Chair of the 2009 National Sportsmanship Day Program (Institute for International Sport, 2009). The annual event, started by the Institute for International Sport, attempts to raise awareness about fair play, sportsmanship and ethics in athletics and society. Students at elementary, middle and high school, and colleges participated in various events and committed to the ideals of sportsmanship both on and off the field/court. Student participants generally write essays addressing sportsmanship and ethics and offer a personal reflection on good or poor sportsmanship experiences. A panel of judges determines winning essays.

Wouldn't it be great if the ideals of sportsmanship were promoted and encouraged on a daily basis? Or at the very least, it would be refreshing if this annual day of sportsmanship was as well-known as another annual March event—March Madness.

The World Sports Humanitarian Hall of Fame

Each major sport has its shrines to honor its hero located in their respective Hall of Fames. Sportspersons also have a Hall of Fame: The World Sports Humanitarian Hall of Fame, located on the Boise State University campus in Idaho. (College Football's The Humanitarian Bowl is played in Boise in honor of this Hall of Fame.) According to their website, the Hall "recognizes individuals and organizations from the world of amateur and professional athletics, who through their humanitarian efforts, distinguish themselves as role models in the community" (World Sports Humanitarian Hall of Fame, 2009).

This admirable Hall of Fame is the creation of Myron Finkbeiner, a former high school and college basketball coach who believes that athletes can and have impacted the world in positive ways beyond their athletic skills (DiCesare, 2005). Finkbeiner, an avid sports fan, grew tired of the media's focus on the negative aspects of sports during the early 1990s and took it upon himself to create a tribute to athletes who act in a humanitarian fashion. Upon his influence, the World Sports Humanitarian Hall of Fame was established in 1994. Beginning with that inaugural year, sportspersons (usually three) are inducted annually. The first three inductees were tennis star Arthur Ashe, known for his fight against AIDS and apartheid; golfer Chi Chi Rodriquez, who created a foundation to support abused children; and decathlete Rafer Johnson, cited for his long-time commitment to the Special Olympics (DiCesare, 2005).

To date, more than 35 sports-humanitarians have been enshrined in Boise, including the 14th annual (class of 2008) award winners, NFL running back Warrick Dunn, cited for assisting single parents to become homeowners through the Warrick Dunn Foundation; NBA player Vlade Divac, acknowledged for his efforts to assist refugees from war-ravaged Yugoslavia through his Humanitarian Organization Divac; and Olympic skier Jimmie Heuga, who assists people with multiple sclerosis (a disease that inflicted Heuga after his Olympic days) through his Heuga Center for Multiple Sclerosis.

If you like to hear positive stories about true sportspersons, visit the World Sports Humanitarian Hall of Fame website and find the links to the numerous athletes who run foundations to help others. Despite the seeming

---

Box 8.1.   Color Me Pink: An Example of Poor Sportsmanship, or Clever Psychological Ploy?

Are there colors that are gender specific? There seems to be a popular belief that the color blue is associated with boys, while the color pink is for girls. This idea is reinforced in most hospital nurseries across the United States; that is, female babies are wrapped in pink blankets and male babies in blue ones. For most people, the idea that girls wear pink and boys do not is a mere social folkway (an informal rule). It is true that boys have been known to tease other boys if they wear pink; although oddly, girls are not teased when they wear blue! But why is it so unmanly to wear pink? And why would any male want to wear pink if he is going to be teased? Maybe he looks good in pink. The movie *Pretty in Pink* references the idea that a girl's best color is pink. The inference is that pink is associated with femininity. And that is why girls wear pink, and boys do not.

The fact that males tease other males when they wear pink reveals a sex-appropriateness connotation to colors. In the sports world, the male preserve, any violation of "codes of masculinity" will trigger taunts similar to Pavlov ringing his bell to get his dogs to salivate. The male locker room is an especially important "safe zone" for male athletes—it is a testosterone environment where males feel the need to constantly show their manliness, often at the expense of others. The University of Iowa's football team, looking for any edge possible, decided to try and psyche out its opponents by painting the visitor's locker room at the University of Iowa's Kinnick Stadium in pink. Today, the walls are pink, the bathroom stalls pink, the ceiling is pink, the urinals are pink, and the carpet is also pink.

Former Hawkeye's coach (1979-1998) Hayden Fry, a psychology major, first had the walls and benches painted pink in 1980, reasoning that the color pink has

(continued)

Box 8.1. (*continued*)

a calming effect on opponents (research has shown that light pink has a pacifying affect). Most visiting football players are aware of the pink locker room and claim that it has no effect on them and that they realize it is merely a ploy in an attempt to psyche them out. Other people are offended by the pink locker room and for different reasons. Former Michigan Head Coach (1969-1989) Bo Schembechler was so upset over the pink lockers that he had his assistant coaches tape over the pink benches and walls with white butcher paper. Schembechler complained to Fry during the warm-ups about the pink locker room and Fry realized that he had gotten "into his head" and psyched him out (because anyone that worried about the locker room was not focused on the game). Interestingly, in the 20 years prior to painting the visitor's locker room pink, the Hawkeye's had won about 40 percent of their home games. They have won nearly 70 percent of their home games in the 25 years that the visitor's locker room has been painted pink.

The color pink was associated with notions of femininity during the November, 2005 Skins Game. Tiger Woods had been teasing follow contestant Fred Funk that be better be careful because Annika Sorenstam might out-drive him on a tee shot (thus challenging his manhood) during the competition. Sorenstam is the leading golfer in the women's professional tour. Funk is known for his short but accurate tee shots and told Sorenstam weeks before the match that he'd wear a pink skirt for an entire hole if she outdrove him. (Thus, Funk and Sorenstam had a prior agreement to participate in a scheme involving the cultural image of wearing pink; unlike the pink locker rooms at the University of Iowa.) On the 3rd hole, Sorenstam outdrove Funk by seven yards (even though because of the angle, Funk's ball was technically closer to the hole). Sorenstam then reached into her golf bag and pulled out a pink skirt and presented to Funk, who them put the skirt on over his pants. He rolled up one-pant leg to expose skin. Sorenstam, Funk, Woods and Fred Couples (the 4th player in the Skins competition) all joked about it. Funk got the last laugh as he won $700,000 during the two day event. Despite the fact that this incident was a more blatant form of sexism (and a female also participated in it), than the pink locker room, there were no public outcries of condemnation.

If pink is a color associated with, among other things, passivity, what color is associated with aggression and winning? The answer is not surprising—red. According to British anthropologists Russell A. Hill and Robert A. Barton of the University of Durham in England, across a range of sports, wearing the color red is consistently associated with a higher probability of winning. The color red is associated with aggression in many animals (witness the color of the cape used by professional bullfighters). The color red may subconsciously intimidate opponents in athletic contests, especially when the athletes are of equal skill and strength. The anthropologists analyzed the results of four combat sports at the 2004 Olympic Games in Athens: boxing, tae kwon do, Greco-Roman wrestling and freestyle wrestling. Athletes were randomly given protective gear and other sports gear. Those who wore red won more often in all four sports (*The Post-Standard*, 2005).

never-ending presence of negativity that clouds sports, there are countless athletes who understand the meaning of fair play and being a good sport. Many of them will never receive proper recognition for the time and effort they put in to charitable activities, but it is good to know that there is an organization dedicated to honoring good sportsmanship both on and off the field.

BEING A GOOD SPORT

Good sportsmanship implies playing fairly and adhering to the letter and spirit of equality before the rules. "Since the athletic contest is designed to determine which competitor meets the challenge best, fair play requires that competitors not intentionally disregard the rules . . . Fair play requires that victory be honorable" (Simon, 1991:39–40). For example, a soccer player who takes a dive in order to cause the opponent to be given a yellow card (penalty) is deceiving the opponent and can be regarded as breaking the rules of fair play and sportsmanship. He or she certainly is not a good sport. Fair play, then, can be understood as respect for the game (Butcher and Schneider, 2001). Respect for the game is demonstrated by following the rules and treating the opponent as a worthy adversary.

Nearly four decades ago, Rudolph Brasch (1970) proposed the following "Ten Commandments of Sport" as applicable to all sportsmen:

1. Thou shalt not quit.
2. Thou shalt not alibi.
3. Thou shalt not gloat over winning.
4. Thou shalt not sulk over losing.
5. Thou shalt not take unfair advantage.
6. Thou shalt not ask odds thou art willing to give.
7. Thou shalt always be willing to give thine opponent the benefit of the doubt.
8. Thou shalt not underestimate an opponent or overestimate thyself.
9. Remember that the game is the thing and he who thinks otherwise is no true sportsman.
10. Honor the game thou playest, for he who plays the game straight and hard wins even when he loses (p.7).

It would seem that these ideals of sportsmanship are just as relevant today and it would be refreshing if more athletes abided by these guidelines.

However, as we know, the primary goal in sport is to win. There are times when the goal to win supercedes fair play. In fact, obtaining a competitive edge, even if done unjustly, is viewed by many in sport as a type of "tactic" rather than cheating.

Cheating: Being a Bad Sport, or Doing what it takes to Win?

Cheating is a form of deviance as such behavior violates the norms and laws of society. Cheating involves deception (e.g., fraud); trickery (e.g., swindling someone of their land); manipulation (e.g., misleading someone through illusions); and dishonesty (e.g., lying on a tax return). An adulterous spouse, a boxer that hits below the belt, an athlete who takes steroids are all examples of cheats. There was a time when being called a cheater led to great stigmatization. It seems that in our "growing culture of shamelessness," however, that an increasing number of people no longer view cheating as deviant and immoral behavior.

Many people start cheating in school. A "Dear Abby" column that ran in 2008 focused on this topic. Former and current educators has shared their experiences with Abby on the predominance of cheating they observed. One of the articles that appeared in the column was written by a seventh-grade Sunday school teacher who claimed that cheating is encouraged by parents. The father of one of the Scouts at her local Scout troop called cheating "just a form of competitive advantage." Is it any wonder that recent research indicates that nearly half of all college students admit to cheating? Business professor Donald L. McCabe of Rutgers University, and his colleagues, found that 56 percent of business students admitted to cheating in at least one of a variety of topics, including cheating on tests and exams, plagiarism, faking a bibliography, or submitting work done by someone else. Business majors were followed by engineering majors (54 percent), physical sciences (50 percent), medical students and health care (49 percent), education (48 percent), law (45 percent), arts (43 percent), and humanities and social sciences (39 percent).

It seems there are cheaters in all walks of life. Which concerns you the most, that future business leaders and lawyers are likely to continue to cheat; or that people going into medicine and health care are likely to continue to cheat? A lot of people cheat in a variety of situations. As a result, is there any wonder why cheating occurs in sports as well?

Whatever sort of reasoning it takes, people find a way to justify or rationalize their cheating. "I have to cheat, everyone else is." "If I don't cheat, I won't get good grades. And how am I going to get into graduate school then?" "The government sticks it to me, so I stick it to the government whenever I can." It goes on and on. Numerous athletes, coaches, personal trainers, owners, and others associated with sport rationalize their cheating as well. As a result, cheating is not always viewed as unsportsmanlike behavior. For example, if an umpire (in baseball) determines that a batter was hit by a pitch and awards him with a free pass to first base and yet the batter knows the ball did not hit him but instead hit his bat, his teammates do not expect him to tell the truth (fair play). This type of deceitful behavior is known as *normative cheating*.

Normative cheating refers to acts of deviance that are, for the most part, accepted as part of the game. In basketball, players commit many fouls that are not called; they are not expected to inform the referees about such infractions. Offensive linemen in football routinely hold their opponents and yet are not expected to report such violations to game officials. Baseball catchers often "frame a pitch" — moving the glove over the plate quickly after catching the ball in an attempt to influence the umpire's call (decision of "strike" or "ball"). Regardless of the fact that such violations are tolerated, such acts represent deviant behavior. In contrast, there are acts of deviance that are not acceptable and are subject to sanctions/punishments. These behaviors are referred to as *deviant cheating*. Regardless of its categorization, cheating represents behavior that violates the rules and therefore, by definition, is deviant; even if it has become normative behavior within a subcultural setting.

Another example of cheating involves lying about one's age. Now admittedly, many people lie about their ages. People under the age of 21 may lie about their age in order to get into a bar or to buy alcohol at a store. Adults lie about their age, usually for vain reasons. In both examples, such behaviors are rendered as a normative form of deviance. However, in youth sports, lying about the age of a participant is very deviant and violates every acceptable code of sportsmanship, fair play and decency. In 2001, Little League Baseball was humiliated by the cheating of a Bronx, New York team that was playing with a 14-year-old player (the age limit is 12) named Danny Almonte. The birth certificate of Dominican Republic born Almonte had been altered to show the boy was 12 years old instead of 14 years old (Cala, 2001). By the time the deceit was uncovered, other Little League teams had already been eliminated from competition and were not allowed to advance. One such team eliminated by the Bronx team was from Orchard Park (Buffalo, New York). The boys who were cheated out of an opportunity to play fairly were obviously disappointed. One boy stated, "Little League should pay us for traveling to a fraudulent tournament" (Geschwind, 2001:A-1).

In 2002, more than a dozen Dominican players playing youth sports in the United States were caught claiming to be a year or more younger than their actual age. The Atlanta Braves general manager John Schuerholz reported that their 2000 National League Rookie of Year, Rafael Furcal, was really 23 and not 21 as they believed. Schuerholz believes that most players from

"Third World countries" (his term) lie about their age (Beaton, 2002:C1). In 2008, Houston Astros shortstop Miguel Tejada admitted to the team's general manager (Ed Wade) that he was actually 33, two years older than he was listed in the club's media guide. The Dominican native first lied about his age when the told the Oakland Athletics (his first MLB team) that he was 17 when he was really 19 years old. And in the 2008 Summer Olympics, heated controversy arose over the actual age of various female Chinese athletes, who seemed to be ineligible because they were too young to participate, even though the official documents produced by Chinese authorities stated they were in fact old enough.

Players often lie about their age at the professional level because youth has a greater appeal to management; they lie about their age at the youth sport level because their older age is a drastic advantage over those a couple of years younger. On the opposite extreme, Marv Levy has admitted that he originally lied about his age (claiming to be younger) when appointed as head coach of the Buffalo Bills (NFL) in 1986, out of fear of ageism. It was only a few years after assuming the coaching job that he admitted he was already in his mid-sixties. Levy's success as Bills head coach contributed to his induction into the NFL Hall of Fame. In 2006, Levy, at the age of 80, was hired as General Manager and Vice President of Football Operations for the Buffalo Bills. He retired when his contract expired following the Bills last game in 2007.

Other examples of cheating in sport include athletes who use illegal equipment, take illegal recreational and performance-enhancing drugs, gamble, and even commit crime. Coaches cheat in such matters as extending practices beyond the allotted time, illegally recording the practices of opponents, and teaching athletes how to circumvent the rules. Owners can be involved with collusion, making secret deals to relocate their franchise, and cheating their athletes out of money. In short, there are too many examples of cheating in sport to try and detail here. Let's just say, when it comes to cheating, sport mirrors society once again.

However, as sports fans, we would like to think that cheating in sports is at a minimum. And we would hate to find out that blatant forms of cheating cost our favorite athlete or team a victory. After all, cheating represents a breach of expected codes of conduct, fair play, and sportsmanship.

ETHICS AND THE CIVILIZING PROCESS IN SPORTS

Since the Middle Ages, society has increasingly attempted to control the behavior of its citizens. Elias (1978) argues that it is necessary for society to adopt and abide by social manners. Without manners civilization is not possible. As Robert van Krieken (1999) explains, "Norbert Elias suggested that 'civilization' involves the transformation of human *habitus* so that violence of all sorts is gradually subjected to greater and more sophisticated forms of management and control, whereas 'decivilization' encompasses processes which produce an increase in violence and a breakdown in the stability and consistency of on-going social relations" (p.297). Enlightenment thinkers argued that a civilized society was a society that had progressed morally and ethically. Civility implies more than simply following the rules; it also involves observing social conventions, protocol, courteousness and politeness. Thus, civility may be defined as formalized politeness.

The civilizing process that began during the sixteenth and seventeenth centuries was first introduced to members of nobility. Numerous books on manners and etiquette were written for the European elites (Elias, 1978). Rules of etiquette for the nobles included the proper way to eat, dress and speak in social circumstances (Arditi, 1998). The civilizing process and its effect on the manners of nobility became a means to distinguish them from the commoners (Varner and Knottnerus, 2002). "A central component of civility was the idea that members of the nobility were expected to demonstrate control and self-restraint; noble breeding consisted of polished manners and proper social decorum" (Varner and Knottnerus, 2002:426). With the rise of the middle class in the Industrial Revolution, such civil notions became more widespread throughout society.

A Freudian perspective of civility involves a belief that society mediates the individual's quest to fulfill the pleasure principle (the *id*) through society's civilizing process (the *superego*). The civilizing process forces individuals to become more self-controlled. Social pressures of self-control include such personal spheres as sexuality, aggression and emotions. The civilizing process creates a stronger superego within the personality of the individual. The Freudian perspective argues that individuals build up tension and become frustrated because their quest for excitement has been hampered. As a result, the state promotes sports as a major method of tension reduction in a "civilized" manner. There are two major flaws with this reasoning. First, as we have already shown, sports do not always provide a cathartic controlled-release of energy. Second, controlling societal behavior does not imply that individuals can no longer have fun and excitement in their lives. As Elias (1986) explains:

> The nature of a civilizing process is sometimes misunderstood as a process in which the restraints or, as it is sometimes put, the 'repressions' bred into people decrease and in which people's capacity for pleasurable excitement and enjoying

life correspondingly decrease. But perhaps this impression is, to some extent,
due to the fact that people's pleasurable satisfactions have attracted less attention as a worthy and interesting object of scientific research than the restricting
rules—than social constraints and their instruments such as laws, norms and values" (p.163).

Elias, Dunning and others have applied the "civilizing process" model to
the study of sports. They noticed significant changes in sport civility beginning during the Middle Ages and continuing, for the most part, into contemporary society.

Civility in Sport

As the nobles of the Middle Ages were being "civilized" they adopted rules
of conduct in their leisurely pursuits. Failure to abide by a specific code of
conduct led to humiliation and the forfeiture of power, privilege and prestige
(Varner and Knottnerus, 2002). "Rules of etiquette and civility defined the social and recreational activities designed for amusement. As early as the
twelfth century, it is documented that the nobility incorporated civilized rituals into their leisurely activities, thereby distinguishing them from the recreational activities of the lower classes" (Varner and Knottnerus, 2002:426).
Elias (1986) notes how the English nobility sport of hunting (e.g., fox hunting) transformed itself (civilly) in order to abide by rules of etiquette. "Civilized gentlemen" let the hounds do the actual killing of the prey while con-
fining their own activity to assisting them and to the anticipatory excitement
of watching the kill.

Guttmann (1986) notes how the violence and death associated with earlier jousting became civilized by the sixteenth century. "Opponents were
usually separated by 'tilts,' that is, by wooden barriers eliminating the risk
of head-on collisions. Since knights passed left arm to left arm, with lances
held in the right hand, their weapons struck their opponents' shields at an
angle which made it less likely for a sixteenth-century knight to be dangerously unhorsed. Jousts were decided not by the mere shock of lance against
armor but by an extremely complicated system of points" (Guttmann,
1986:37).

The sports of the commoners were also being civilized. Medieval folk-
football, a very violent game where matches between teams of excess of
1,000 participants on each side were commonplace, was transformed into the
modern games of soccer and rugby (Dunning, 1986). The civilization
process of Medieval sport was an ongoing process into contemporary times.

Dunning (1986) argues that modern rugby is civilized by four primary characteristics:

1. A complex set of formally instituted written rules which demand strict control over the use of physical force.
2. Clearly defined intra-game sanctions, that is 'penalties,' which can be brought to bear on offenders and, as the ultimate sanction for serious and persisted rule violation, the possibility of exclusion from the game.
3. The institutionalization of a specific role which stands, as it were, 'outside' and 'above' the game and whose task is to control it, that is that of a 'referee.'
4. A nationally centralized rule-making and rule-enforcing body, the Rugby Football Union (p.230).

These four characteristics of civility are stables in contemporary sport ideology. Further, with the exception of the relatively recent phenomenon of soccer hooligans, soccer and rugby are far more civilized sports than medieval folk-football. Dunning and Sheard (1979) view soccer hooligans as the least affected by the civilizing process.

By the twentieth century, most sports were relatively civilized; at least in terms of adhering to a set of written rules, established sanctions for violating the rules, referees and officials to enforce the code of conduct specific within each sport, and a governing body to oversee the entire process. Some sports are far more "civilized" than others and therefore embrace rules of etiquette and proper decorum. Tennis demands that spectators be quiet while players serve and volley. Golf also demands "proper" behavior by its spectators. Golf also stresses to its players a certain code of conduct. In golf, "Rituals of civility were clearly important because such rituals involve behavior defined as positive restrictions. These positive restrictions include practice, proper behavior, control, obedience to the rules, concentration, accuracy, courteousness, and good judgment. Negative restrictions for designating appropriate conduct include: do not interfere with others, avoidance of forceful or aggressive behavior, anxiousness, cheating, prideful activity, neglecting club rules, complaining, loss of control, and being self-centered" (Varner and Knottnerus, 2002:431,433). With all these criteria, it is easy to understand why golf was never popular with the masses in the early twentieth century. The original members of the United States Golf Association (USGA) were "businessmen, prominent, wealthy, and well-educated; individuals who could control their leisure time" (Varner and Knottnerus, 2002:431).

Narrative 8.1.   An Interview with Gordon Marino, a Professor of Philosophy at St. Olaf College and the Curator of the Hong—Kierkegaard Library. (He is also a former boxer)

1. How did you get involved in boxing?

My grandfather was a boxer and he used to talk about the sport to me as a young boy. In my adolescent mind, much of sport in general seemed to me to be tied up with the question of who can beat up whom. Boxing seemed of the essence to me. Also, I grew up around a good deal of violence—so the feeling of being able to protect myself was very attractive. I was no stranger to rage either and boxing seemed a good outlet for that.

As for the actual mechanics, I got involved in amateur boxing at around 16 but I was always juggling it with football and baseball. I went to college—first Bowling Green State University, hoping to make it to the NFL. When it was clear that that was not going to happen, I transferred to Columbia University. There were some great gyms in New York. I went down to the Gramercy Park Gym on 14th St. where Floyd Patterson and Jose Torres used to train with Cus D'Amato. Later I went to the Solar Gym on 28th St and signed a pro contract. I was mostly a sparring partner for some top contenders. I had a bad contract or rather a very bad manager. I tried to switch to someone else but he had me tied up and that was the end of my boxing career.

2. What do you say to critics who argue that boxing is not a "true sport"?

I'm not sure what a true sport is. I am not inclined to believe that there is something akin to an "essence" of sports. However, if critics mean that in boxing the aim is to hurt someone as opposed to trying to win—I think that is wrong. The aim is to have your hand raised at the end. Of course, some boxers might come into the ring with "bad intentions" but there are linebackers who have the same kind of attitude. Sometimes it is just to get oneself psyched up. And sometimes it is an unsportsmanlike attitude—but the fact that some participants have the wrong spirit does not mean that boxing, football, or what have you, are not sports.

3. How does boxing relate to your profession of philosophy?

Going back to Socrates there is a good deal of sparring in philosophy—and some combat as well—such as in colloquia. It is true that philosophers are not in danger of bodily harm but in these scrapes people do have their sense of self bloodied and that can sometimes seem a lot worse than a bloody nose. After all, people in philosophy are very strongly identified with their minds and being made to feel stupid does not exactly seem like a feather punch. Boxing also helps to teach a person how to look for openings, pace yourself, read levels of aggression in others and, when necessary, to mobilize your own aggression. That can be very helpful in realm of intellectual frays.

4. What virtues do you think can be learned in the ring?

Boxing provides supreme instruction with regard to courage. It provides a safe workshop in which you can actually get some practice at dealing with very intense levels of fear. I once questioned George Foreman as to how he could reconcile his Christianity with his love for boxing and with the fact that he was actively engaged in teaching young people how to fight. Foreman chuckled in his inimitable way and said that it was easy to reconcile the two. Christianity is all about peace, he said, and in boxing you develop control of your emotions and that makes people much more peaceful, much less inclined to go out and DO something stupid.

Also, in ethics there is a lot of abstract blather about respect. And yet, when you try to flesh this concept out, it is seldom clear what we mean by the term. To me, going back to Kant, respect has always had a rather chilly connotation. I think that there has to be an affective component to it as well as a conceptual sense that we are all persons. There is a feeling between boxers—especially after they have fought, that for some reason or other seems to come close to what respect involves. It is a strong admixture of affection and admiration. Indeed, if you thought of emotions as birds then you would have to say that the feelings that exist between boxers is a rare and, well, beautiful bird.

5. Professional boxing suffers from financial improprieties. What do you think can be done about this?

I am certainly in favor of a national boxing commission. There is not enough oversight—and the sanctioning bodies WBC, IBF, WBO, WBA etc, (otherwise known as "Alphabet soup" in boxing) are not able to police promoters. Just the opposite, many boxing insiders insist that these governing bodies are themselves governed by the Don Kings of the world. All this is not to say that the promoters are all bad. There are enormous financial risks in promoting boxing and without these guys there would be no professional boxing.

I am encouraged by the existence of Golden Boy Promotions. This is a company largely run by boxers. In fact, it was started by the Golden Boy himself—Oscar De La Hoya. De la Hoya has also signed up champions Shane Mosely and Bernard Hopkins as partners. Within a matter of a few years, Golden Boy has become a major force in promoting fights and that is good because the company seems to be all about empowering boxers.

6. In what ways might boxing be therapeutic?

As I mentioned earlier, people who stick at boxing do feel safer in the world—more at home in themselves. Primitive as it may seem to some, it does not hurt a person's self esteem to know, or at least believe that they can handle themselves in a violent situation. Also, anger is probably more taboo in our society than sexual feelings. Still, virtually every big box office hit has murder and mayhem in it, which might suggest that there is a little more rage in people's heart than they would care to admit. Boxing helps cough that up—helps people realize that they can express some of their not so pleasant feelings and no one is going to die. Finally, the sweet science requires a great deal of discipline and the control of one's emotions.

During the twentieth century, each clubhouse would hire a golf "professional." The professional was not one of the athletes on the tour, but rather someone good enough to teach others how to golf. To the scorn of the golf athletes and the wealthy, these golf professionals did not teach the rules of etiquette to those interested in sport; rather, they taught the technical skills of the game. As an interest in golf grew, public golf courses were opened for the "less-privileged" classes and those who lacked a commitment to the rules of civility. For the "old guard" of civility in golf, "The lower-class golfer, public player, caddie, and the professional were described as improper, impulsive, loud, and experiencing difficulty following the rules of the game" (Varner and Knottnerus, 2002:434). Today, the Professional Golf Association (PGA) demands a high level of civility (by athletes and spectators). This same level of civility is often lacking at golf venues other than the professional tour. Non-tour golfers often curse, drink alcohol, complain, lose control of their temper, act self-centered, throw their clubs in anger, and commit other violations of civility.

Most of the major sports, such as football, hockey, and basketball, also promote rules of civility. The NFL for example has outlawed many types of formations and placed restriction on tackling (especially tackling the quarterback). The NHL has instituted a number of rules limiting fighting (e.g., the "third man in" rule). Nonetheless, many sports remain violent and encourage physical actions on the part of the participants. The huge popularity of football in the United States indicates that the masses still enjoy violent spectacles.

Despite the level of built-in physical aggression associated with modern football, it is a much more civil game now than compared to the past. Still, football possesses elements of raw, physical and confrontational battles that spectators and fans feel viscerally. Add the components of loyalty and identity to this mix and one begins to understand the passion many Americans have for the game. Sports like football that involve physical contact are intended to serve as a safety valve for a species that still, in spite of civility and the socialization process, possesses a survival instinct that is fueled by aggression. Civility and aggression are usually at odds with one another. And sports fans are often caught in the middle. On the one hand, fans are supposed to cheer and act lively while watching sports such as football. On the other hand, they must do so in a civil manner. Some fans have a hard time understanding where to draw the line. Enter the agents of civility.

Agents of civility (e.g., sports league officials) are those persons/institutions that make clear the distinction between arbitrary constructs of civility and specific rules of behavior that must be followed. The NFL, for example, has a number of clear rules of proper conduct (civility) it expects all

Although a violent sport, most contact in football is deemed acceptable. (Courtesy Cardinal Sports Imaging)

spectators to abide by. This code of conduct was updated in 2008 and includes bans on:

- Behavior that is unruly, disruptive, or illegal.
- Drunkenness and signs of alcohol impairment that result in irresponsible behavior.
- Foul or abusive language or obscene gestures.
- Interference with the progress of the game, including throwing objects onto the field.
- Failing to follow instructions of stadium personnel.
- Verbal or physical harassment of fans of the opposing team (NFL, 2008).

Anyone who has attended an NFL game will tell you that many of these rules are violated regularly, more so in certain NFL cities than others. It may also seem a daunting challenge to enforce all these rules as it is relatively difficult to catch spectators in the act. However, the NFL has a partial solution to that problem as well—they go after the season ticket holders. NFL clubs generally have a written clause in their contracts with season ticket holders that hold them responsible for the behavior of the person sitting in their seat. That is, if a season ticket holder gives/sells their ticket to someone else and they act unruly, the season ticket holder may be forced to give up his or her season ticket. (Note: one of the authors is an NFL season ticket holder and his contract clearly states that this is the case.)

Contemporary individuals should not need "codes of conduct" from sports leagues. They are supposed to already possess internalized codes of restraint and respect for others which obligates them not to harm others. Most people affiliated with the sports world, including spectators and fans, athletes, coaches, and officials, behave in a civil manner. Contemporary moralists, including some sociologists, ponder whether violent sports have a place in modern civil societies; especially societies which attempt to impose a civilizing protocol among its citizens. Others address the ways in which athletes, coaches and fans can still achieve a virtuous life through their participation in sport. Randall Feezell, for instance, is a professor of philosophy at Creighton University as well as an athlete and coach. In discussing the importance of "character" and sportsmanship, he writes:

> First of all, I associate character with a kind of strength that forces one properly to take responsibility for certain negative events that befall a person. Such events might make one look bad in the eyes of others and oneself. It is the courage to take responsibility for defeat and failure when appropriate, to be honest about one's self. I know of no neat virtue term that sums up this quality, but

it is obviously a kind of responsibility. It is akin to a kind of self-reliance, and its opposite is the perpetual whiner, blamer, and excuse-monger. John McEnroe's lack of this quality is expressed in his constant paranoid complaints to officials, as if he has experienced more unfair and incompetent officiating than anyone in the history of tennis. Lack of this quality is apparent throughout the sports world when officiating is blamed for defeat (Feezell, 2004:139–140).

Many ethicists see a return to a "virtue ethics" approach as a rejection of moral theories based simply upon learning and applying rules. Virtue ethics stresses the importance of character development, including harmonizing of one's personal traits, applying good judgment, and having a sense of pride in doing one's best, rather than necessarily winning or achieving public recognition. While civility may be under attack, it is also clear that athletes, coaches and spectators who violate such norms do receive public criticism and, if extreme cases, are prosecuted for their infractions. It is by no means the case that a "winner take all" attitude permeates modern society to such an extent that boorish behavior, violence and cheating are generally acceptable practices. (We'll return to this in the final chapter.)

SPORTS AND LEISURE IN PRISON

Persons that act in a civil manner may find their behaviors acknowledged by various humanitarian associations. Athletes, for example, may be inducted into the World Sports Humanitarian Hall of Fame. Conversely, athletes who violate the rules of the game are subject to various sanctions when such transgressions are discovered. Anyone, for that matter, who is caught breaking a rule, is subject to punishment. People who violate formal norms, known as laws, are subject to more serious form of punishments, including incarceration.

Despite the best efforts of the agents of civility, and using current U.S. incarceration rates, many Americans are not acting in a civil manner. Based on a 2008 report from the Pew Center on the States, more than one in 100 American adults were incarcerated in 2007 (Liptak, 2008). This was the first time in the nation's history that more than one percent of adult Americans were in jail or prison. Of the 230 million U.S. adults, 1.6 million are in prison and another 723,000 are in local jails; thus, one in every 99.1 adults is behind bars (Liptak, 2008).

Historically, prisons were viewed as institutions that stressed callous punishment and personal deprivation over inmate rehabilitation. As a result, leisure and sports programs for inmates were seldom allowed. Over the past few decades, however, recreational activities were introduced as a means of alleviating the monotony of prison life and as a safety valve to release inmates' built-up emotions and frustrations. The introduction of sports and leisure in prison reflects the movement of treating the incarcerated more civilly. This movement is also reflected in the relabeling of prisons to "correctional facilities." In other words, the focus has shifted from punishing inmates to rehabilitating (correcting) them.

Sporting Activities in Prison

Recreational and leisure activities in prison include calisthenics; jogging; walking; playing cards, checkers, chess and board games; arts and crafts; watching movies and television, including sports; taking music and signing lessons; and just hanging out with other inmates. Like civilians, inmates enjoy playing a variety of sports. Among the more popular sporting activities include, weightlifting, basketball, softball, handball, volleyball, flag football, and soccer. Pole-vaulting is not allowed!

Some prisons have relatively elaborated sports programs that allows for civilian spectators or civilian opposing athletic teams. For the inmates, participating in a sporting activity that involves contact with civilians is a sign of good behavior. They must maintain the strictest adherence to the ideals of sportsmanship or they risk losing all their sports and recreation privileges. The ability of prison officials to be able to dangle this carrot in front of inmates assures their cooperative behavior in general lockup as well. The opportunity to interact with civilians is a major self-esteem boost as well. For example, all athletes like to hear applause, but inmates really like to hear it from civilians. Perhaps one of the best examples of inmates and the community benefiting from a prison sports program is the Angola (Louisiana) Prison Rodeo.

The Angola Prison plays host to an annual rodeo that is billed as the "Wildest Show in the South!" The Angola Rodeo is the longest running prison rodeo in the nation, having started in 1965 (Angola Prison Rodeo, 2008). Although there were still no stands at the time (spectators sat on apple crates and the hoods of their cars to watch the performances), the 1967 rodeo became the first one opened to the general public (on a limited basis). A 4,500-seat arena was opened in time for the start of the 1969 rodeo. As the years passed, the rodeo continued to grow in size, adding events and sponsorships. The official Professional Rodeo Cowboys Association rules were adopted in 1972 and as a result, the Angola Prison Rodeo is recognized as a professional rodeo. The rodeo is held twice a year, in April (2 dates) and October (every Saturday), rain or shine. Today, the grandstand seats 7,500 spectators and routinely sells-out (Angola Prison Rodeo, 2008).

Other prison sports programs involve civilian sports teams that are willing to go behind bars and play against inmate teams. It takes a relatively brave person to be willing to go inside a correctional facility and come close enough to inmates that they can literally reach out and touch someone. Civilian teams that play sports against prison teams must, obviously, compete on the "home" field of the prison team. It can be quite intimidating for civilians to play sports behind prison walls. The sound of the big heavy doors closing instills a sudden sense of reality. (One of the authors taught his very first course in a prison, and can attest to this!) Civilian ball players want to win, but many are fearful of playing against inmates and realize the importance of guards. In "Narrative 8.2," Carolyn Agle (a former student of Tim Delaney's) describes her experiences playing softball against a prison team at Collins Correctional Facility (NY). Agle was the only female on the softball team. Although she recalls many "cat calls" from the men (the

---

Narrative 8.2. An Interview with Carolyn Agle, 20, college student and NCAA softball player

A softball player's account of playing on a recreational softball team that played against a prison team at Collins Correctional Facility (NY).

1. What was your first reaction when you were told that you were playing a game behind prison walls against an inmate team? Had any of your teammates ever played a game in prison before?

   When I was first asked by my friend to play softball against prisoners, at the prison, I was nervous, but thought that it would be fun. My friend Matt had originally asked me to be on the team because he needed a pitcher, and I play softball and am a pitcher so he thought we would be an advantage—that is, until he told me it was modified pitch and slow pitch. I don't think the actual real nervousness of it all hit me until my friend Shea and I were driving to the game; we talked the whole way about how nervous we were but made jokes about what would happen to try and not be as worried. When I found that I was the only girl on the team I became more nervous. All of the guys on my team pumped me up though so I wouldn't be worried. My teammate, Matt, the one who set up the game, works at the correctional facility so he has played games versus the prisoners before.

2. Did any of your friends or family members express any concerns over your playing in the prison game? Did they offer you any advice?

   My mom was nervous about me going into the prison and especially because I was the only girl. I think she knows that I can hold my own but she was just worried about security issues and how all of the male prisoners would treat me, especially verbally. My dad thought it was cool and was making jokes about it

---

(continued)

Narrative 8.2.   *(continued)*

and just told me to do well. My step dad probably had the funniest advice. When my friend Shea and I were at my house before the game, my step dad told him that he better wear his cup on backwards to prevent any "problems." Referring to getting taken advantage of, if you know what I mean! It was funny, we all laughed; because Shea is really good looking and all of the teammates knew that the inmates would love him and pick on him the most.

3. What was it like being the only female on the team? Did you feel intimidated or scared being around male inmates?

   It was actually really fun being the only female on the team. Once I got on the field and the prisoners came out I think they were all thinking that I would be an easy out and the weakest player on the team, and that was not the case. I would absolutely do it again being the only girl on the team. There were times that I felt intimidated being around the male prisoners because I played right field and about 20 feet behind where I stood was the caged in area where the weights were, so the prisoners were working out right behind me. In addition, they would all walk *through* the outfield to get to the work out area instead of going around and they were walking within 5 feet of me and some of them would make comments, but it was funny.

4. Describe how you felt as you approached the prison. How did you react when the prison gate locked behind you? Describe the prison setting (e.g., barbed wire fences? Tall walls? Guard towers?)

   As I approached the prison I stayed by Shea and really didn't say much, all of us kind were silent because this was real and actually happening, all of the talk now came down to reality of walking into a prison. I was nervous and anxious, I think I was just nervous because I didn't know what to expect, and then once we were getting briefed by the woman who coordinates the prisoner's games versus other teams, she told us that once we got into the "yard" there would be upwards of 500 prisoners out there with us. Then I became very nervous, because I only expected the prisoners that we were actually playing to be out on the field, but the hours that we were there was also the inmates free time. When the prison gate locked behind us, I was like well, there's no turning back now. I was also excited though just because I love to play and I was curious to see how the male prisoners would react to having a girl on the opposing team. The prison setting included several windy tunnels and sidewalks to get to the yard and there were also a lot of brick walls and barbed wire fences .There were a lot of guard towers as well, however there were some really nice trees and shrubbery so I as surprised that it actually looked fairly nice and well-kept inside the prison.

5. What kind of instructions were you given by prison officials in regard to your behavior while behind bars?

   The instructions that we all were given before we went in was to make sure that all of our belongings (cleats, sneakers, gloves, any bags) needed to be checked. After we all signed a lot of forms and handed over our driver's licenses we got visitor passes that we had to keep on us until we played (we could take them off while playing). But, the guard explained to us what to expect and warned us that inmates may place items in our bags or shoes and that we could get in serious trouble even though it was not our fault. So basically, we had to be cautious and smart about the experience and just protect ourselves. The guard really didn't tell us anything that we couldn't do, he just warned us about the inmates taunting (e.g., talking smack) us and that it was all just in competition and fun.

6. Were there any inmate spectators at the game? If so, were you harassed by any inmates? Were any of your teammates harassed?

There were about 500 inmates in the yard at the time and most of them lined up along the third base line because that was the inmate side, but some lined up on the right field line as well. Many of the inmates watched the game and all of them yelled comments to the pitcher, "you got nothing,'" "he throws like a girl," etc. Also, they all made comments when our players were up to bat, especially me because I am a girl. The inmates would yell to their pitcher to go easy on me and that I was an "easy out." This really didn't bother me because I knew that I would do fine. So, after a few at bats for me, they realized that I could play with the guys and kind of left me alone at the plate. However, when I was in right field and the inmates were walking through to get to the workout area, they would say, "what's the score, I hope you guys kick their asses!" and I responded, "yeah, me too!" The only thing that really freaked me out though was when one of the inmates walked by me and said, "Hey Carolyn, how are doing?" I was like, "uhhhhh, good." I was really scared that he knew my name and I was wondering how he could have known that, so that worried me. Also, when I was in right field, the prisoners on the right base line would yell to me to back up because a lefty was up, and would ask me the score and stuff like that. The one time I ran down a fly ball and caught it the inmates all went wild—I think it was because a girl got a guy out, that whole gender thing. But it was an AWESOME feeling! The funniest thing to happen was when I got a single, I'm on first, Shea is at the plate and hits it to shortstop, so of course, I am running to second and they try to turn two (a double play) and I am called out. Then ALL of the inmates that were standing on the third base line were booing because I got thrown out. I was confused why they were booing because I thought they wanted to win. When I returned to my dugout all of my teammates were laughing and I asked what was so funny. That is when I learned that the inmates were booing because they didn't want me to get thrown out because they wanted to watch me run to third base and remain at third base so that they could "check me out." Hahahahahaha, so I thought that was kind of funny, typical guy behavior! But at the time, I was so naïve and didn't realize that was the reason.

(*continued*)

Narrative 8.2.   (*continued*)

7. How many correctional officers were nearby?

    There were a few correctional officers up in the bleachers, and down on the field in the dugout areas there were 3 officers and the woman coordinator of the game. We were only two women there. When I was out in right field, one officer would stand near me in the foul area of right field, but they didn't do that for anyone else, even the guy in left field who was very close to the throng of inmates cheering on their fellow inmates. I felt safe the whole time. Once the game started that was all I really focused on. I had a really great time.

8. Who won the game? How did you do personally? Will you play another game behind prison walls?

    We played 4 innings of modified pitch and 4 innings of slow pitch. We lost by a couple of runs. We were all mad that we lost but we knew going into it that the prisoners take these games really seriously and also they play together all the time because they have nothing else to do. So we were all happy that we played a close game with them. I ended up going 5 for 5 and scored 4 runs. So, I showed those inmates that I could keep up with the boys! I would most definitely play another game behind prison walls; I had such a great time, and got some good practice too!

9. Would you recommend this experience to other athletes in other sports under properly supervised conditions? Why or why not?

    I would absolutely recommend this experience to other athletes in other sports under properly supervised conditions. I think that this was a great experience to learn about prisoners and to realize they really aren't so scary. So many people have the preconceived notion that they are horrible people, but they are really nice and I think a lot of people just think they all did violent crimes, however that is not always the case. This experience would be great for any athlete because it gives them a chance to play at a competitive level, because the game was not easy or a blowout by any means. In addition, you get to learn about yourself and how you can perform at different levels and in strange situations. Overall, this was a great and fun experience and I would do it again with no questions asked.

---

inmates stood on the third base sideline and they were especially disappointed when she was ruled out at a close play at second base—because she would not find her way to third base) her overall experience was a very positive one.

FINAL THOUGHTS

There's an old saying: it isn't if you win or lose; it's how you play the game. While that may sound trite in today's increasingly competitive world, it still rings true for those who love sport, especially for what it can do in helping to build character and unite people for a common cause. Sportsmanship, while a battered concept, remains a worthy virtue.

Surely one of the main reasons we continue to love sport is because of the challenges it presents: allowing us to test ourselves to learn what exactly we are capable of achieving. Cheating, particularly when the stakes are high, will always be a temptation, and there is no lack of examples of athletes and other sports officials who have been found guilty of such behavior. Nonetheless, it is impossible to separate the love of sport from the desire for honorable performances, and we hope that these preceding chapters, as well as the final one to come, have demonstrated that sportsmanship is alive and well in the twenty-first century.

Chapter Nine

Why We Love Sports

The point was made earlier, but it is worth repeating: billions of people around the world love sports. Yes, there are troubling aspects about the institution of sport, but there are problems with every social organization. Sports adherents recognize the negative issues but prefer to concentrate on the more positive ones.

As we have discussed throughout the book, Americans are among the billions who love sports. And there are at least as many reasons for this affection as there are examples of sports. Although many of us follow more than one sport, nearly everyone has a favorite above the rest. We think about our favorite sport year-round but during the season we often immerse ourselves with its goings on. Some fans dream about sporting events. You know that dream, the one where they wave the checker flag as you finish first at the Daytona 500; or the one where you score the winning touchdown in the Super Bowl; or maybe when you win an Olympic gold medal in the 100 meters. Not only do a number of fans dream about sports, some actually fantasize about them. Luckily for them, there are fantasy-driven sports. For example, sports fans can go to "fantasy camps" where they train like real professional athletes and are afforded an opportunity to play with, or against, current or (more likely) past athletes. If actually playing the sport is not an option, there are Internet-based "fantasy sports leagues" that adherents can partake.

Nearly all major sports, and especially team sports, have fantasy sport leagues. These leagues allow participants to "draft" real (current roster) players so that they can form their own teams. In this regard, participants can fantasize that they are a Team Owner or a General Manager of a sports franchise. The "draft parties" themselves can be quite elaborate and many fantasy sports participants gather at a bar and "socialize" while the draft occurs. Eventually, each participant has drafted enough players to complete his or her roster. When deciding which player to draft, the fantasy sport participant is trying to ascertain which individual players will have the best statistics for their position. In other words, it does not matter if the real-life player's team loses as long as that player had a good game. In this manner, the fantasy sports world is the exact opposite of real life team sports wherein the most important thing is team victory, not individual statistics. However, the use of individual game statistics is a critical element of fantasy sports leagues, as they are infused into each participant's fantasy team. Points based on performance are calculated so that "winners" and "losers" can be determined. Imagine how the "losers" feel about losing in their own fantasy world!

Although there are many options of fantasy leagues that people can choice to participate in, most major sports leagues promote their "official" fantasy league. For example, in 2008, the NFL promoted "NFL Fantasy 2008" on its website. A number of fantasy draft tips were made available to those interested in joining the league via a wide variety of links. Among the helpful hints: "Top 100" player rankings; "Key sleepers" for 2008; an NFL-based mock draft to help prepare for the real fantasy draft; and NFL.com's fantasy football magazine. Armed with this information a fantasy sports enthusiast is set for the season. Each week throughout the season, fantasy sport participants are provided with running point totals. Trades can be made as well as new acquisitions. Thus, it is very important to keep up with the statistics of all NFL players in case one of your fantasy players is injured in real life and has to be replaced on your roster.

There is a certain amount of intrigue involved with fantasy sports leagues. Participants are quite aware of statistics, but—like the sports gambler discussed in chapter 7—are less concerned about the real teams' win-loss record. To be fair, most fantasy sports participants, unlike sports gamblers, maintain an interest in their favorite team.

As much fun as a fantasy world can be, it is the real world of sports that is our top concern. And for the most part, sports bring us the desired diversion from the everyday stress of life.

FEELING GOOD ABOUT SPORTS

The vast majority of people who participate in sport have a positive experience with it. This includes both athletes and fans who have suffered through the agony of defeat. And some sports fans know about the agony of defeat better than others! In this regard, once again, sport reflects life. Sometimes you win; sometimes you lose (with some winning and losing more often than others). Usually the rules are fairly applied, but sometimes they are not. Sport, like life, is not always fair. Just as we cannot give up on life, we cannot give up on sports, for occasionally bright moments and events occur that give us hope. And isn't that the meaning of life—to live for euphoric moments that propel us from the mundane? Sports provide many of these moments of exhilaration and that is just one reason why we love sports.

Undoubtedly, each reader has his or her own reason(s) for feeling good about sports. (The authors would love to hear your reasons why you love sports, so feel free to contact us!) Participants enjoy sports for such reasons as enjoyment of personal and/or team achievement, a healthy workout, and fair competition. Among the primary reasons that fans love sports are the tradition and history associated with sports; the spirit of cooperation among teammates; competition between athletes, especially elite athletes; the temporary escape from the everyday, mundane world that sport provides; the entertainment factor; and the idea that sports provide us with a reason to hope and persevere. Furthermore, cheering for a particular athlete or team (especially the "home" team) provides sports adherents with a sense of identity.

Some fans love sports and games so much that they combine the two. Beach balls are more common at Los Angeles Dodgers games than they are at the beach. (Courtesy Tim Delaney)

There are times when the positive aspects of sport participation and the desired ecstatic feelings of fans coincide. That is to say, sports fans and athletes share a euphoric moment in time together, and memories of such an event will always bring a smile to their faces. When this harmonic convergence occurs we are all reminded that sports, in its purest form, serve a vital, positive service to society.

There are many examples of positive sports stories and each of them represents an explanation as to why we love sports. We would like to share a few of these "feel-good" tales. The first is a Cinderella-type yarn. Using the expression "Cinderella" to describe any account implies that a positive outcome would defy the odds. It should be noted that although the media enjoys using the Cinderella analogy, most athletes do not like such a label attached to their accomplishment as it seems to cheapen their abilities. Such is the case with Fresno State's successful, underdog, run through the 2008 College World Series (CWS). The Bulldogs were the lowest seed to ever win an NCAA championship in any sport. It was also the first men's title in any sport. The Fresno State women won a softball title a decade earlier in 1998.

Things did not start out well for Fresno State as the team lost 12 of their first 20 games. Their remarkable run began when the Bulldogs qualified for the NCAA field of 64 after winning the Western Athletic Conference tournament. Fresno fought off elimination in the regionals and super regionals, and became the first No. 4 regional seed to reach the CWS since the tournament expanded in 1999 (Olson, 2008). In Game 3 of the CWS (the last game), Fresno State defeated Georgia 6-1. Bulldog players and fans erupted in elated joy. And people who enjoy watching underdogs achieve the seemingly impossible basked in the Bulldog glory.

The Olympics almost always provide us with examples of underdogs achieving victory, moments of glory, and opportunities to display pride in one's citizenship. Perhaps the most thrilling aspect of every Olympics is the Opening Ceremonies, wherein, athletes wearing their national colors walk into the stadium proudly representing their country. Each national team also designates an athlete to carry their national flag during this "Parade of Nations." For the 2008 Beijing Summer Olympics, the United States selected Lopez Lomong, a long distance runner (1500 meters). Lomong was not born in the United States, but his patriotism toward the United States is unquestioned.

Born in the Sudan, Lomong was separated from his birth family at age 6 by the Sudanese government that tried to recruit him to join its army. He spent his next 10 years in a refugee camp in Kenya. Lomong and other Sudanese refugees came to be known as the "Lost Boys." In 2001, Lomong found himself adopted by Robert and Barbara Rogers, of Tully, New York. The

Rogerses also took in 5 other Sudanese refugees. Elected by U.S. Olympic team captains, Lomong feels honored to carry the American flag. Speaking of the United States as the "land of opportunity," Lomong states, "There's no greater honor . . . than to represent this country" (Sieh, 2008: A-6). Realizing what Lomong has gone through in his short lifetime, he is already a winner. Even though he did not ultimately qualify for the 1500 meters final, the fact that he was proud to represent his adoptive country in the Olympics makes us all feel good to be fans of sports.

Another feel-good story of sportsmanship took place during a college soft-ball game in Ellensberg, Washington on April 26, 2008. Sara Tucholsky of Western Oregon hit what appeared to be a three-run homer, the first such home run ever for her. In her excitement she missed first base on her run and, turning around to touch the bag, twisted her knee. As sportswriter George Vescey of *The New York Times* reported: "Pam Knox, the Western Oregon coach, made sure no teammates touched Tucholsky, which would have auto-matically made her unable to advance. The umpires ruled that if Tucholsky could not make it around the bases, two runs would score but she would be credited with only a single" (Vescey, 2008:C13). Amazingly enough, Mallory Holtman, the first baseman of the rival Central Washington team then asked the umpires if it would be okay if she and some of her fellow teammates car-ried Tucholsky around to touch each of the bags. "The umpires", Vescey con-tinued, "huddled and said it would be legal, so Holtman and the Central Washington shortstop, Liz Wallace, lifted Tucholsky, hands crossed under her, and carried her to second base, and gently lowered her so she could touch the base. Then Holtman and Wallace started to giggle, and so did Tucholsky, through her tears, and the three of them continued this odd procession to third base and home to a standing ovation" (Vescey, 2008:C13). This unusual demonstration of sportsmanship received national attention. When asked what motivated her to come up with the idea, Holtman credited her coach, Gary Frederick, who had taught her that winning isn't everything. Indeed, Western Oregon went on to win the game, 4-2. But in this case, it's clear that all the participants were winners.

A similar experience occurred on May 15, 2008 in a game between the St. John Fisher Cardinals and the State University of Oswego Lakers (coinci-dentally enough, the home schools of the two authors of this book). In the top half of the ninth inning, in a game that would decide who win the Eastern College Athletic Conference tournament, host team Fisher was trailing by 9-5. Lakers' player Dan Pecora, a junior at Oswego, hit a line drive down the third base line. Pecora watched in horror as the ball hit Oswego manager and third base coach Frank Paino on the side of his head, dropping him to the ground, where he instantly lost consciousness. Fisher coach Dan Pepicelli was the first person to reach him, yelling to Cardinals athletic director Bob Ward to call 911. An ambulance soon arrived and, while Paino (who—while sore for a few days—was soon back on his feet with no lasting injury) was taken to a nearby hospital, the Fisher players and coaches huddled together. After a few minutes of discussion, they agreed to concede the game to Oswego. "The gesture," wrote Kevin Oklobzija of the Rochester *Democrat and Chronicle* newspaper, "which ended Fisher's season and NCAA Tournament hopes, truly defined amateur athletics. The Cardinals finished with a 25-14-1 record. 'It was a lesson in the rules of the game of life,' said Marilyn Montesano, a teacher at New Hartford High School near Utica, whose son Marc was playing in the outfield for Fisher. 'My son learned a life lesson I could not have taught him'" (Oklobzija, 2008:A3). Indeed, it was a lesson that soon swept through both campuses. "For the players," Oklobzija continued, "the minutes and hours that followed—from the time Paino was struck to the time they learned his injuries weren't believed to be serious—were traumatic but precious. Players cried. Parents cried. Players prayed. Parents prayed. And college baseball players grew as people" (Oklobzija, 2008:A3). The story also received national attention, and was featured on ESPN, which quoted Fisher's pitcher Justin Lutes, a graduating senior whose pitch had been the one Pecora connected with, and—like seven other of his fellow seniors— whose college career thus came to an end: "It isn't exactly the dream I had about how I wanted to go out. But there was a lesson that we all learned. People may think that sports is their life. But when you see somebody's life flash before you, you realize there are bigger things in the world than a baseball game" (Drehs, 2008:3).

One other story we would like to share involves a mildly autistic (former) high school student-manager at the Greece Athena High School in Rochester, New York, named Jason McElwain, or J-Mac as he is popularly known. You may have heard about Jason's story as he was a 2006 ESPY Award winner in the "Best Moment" category. His achievement on the basketball court beat out Kobe Bryant's 81-point performance with the Lakers earlier that season. So what makes McElwain's story so interesting? We believe that there are two "feel good" aspects worth particular mention: first, that Jason was able to play in a game at the end of his senior year in high school and second, the sportsmanship displayed by the opposing coach.

Let's start with J-Mac's big night on the court. It was "Senior Night" on February 15, 2006. McElwain was never quite good enough to make the basketball squad but he wanted to be a part of the team anyway. As such, this autistic boy became the student-manager. Still, he always wanted to play in a real game with his teammates. On the day of "Senior Night" Jason's coach, Jim Johnson, informed the student-manager that he would be allowed to "dress" that evening (he was allowed to wear the basketball uniform and sit on the bench as a player). Although his coach could not promise Jason that he would actually play in the game, he remained optimistic. Word spread throughout the campus and before long, the popular student had the entire student body at Greece Athena behind him. At game time, the stands were packed with students—many of whom had cut-outs of McElwain's face on Popsicle sticks and posters bearing Jason's name—as well as his family and community members.

Everything was working in J-Mac's favor as Athena built a big lead over their opponent, the Spencerport Rangers. With about four minutes remaining in the game, McElwain's coach signaled for him to go in (to the game). The fans were raucous. After missing his first shot but still receiving support from his teammates and fans, McElwain swishes a three-point shot. The crowd goes absolutely fanatical. Another possession and another three-pointer by Jason. Those assembled in the gym could hardly contain themselves. Jason would go on to make 6 of 10 three-point shots and 7 for 13 in all during his four minutes of play. When the final buzzer sounded, the Athena spectators stormed the court and carried Jason on their collective shoulders. A homemade film of the game found its way to ESPN and before long Jason's exploits were all the rage in a wide variety of news programs. Proponents of mainstreaming autistic children viewed Jason's accomplishments as inspirational. Yes, there are many reasons to enjoy this story. Jason's determination and dedication are admirable. Giving hope to autistic kids and parents is marvelous. Jason's coach giving him a chance to play on Senior Night is touching and a wonderful sign of sportsmanship.

However, a great deal of sportsmanship was displayed on both ends of the court as the Spencerport boys' basketball team, coached by Josh Harter, should also be acknowledged for being good sports. Consider that, typically, when an opposing player finds the hot hand, the coach will design a defensive tactic to stop him. To their credit, Spencerport did not simply give McElwain unchallenged shots, but they did not aggressively cover him, nor did they commit hard fouls. Spencerport enabled this magical moment to occur. And this point was not lost on a number of Greece Athena parents, as they initiated the presentation of a "thank-you" plaque to Spencerport basketball coach, Harter, and his team for adhering to the sportsmanship ideal. (See Narrative 9.1 to learn more about Josh Harter and his perspective of this game and coaching philosophy.)

Sport participation was a very positive experience for Jason McElwain despite his autism. It should, however, be pointed out that Jason is labeled as a "highly functional" autistic person and Jason's experience with sports, especially being touched and lifted by his teammates, schoolmates, and strangers from the community, may not be a common outcome for autistic youth who are not as "highly functional."

Narrative 9.1. An Interview with Josh Harter, Coach of the Spencerport Rangers

1. How did Coach Johnson approach you before the game, to let you know he was planning to put J-Mac in?

   Jim called me about a month before the game to ask if the opportunity presented itself, would it be okay with me if J-Mac was put into the game. I've known Jason for the 4 years that he has been the team manager. He's a great kid and I thought it would be the opportunity of a lifetime for him. I was all for it.

2. How did you advise your team to play against J-Mac?

   We spoke about it briefly before the game. My players noticed that J-Mac was wearing a uniform. My kids asked me about it, and I told them if the opportunity presented itself, that he'd play in the game. When J-Mac checked in at the table to enter the game the crowd erupted; it was during this timeout that I instructed the team to keep the integrity of the game. When it was game time, my team did a phenomenal job displaying a character of generosity in finding joy in J-Mac's success. The ability to do that will be an asset throughout life.

3. There was a delicate balance—you wanted to give him that opportunity, but not let up completely. What was the correct sort of pressure in this situation?

   It was a spontaneous and unique situation for my players. They were in a situation where, after he hit one or two, they were asking "What do we do now?" I remember one kid in particular who was guarding him looked over at us and we were clapping, which kind of gave him the go-ahead to allow the situation to occur. That's what was so nice about it. When you cross the court after Jason hit his third, you saw our fans clapping more than anyone. That was awesome. Then when he hit four and five, I said "Wow. I can't believe this is happening!" But when all is said and done, I remember at the conclusion of the game I grabbed my team when I saw the crowd coming down. My first response was to make sure I got them off the court so they didn't get hurt. But as I was trying to do this, Athena parents were grabbing our kids, hugging and thanking them. It was such a great feeling. We lost the game by 36 points. It was a pretty good game early on, but with 4 minutes to go, the game was pretty much over. In our post-game meeting, I told the kids I was proud of how they handled themselves. They're the type of kids who can take joy in others' success. We do a lot of community stuff, where they are great with other kids. We run a 12 week basketball program for grades kindergarten through second grade, so they are teaching and coaching themselves. It's a great experience for them as mentors. I think this makes them better people. We fundraise for the American Cancer Society, which is another opportunity for them to give rather than receive. We do a point/pledge system where they fundraise based upon how many points we get in a game. And we have a fundraiser game in honor of a boy who passed away who was in our program seven years ago. He died of a heart attack, and his parents have a scholarship fund that we assist in.

(continued)

Narrative 9.1.   (*continued*)

4. How important was the game overall? Is there a strong rivalry between the two schools?

    They are rival schools. Athena is always in the top of the division, and we are always trying to beat them. It was our final regular season game. Athena went on to play in the championship.

5. It's a hypothetical question, but if you hadn't been behind by so many points, would that have made a difference regarding how Jason was covered?

    If it was a winnable situation, if the game was on the line, then that would have made a difference. We are all playing to win. I think the circumstances allowed for Jason's moment to happen. I was delighted when the Athena players presented us with a thank-you plaque. It shows the class of Jim Johnson, their head coach, and their community. It was unnecessary but greatly appreciated.

6. Had you anticipated the attention that the J-Mac story would receive?

    I had no idea. The national recognition has been unbelievable. What amazed me was when I got a phone call from my cousin who works in Singapore. He said "Josh, I've seen you on the news four or five times. It's all over the place here in Singapore." Coach Johnson called to tell me a Japanese TV station came to interview him. That's when I knew this story was big!

7. If a movie is made of this, do you have anyone you'd like to play you?

    I always say I'd like Brad Pitt. Or I'd like to play myself. I'd do it free of charge!

8. What does the word "sportsmanship" mean to you?

    It's a culmination—for an athlete it means respecting yourself, your teammates, your opponents and respecting the game. We preach a lot in our program that we want to be good people first. When kids leave my program, if I know they are caring people, then that's what I'm most proud of. We also strive for academic excellence. Sportsmanship means to compete hard, be a good winner and a good loser. When the game is over you need to be a good person, and show class. I'm proud to say our kids have done that, resulting in us winning the county sportsmanship award the past three seasons.

9. What are your reactions to the overall effect of the J-Mac story?

    Not only was it great for two communities, Athena and Spencerport, it was great for the whole nation. It was a story of hope. I saw a special before the NBA finals about J-Mac and the impact it had on a former Division I athlete who has an autistic child. That was remarkable. His team, the University of Richmond, beat Syracuse, in the biggest upset in NCAA history. He stated in the special that his greatest sports moment wasn't his winning that game, but it was the J-Mac story. It gave him hope for his son. That was really moving. And there's no question this will have an impact on my own coaching. Head coaches are often guilty of forgetting the big picture, just focusing on wins and losses. This will always give me a perspective on life that is bigger than any game. It demonstrates how far-reaching the effect is when you do the right thing.

SPORTS PARTICIPATION AND AUTISM

As we mentioned, J-Mac's accomplishments on the basketball court serve as inspiration to many, including parents of autistic children who hope that sport participation will help to integrate their children into the mainstream school systems. Although sport participation is generally a good thing to encourage, organized sports may not always work out with autistic children who are not highly functional.

What is autism? Autism is a behavioral type of spectrum disorder that is usually detected in early childhood, especially now that awareness is on the rise. Autism can inflict any person regardless of race and ethnicity or social class. The exact cause of autism is unknown but the majority of researchers in this area agree that the central nervous system does not develop normally in an autistic person. Autistic persons are overly sensitive to certain stimuli and under sensitive to others. An autistic person may have problems with verbal and nonverbal communications and withdraw into their own private worlds. In general, there is a basic lack of emotional contact with others. A number of organizations, including the Doug Flutie, Jr. Foundation for Autism (named after Doug Flutie's autistic child, Doug) exist in an effort to raise awareness of autism and in hopes of conquering autism.

Playing organized sports may present a challenge for autistic children because of their general lack of communication skills with others, difficulty understanding the rules and guidelines associated with sports, and their self-imposed social isolationism. However, autistic children by and large enjoy participating in a number of recreational activities; especially individual ones. Long distance running, for example, is enjoyed by a number of autistic people because of it is a solitary, repetitive action that requires determination and stamina; traits characteristic of most autistic persons.

That sports and recreation can benefit persons with autism and families with autistic children is another reason why we love sports. We also love sports because they are beneficial to people with physical impairments.

SPORTS FOR THE PHYSICAL IMPAIRED

People with physical impairments face a number of challenges in life. Sport participation represents one of these areas. For example, people who develop arthritis in their knee(s) may find that they can no longer run. If they wish to remain physically fit through sport and recreation, biking and swimming may have to replace running and playing basketball. Athletes who accumulate a number of injuries over the course of their playing careers may find that they can no longer compete at the level they once did. In cases such as these the very identity of the recently physically impaired person is altered.

Persons with more severe disabilities and those born with physical impairments (e.g., no arms or legs, blindness, etc.) may never have the chance to play sports in a traditional manner. But that does not mean that they will be excluded from sport participation. Instead, they may play sports that have been modified to fit their needs. And just as able-bodied person play sports for enjoyment, competition, mental and physical health, and for fun, so too do persons with physical impairments.

National Wheelchair Basketball Association

There are many sports and recreation options available for the physically disabled, including team and individual sports. One of the more popular team sports for the physically impaired is basketball; more specifically, wheelchair basketball. Thanks in part to the National Wheelchair Basketball Association (NWBA), a number of men, women, and children with a physical disability are able to play organized and competitive basketball. According to its website, the NWBA (2008A) is comprised of over 200 basketball teams within twenty-two conferences. The NWBA was founded in 1948 and today consists of men's, women's, intercollegiate, and youth teams throughout the United States and Canada. Wheelchair basketball was created primarily to give returning war veterans who were paralyzed and confined to wheelchairs something competitive and sporting to do. Many of these veterans were frustrated over their recently impaired bodies and altered sense of selves and needed a release valve to alleviate stress and aggravation. Although many impaired veterans found solace with such sports as ping pong, bowling, swimming, and volleyball, those with more energy wanted an opportunity to play action sports such as softball, touch-football, and basketball. The California Chapter of Paralyzed Veterans of America and the New England Chapter of the same organization both claim to have created wheelchair basketball in 1946 in various Veterans Administration Hospitals. Two years later, the organizations were merged under the NWBA.

Today, the NWBA maintains a commitment to its mission statement: "In our pursuit of excellence, the National Wheelchair Basketball Association provides individuals with physical disabilities the opportunity to play, learn, and compete in the sport of wheelchair basketball" (NWBA, 2008B). The NWBA also maintains a commitment to five core values:

- We value unequivocal excellence in all aspects of the organization.
- We strive for excellence with integrity and respect.
- We recognize our rich tradition as a solid foundation.

- We celebrate the development of our members and our community.
- We believe in the pursuit of competitive excellence always.

The Paralympics

Around the same time, and for the same primary reasons, that wheelchair basketball was established, sporting events for World War II veterans with spinal cord injuries were established. First organized in 1948, by Sir Ludwig Guttmann, paraplegic sports competitions were held in Stoke Mandeville, England. Four years later, the Netherlands sent participants to compete at the Games, thus creating an international paraplegic sporting movement known as the Paralympics. In 1960, Rome held the first official Paralympic Games in the style and tradition of the Olympics. That year there were over 400 athletes from 23 countries. Today, there are over 4,000 athletes from more than 140 nations competing in the Summer and Winter Paralympics. The Paralympic Games are also held in the same cities, at the same time, as the Olympics. Winning a Paralympic event, much like an Olympic event, requires hard work and dedication.

Just like the Olympics, the Paralympics are governed by an international body, called the International Paralympic Committee (IPC). According to its website the IPC (2008) serves as the International Federation for nine sports, for which it supervises and co-ordinates the World Championships and other competitions. The IPC is committed to enabling Paralympic athletes to achieve sporting excellence and to developing sport opportunities for all persons with a disability from the beginner to elite level. The IPC also promotes the Paralympic core values of courage, determination, inspiration, and equality.

In the 2008 Natalie du Toit, a swimmer from South Africa and a 2004 Paralympian gold medal winner, became the first female amputee to qualify for the Olympics, placing 16th in a field of 24 in the 10,000 meter swim. And Kelly Bruno, a amputee since the age of six months and a Paralympic champion track star, has become a world-class triathlete and Ironman competitor. Joshua Robinson writes that "long before Bruno's athletic ability catapulted her into the elite ranks, she used sports like soccer, basketball and baseball to prove that she could just be average. 'Especially during a lot of those years when you're trying to fit in, you want to be like everyone else,' she said. 'I obviously wasn't'" (Robinson, 2008:C15). That's putting it mildly!

The Special Olympics

There also exists an international sporting competition for people with mental disabilities (including autism)—the Special Olympics. According to its website, the Special Olympics (2008) is an international nonprofit organization dedicated to empowering individuals with intellectual disabilities to become physically fit, productive and respected members of society through sports training and competition. The Special Olympics offers children and adults with intellectual disabilities year-round training and competition in 30 Olympic-type summer and winter sports. The Special Olympics currently serves 2.5 million people with intellectual disabilities in more than 200 programs in over 180 countries. The goal of the Special Olympics is that children and adults with intellectual disabilities will develop improved physical fitness and motor skills, greater self-confidence and a more positive self-image. "They grow mentally, socially and spiritually and, through their activities, exhibit boundless courage and enthusiasm, enjoy the rewards of friendship and ultimately discover not only new abilities and talents but 'their voices' as well" (Special Olympics, 2008).

As with the two previously discussed versions of the Olympics, the Special Olympics are also held in the Summer and Winter. The organization is dedicated to providing its participants a safe environment to compete.

Technology and Sport Participation

Thanks in part to technological advancements, an increasing number of disabled persons are playing sports at an elite level. Biotics are being used to improve the quality of artificial legs and arms. Wheelchairs are specially made for speed, control and stability. And prosthetic racing blades are being used by sprinters. In fact, one world class athlete, South Africa's Oscar Pistorius, a double-amputee sprinter, is so fast that a number of able-bodied athletes argue that he has an unfair *advantage* over them. Pistorius, known as the "Blade Runner," is so fast that he competed for his national team's Olympic qualification. However, the International Association of Athletics Federations (IAAF) barred the runner from the Olympics and any other able-bodied competition because it was determined that his prosthetic racing blades gave him an unfair advantage. Specifically, the IAAF issued the ban because of its clause that forbids the use of "any technical device that incorporates springs, wheels or any other element that provides a user with an advantage over another athlete not using such a device." The Court of Arbitration for Sport (CAS), though, overturned the IAAF's decision and allowed Pistorius to proceed with his tryout. In its ruling the CAS claimed that the IAAF had not provided sufficient evidence to prove that Pistorius's prostheses give him an advantage over able-bodied athletes. As it turned out, Pistorius did not qualify for the 2008 Beijing Olympics.

Innovator, and two-time (2002, 2006) Paralympic Gold medalist (downhill) Kevin Bramble, has revolutionized sit-skiing with his customized sit ski. Bramble may have become the best able-body skier if it were not for a 1994 skiing injury that left him with a broken back (he is paralyzed below the waist). An ultimate competitor, Brambe taught himself how to ride a sit ski in 1997. He also taught himself to weld. With his welding knowledge, Bramble "changed the geometry of the four-bar suspension and paid the Swedish company Ohlins to custom-build a shock absorber from its snowmobile line to fit his dimensions . . . A month after he built his protype, he rode it to victory in the 2002 Paralympic downhill" (Berg, 2006: C19). In the 2006 Paralympic Games, 7 of the 10 sit skiers on the U.S. disabled team rode Bramble's customized sit ski. Bramble won the event for the second straight year.

Today, Bramble builds his sit-skis for sale. Bramble's innovation is so revolutionary that the IPC is keeping a close eye on him because they feel his technologically-advanced sit ski gives him an unfair advantage over other paraplegics. For a closer look at the role of technology in sport see "Popular Culture and Sports" Box 9.1.

Box 9.1. Technology's Impact on Sport

A basic aspect of popular culture is the realization that it represents the here and now. In that regard, what was popular yesterday, is not popular today; and what is "popular" (e.g., tastes in music, language and slang, and media stars) today will be replaced by something new tomorrow. Technology has a great influence on popular culture as well as sports. Kevin Bramble's innovative sit ski has transformed that sport, just as tricked out wheelchairs have allowed Aaron Fotheringham the ability to do a "360" back flip.

Technology has completely changed the game of golf as today's golfers have numerous advantages over those from the past. These advantages include dramatic changes in the design of golf clubs and golf balls. Is it any wonder golfers hit the ball so far, so easily. NASCAR has introduced so many changes in auto design that today's cars have little resemblance to those of the past.

Many athletes have introduced technological forms of training that include a variety of performance-enhancing devices including the consumption of steroids and other chemicals. Genetic engineering, in the form of genomics, represents the newest form of techno cheating. While gene therapy has been used to treat disease, the introduction of such technology as a form of performance-enhancement is relatively new. However, it may just be a matter of time before we see a race of genetically supercharged athletes. "Speed, strength and endurance—the qualities by which athletic competition defines human differences—would become the results of deliberately controlled processes" (Nesmith, 2007: C-1). Thomas Murray, president of the Hastings Center, an institute devoted to bioethics, claims that there is no such thing as a "shortstop" gene, per se, but as the science of genomics

(continued)

Box 9.1. (*continued*)

progresses, "there is talk of using genetic engineering to insert into human beings genes responsible for traits known to be important to sports performance" (Nesmith, 2007: C-3).

Technology assists humans in many areas of life, and especially in healthcare. People with heart problems, for example may be fitted with a defibrillator—an electrical device used to counteract fibrillation of the heart muscle and restore normal heartbeat by applying a brief electric shock. More than 100,000 defibrillators are implanted a year in people at risk of a life-threatening irregular heartbeat. An installed defibrillator and living a sensible lifestyle will extend the life of those with heart problems. An implanted cardioverter defibrillator (ICD) constantly checks for abnormal beats and automatically zaps the heart to short-circuit any dangerous arrhythmia in senses forming (*The Citizen*, 8/21/07: C5). A "sensible" lifestyle generally includes not participating in competitive, physical sports. Lots of patients ignore these guidelines and play physical sports anyway. A new nationwide registry is recruiting these athletes in an attempt to track their successes and failures. Athletes playing with a heart-zapping defibrillator implanted in their chests risk being shocked during play because of their accelerated heart beats. It is estimated that as many as 40 percent of athlete-patients have experienced ICD shocks while participating in their sports. However, it is the ICD that allows such people the opportunity to live and play sports.

There is a cliché that states, "Clothes make the person." Believing in such an expression often reflects one's superficial personality but, clearly, there are times where dressing appropriately for the situation is more than a suggestion of protocol. In sports, the look of a certain uniform can either enhance the reputation of the team, or athlete, or make the wearer look less-than professional. However, there are times where wearing the right clothes may actually help athletic performance. This is especially true in sports like biking where wind resistance comes into play. Swimmers must overcome the resistance of water and as a result, they look for swimwear that may provide them with an advantage over the competition. Recently, Speedo has developed such a high-tech uniform. Known as the LZR Racer swimsuit, this revolutionary style swimsuit has boost the times of the fastest swimmers in the world. Although some nations, most notably Italy (mostly because they are locked into long-term contracts with Speedo's rivals), have cried "foul" and used such terms as "technological doping" when referring to these suits, the IOC ruled (in 2008) the LZR Racer could be worn by athletes in the 2008 Beijing Olympics. The suits are so tight that athletes need assistance just to put them on. But true to Speedo's claim, a number of swimming records have been set by athletes who were wearing these technologically-advanced suits.

Although it is nearly impossible to predict what the next wave of technology will bring to the world of sports, one thing is for sure; something new is being researched and developed right now.

Bramble is not alone when it comes to blazing new trails in sports achievements for physically impaired persons. A search of websites will provide a number of stories of individuals overcoming physical (and mental) challenges. One of the more intriguing persons is a teenager, Aaron Fotheringham (born 1991). Aaron is "confined" to a wheelchair due to spinal bifida, but he hardly lacks for athletic prowess. Fotheringham has a tricked out wheelchair that allows him to compete with skateboarders on their ramps. He has successfully accomplished a "360" back flip in competition. Aaron has caught the eye of many people and now has his own sponsorship deal. His goal is to compete in the X-Games on the Mega Ramp. Aaron's tricks are so hardcore that he refers to his wheelchair skating abilities as "extreme sitting" or "hardcore sitting." Don't try telling this young man that he cannot perform sports because he is physically impaired.

THE BENEFITS OF SPORT PARTICIPATION AND PHYSICAL EDUCATION

Throughout this book we have demonstrated a number of reasons why people love sports. Many people find enjoyment as sports fans and others also like to actually partake in sports. In this chapter, we have highlighted a few benefits of sport and recreation participation for physically and mentally impaired persons. Among the links shared by able-bodied and disabled persons with sport participation is the idea that such activity helps to release stress and tension. Furthermore, people feel good about themselves after they have completed some sort of physical activity, especially competitive sports.

Sports, recreation, and physical education should be promoted for other benefits they provide participants, including fitness and good health and academic achievement. In other words, sports benefit the body and the mind.

Fitness and Good Health

We all know that, as adults, we are supposed to exercise at least 30 minutes a day, five days a week. The medical profession has done a great job of getting the word out on the benefits of regular cardio vascular exercise for the overall good of the physical body. It is not a matter of simply feeling great afterwards; keeping physically fit, so the experts claim, helps us to live longer, and better lives. Children, because of the enormous energy they possess, are capable of hours of daily physical activity.

And children seem naturally attuned to the idea of running, jumping, and throwing—all of which are characteristics of athletics. It's what they do. Or, at least it is something they used to do. During the past decade more and more kids are falling way short of the normal daily exercise required to maintain healthy, trim bodies. The main reason is a changing way of life that encourages a sedentary lifestyle centered on playing video games, watching television, and surfing the Internet. And although the alarm has been sounded lot and clear, parents and school administrators, apparently, have not heard—there is a growing obesity problem in the United States (as well as in many other nations).

Anywhere you go, there are obese people. It is one thing for older adults to be overweight, but it's an entirely different thing that so many young people are overweight and obese. There are more than 9 million children and adolescents (16% of the U.S. population) who are overweight or obese. This figure is nearly four times higher than 40 years ago (Clinton, 2005). Some small children are so obese they cannot fit into car seats; thus risking their immediate safety. The additional weight that young people carry around with them may cause numerous physical health problems in adulthood including, high cholesterol, high blood pressure, type 2 diabetes, heart disease, stroke, and premature death. "If childhood obesity continues to increase, it could cut two to five years from the average lifespan. That could result in our current generation of children becoming the first in American history to live shorter lives than their parents" (Clinton, 2005:5).

And the news gets worse as children become teenagers. While 90 percent of 9-year-olds get a couple of hours of exercise most days, fewer than 3 percent of 15-year-olds do. Further, fewer than a third of teens get the minimum government recommended amount of exercise—an hour of moderate-to-vigorous exercise, like cycling, brisk walking, swimming or jogging (*The Citizen*, 7/16/08:B6).

In short, a growing number of children at all ages are not exercising enough. Add to this the increasingly unhealthy eating habits of many youth, and the reason we are facing an obesity problem in this country becomes quite clear. As with nearly all problems, there is a solution(s) to the growing obesity problem in the United States. It begins with the children themselves. They must exercise more, eat less junk food, and reduce the amount of time spent playing with electronic devices. Parents must oversee and enforce these guidelines. And the schools must eliminate junk food venting machines, provide healthy foods and most importantly, mandate physical education programs. With the costs of health care and hosts of problems associated with obesity physical education courses in the schools should rank up there in importance with the other basics of education: reading, writing, math, and the social and natural sciences.

The finger of responsibility is directed at adults as well as the drop in physical activity continues into adulthood. That is, as people age, they exercise less. That in itself is not overly newsworthy as adults have to work and they have other commitments. Plus, adults do not possess the energy levels of children. However, once again, a sedentary lifestyle in adulthood may lead to obesity. And the Centers for Disease Control report that 112,000 deaths occur each year as a result of obesity. This figure is nearly three times the number of deaths from all drugs and alcohol. The economic costs are just as astounding. Direct health-care costs of obesity have ascended from $52 billion in 1995 to $75 billion in 2003.

Thus, as previously stated, it is important for adults to exercise a minimum of 30 minutes per day. And adults should do this while they still can, as eventually it becomes increasingly difficult to exercise. That is, the aging process eventually compromises the physical capabilities of most older adults. Keeping in shape, however, is one of the best courses of action to combat the aging process. In this regard, we can love sports (and recreation) because it helps to keep us "young" and healthy as we age.

It might be worth mentioning to those adults inspired to start playing sports again that they should also know their limitations. That is, it is a great idea to exercise, but be reasonable in your choice of a particular activity. Research has shown that an increasing number of aging "baby boomers" still think they can perform as they did thirty years ago. "A Bureau of Labor Statistics survey found that infirmities associated with athletic activities caused 488 million days of restricted work in 2002. Sports injuries among baby boomers increased a whopping 33 percent in the 1990s according to the Consumer Product Safety Commission" (Hubert, 2007:E-2). During the 2000s, the number of injuries to adults past 40 but insisting on playing as if they are in their 20s was so significant that it lead to the term "boomeritis." That is, Baby Boomers with a variety of ailments exacerbated by playing sports.

Some adults may be surprised that if they decide to join a gym to lift weights that their grunting will not be allowed. The Planet Fitness chain, for example, has a strict "no-grunting" policy in its fitness centers. Weight-lifters who like to yell out with a big grunt as a sign of exertion are being told at an increasing number of fitness centers to cut it out! Research in the so-called "effort grunt" doesn't reveal much of a physiological advantage. However, exercise physiologists think that grunting prior to an explosive act can help an athlete mentally prepare for the exertion of force. Many athletes incorporate a grunt as a part of their athletic ritual; it is a part of the total package of concentration (Cromley, 2006). It is commonly believed that men are more likely to grunt when exercising than women. However, anyone who has ever watched Maria Sharapova play tennis will agree that women are capable of grunting as loud as any man.

The Relationship between Physical Activity and Academic Achievement

While educators debate the link between physical activity and increased academic achievement in school, recent research suggest that the case is getting stronger. "Seven or eight years ago, studies offered mixed results on the question of whether exercise can boost brain function in children and adolescents. Experts are beginning to contend, however, that the case is getting stronger" (Viadero, 2008: 14). According to John J. Ratey, a clinical professor of psychiatry at Harvard Medical School, today, there is no doubt about the link. However, as Ratey explains, "The exercise itself doesn't make you smarter, but it puts the brain of the learners in the optimal position for them to learn" (Viadero, 2008). Thus, exercise stimulates the student's mind to function at a peak level.

Students who play a sport are learning discipline and teamwork. Discipline helps a student to study. And because the team is depending on each of its

Orange clad fans pack the Carrier Dome, home of the Syracuse University Orange. (Courtesy Tim Delaney)

players to remain academically eligible, studying and attending class brings with it added importance. Hard work and good grades in high school helps a student reach college. Once in college, the good study habits athletes learned in high school tend to carryover. And on the average, college athletes perform better (higher graduation rates) than non-athletes.

THE MEDIA: FEEDING OUR THIRST FOR SPORTS

Sports have been a part of nearly every society's culture throughout human history. During most of this history, sports were dominated by local customs and possessed a following that was pretty much localized. The advent of the mass media changed this.

The Sports Media

The mass media refers to the medium by which large numbers of people are informed about important events in society. The mass media grew from its humble beginnings—the printing press—to its current ubiquitous existence. The mass media consists of television, radio, motion pictures, newspapers, books, periodicals, magazines, sound recordings, and the Internet.

Sports coverage can be found in all aspects of the media. But it is television that quenches our thirst for sports most adequately. The sports media provides many functions for sports fans, including: providing information, such as scores, statistics, and highlights; interpretations, in the form of expert analysis; entertainment; excitement, every day there is always something to make us say, "Wow;" and an escape and diversion from the everyday.

Sports fans are pleased to have the media cover sporting events. It almost seems impossible to think of sports without media coverage. Sports fans often come to identify with the "voice" of their favorite team, the radio and/or television announcer. Sports talk show hosts, analysts, and sports broadcasters on popular shows like ESPN's "SportsCenter" become mini celebrities in their own right. One such popular SportsCenter broadcaster is Steve Levy. As Levy explains (see Narrative 9.2) just knowing that you are speaking to millions of people is exciting and although the perks are not as plentiful as some fans might think, "Super bowl tickets become a little easier to get."

The future, as they say, is not predetermined. At least none of us has a script of future events. But it would seem reasonable to assume that sports will remain as a fixture of humanity indefinitely. The media will continue to fuel our passion for sport through innovative technology. And technology will

**Narrative 9.2.   An Interview with Steve Levy,
ESPN SportsCenter anchorperson.**

Levy was hired by ESPN in August 1993. Before working at ESPN, he first went
on the air on WNBC radio in New York City and his first on-air television job was
with MSG-TV.

1. What courses did you take in college that helped prepare you for your job in
    broadcasting? What curriculum would you recommend for students today?
    Many ex-athletes find jobs in broadcasting without a degree in that field. Do
    you need a degree to get a job in broadcasting?

    I remember taking broadcast performance, journalism and general com-
    munications classes that were helpful. Equally helpful was the opportunity
    to become immediately active in the campus radio, television, and newspa-
    per. I would recommend a combination of all the above. As for needing a de-
    gree to get a broadcasting job, no one has ever asked to see my degree, so I
    probably didn't actually need it, but going for a communications degree
    helped me narrow my focus. As for ex-athletes, that's a totally different is-
    sue. An ex-athlete will be allowed to broadcast strictly because he or she is
    an ex-athlete. The better athletic career they had, the less they have to do
    well as a broadcaster. Conversely, if you were a fringe pro athlete, you bet-
    ter have some broadcasting skills to make it. That being said, an ex-athlete
    who had a degree in communication or broadcasting would have an edge
    over one who did not.

2. What are the most important qualities that an individual should possess if he or
    she were considering a job in broadcasting?

    Be prepared to start at the bottom whether that's in a small market or behind
    the scenes. Patience and perseverance are key. It can take a while to succeed
    and you have to show initiative while not crossing the fine line between being
    aggressive and being a pain; which is very difficult to do at times. Being well-
    spoken is obvious; being well-read is also a key. The ability to think and react
    quickly when things go wrong would also be high on the list. It is important to
    have the ability to write, even if you are a broadcaster. And, the ability to type
    will make your life a lot easier.

3. Many people believe that ESPN anchors live exciting lives (e.g., attending
    many sporting events, meeting athletes and celebrities). Is this true?

    Most of the time it is exciting. The red light coming on, knowing that you
    will be speaking to millions is exciting. We do get to meet people we ordinar-
    ily would never get to meet. People recognizing you can be fun. Super Bowl
    tickets become a little easier to get (although not as easy as you might think).
    Half of the calls I field everyday are somehow ticket related. We are afforded
    some other opportunities and perks that only come our way just because we're
    on TV.

4. What is the "typical" work day for a sport anchor at ESPN? Students wonder whether you have time for your family or does your job demand long hours?

   Every other month, my work day begins at 6:00 p.m. and ends around 4:00 a.m. The other months I'm in the office at 3:30 p.m. and out around 1:00 a.m. I also work weekends and holidays. Since I am single, time for my family is not an issue but most of my colleagues are married with kids and I don't know how they do it all. I hope to find out one day!

5. What is the starting salary for a sports anchor?

   Starting salary really depends on what market you start in. It's just so wide-ranging. And, no one starts "on the air" at ESPN.

6. Do you do your own research on players and stories? Or do you have assistants and staff members or some combination of both?

   At ESPN we have a full-time staff of researchers; there are probably 15 people in that department. They provide us with just about everything and then its up to us to put them into our own words and deliver the information. We do write all our own material, which most people don't realize. Sometimes we'll come up with an idea and give it to the researcher and they'll come back with the answers to our questions.

7. Do you think it is important that ESPN anchors have a background in sports themselves? It is necessary that they have been athletes in order to understand the athletes they are covering?

   I do believe it's a great asset to be raised with sports to get into sports broadcasting. One does not have to necessarily have played the game but to have grown up following the game is a great help. You can read and research forever but it's not the same as if you grew up on it. Again, being an athlete would help you understand what the athletes you are covering might be going through; but it is not a necessity. I find that most sports broadcasters were average to poor athletes themselves growing up (myself included). But, that does not prevent you from loving the sport. If you can't play, broadcast! That's the closest you can get to the action. Getting paid to be around sport without the risk of injury is a positive.

8. How important do you think it is for athletes to be role models? Is athletic ability sufficient or should the character of the athletes also be taken into consideration in evaluating them in the media?

   I do believe it is very important for athletes to be role models. Even if they don't want to be, they are and that's part of their job. They take all the money and with that comes this added responsibility. They are performing in front of so many young people; they don't really have a choice about being a role model. The choice they do have is to be a good role model. I find athletes who disagree with that only do so after they've been in some trouble. As for the media evaluating athletes, our audience, the public, demands so much information and there is so much competition out there among the media; I think that's the

(continued)

Narrative 9.2.   (*continued*)

reason you hear so much about athletes beyond just their athletic ability and getting into their personal lives. As for evaluating them, for example, should this guy
be a pro bowl quarterback, that is based strictly on his on-field talent. Now, I am
human, and if I have a vote and 2 quarterbacks are equal in ability and 1 guy is a
good guy off the field and other is a bad guy off the field, I would allow that to be
tie breaker.

9. Does media coverage actually have an effect on the games, or is it primarily
    impartial?
    I don't believe media coverage has an effect on the outcome of the game. It
    can affect aspects, the crowd, the TV coverage, sales of merchandise, etc. In
    the case of college football, I believe the media can sway the rankings.
10. How has media coverage of sports changed in the past ten years? What to you
    anticipate the changes will be in the next ten years?
    The change in the past 10 years gets back to something I mentioned earlier.
    There is so much competition in the media, especially with the explosion of
    cable/digital TV. I remember growing up with 13 channels and now we have
    500 or something like that. And it's because of the hunger of the audience —
    and that the audience wants more choices and more information — that's why
    we do more in-depth interviews and features and try and get behind the scenes
    and into the athlete's life. Anybody can give the score and stats, and all that
    information, thanks to the Internet, is now instantaneous. As for the changes
    in the next 10 years, well, everything will be broadcast in HD and everyone
    will have HD TVs. You will see cameras and microphones in places you never
    thought possible. Players will have to be more accessible because their teams
    and leagues will demand they do so. This is due in part to allowing sports
    leagues to command ridiculous dollars for the television rights from networks
    like ESPN.

---

affect sports. That sport will continue to evolve has already been demonstrated through its thousands of years of existence.

Sports fans will continue to root for their favorite teams and players. This
is particularly true for national and international events, and—as has been
pointed out several times throughout this book—the Modern Olympics continues to be a primary means of showcasing the abilities of some of the
world's finest athletes.

One of the highlights of the 2008 Summer Olympics was the amazing
string of records which swimmer Michael Phelps achieved. The entire world
was riveted by his achievements. In the 112 year history of the Modern
Olympics, over 100,000 athletes have competed, but only 1 person—
Phelps—has won 8 gold medals at one venue. His 16 total medals are the

most for any male, second most for any Olympian. He has 14 gold medals, more than any other modern Olympian. And, best of all, he is planning to compete in 2012, where he is likely to set even more records. Phelps united all Americans, regardless of race, religion, gender, SES, age—everyone wanted to see him win. While it is true that sports is more than just an obsession with winning, there is something truly stirring about the breaking of athletic records. In fact, even Mark Spitz, the previous gold medal record holder (with seven from the 1972 Summer Olympics) was rooting for Phelps!

It's also important to point out that sometimes good sportsmanship *does* receive the recognition it deserves. In 2008 the NCAA Committee on Sportsmanship and Ethical Conduct (CSEC) selected softball student-athlete Mallory Holtman of Central Washington University and the St. John Fisher College's baseball team as the national 2008 NCAA Sportsmanship Award winners, for their exemplary behavior which we discussed earlier in this text.

We love winners; we love excitement; we love the camaraderie of being together with fellow fans; we love a heated rivalry; and most of all, we love a good game. We hope that this book has demonstrated some of the vital ways in which sport has improved the human condition and given joy to countless numbers of people.

Bibliography

Adams, Natalie and Pamela Bettis. 2003. *Cheerleader! Cheerleader!: An American Icon*. New York: Palgrave Macmillan.

American Sociological Association. 2005. "Reflecting on ASA's Centennial Year, 2005." May/June: 1.

Angola Prison Rodeo. 2008. Available: www.angolarodeo.com

Arditi, Jorge. 1998. *A Genealogy of Manners, Transformations of Social Relations in France and England from the Fourteenth to the Eighteenth Century*. Chicago: University of Chicago Press.

Arnold, Serena. 1980. "The Dilemma of Meaning," pp. 5–18 in *Recreation and Leisure: Issues in an Era of Change*, edited by Thomas Goodale and Peter Witt. State College, PA: Venture.

Babe Ruth League. 2005. Home website. Available: http://www.baberuthleague.org.

Baker, W. J. 1982. *Sports in the Western World*. Totowa, NJ: Rowan & Littlefield.

Banks, James. 1997. *Teaching Strategies for Ethnic Studies*, 6th edition. Boston: Allyn & Bacon.

Beaton, Rod. 2002. "Age May be Off for Hundreds in Baseball." *USA Today*. February 26:C1.

Bell, J. Bowyer. 1987. *To Play the Game*. New Brunswick, NJ: Transaction Books.

Bellis, Mary. 2008. "Hacky Sack." Available: http://inventors.about.com/library/inventors/blhackysack.htm.

Berg, Aimee. 2006. "Build It, So He Can Be a Daredevil." *The New York Times*. December 13: C19.

Black, Lewis, 2008. *Me of Little Faith*. New York: Riverhead Books.

Blais, Madeleine, 1995. *In These Girls, Hope Is a Muscle*. New York: The Atlantic Monthly Press.

Borte, Jason. 2000. "George Freeth." Available: http://www.surfing.com/surfa2/freeth_george.cfm.

Bowen, William G. and Sarah A. Levin. 2003. *Reclaiming The Game: College Sports And Educational Values*. Princeton, NJ: Princeton University Press.

Brady, Erik. 2002. "Cheerleading in the USA: A Sport and an Industry." *USA Today*. April 26–28: 1A.

———. 2002. "Title IX Hits Middle America." *USA Today*. June 13:1A, 2A.

Brasch, Rudolph. 1970. *How Did Sports Begin?* New York: David McKay.

Burton, Stephanie. 2006. "Rah! Rah! Rah! Sis, Boom, Ouch!" *The Post-Standard*. March 14:E1.

Butcher, Robert and Angela Schneider. 2001. "Fair Play as Respect For the Game," pp. 21–48 in *Ethics in Sport*, edited by William Morgan, Klaus Meier and Angela Schneider. Champaign, IL: Human Kinetics.

Byers, Walter. 1995. *Unsportsmanlike Conduct: Exploiting College Athletes*. Ann Arbor, MI: The University of Michigan Press.

Cala, Andres. 2001. "Dominican Investigator Finds Almonte is 14." *Buffalo News*. August 31:C9.

Carroll, John. 1999. *Red Grange and the Rise of Modern Football*. Chicago: University of Illinois Press.

Chappell, Linda Rae. 1997. *Coaching Cheerleading Successfully*. Champaign, IL: Human Kinetics.

Chu, Donald. 1989. *The Character of American Higher Education and Intercollegiate Sport*. Albany, NY: State University of New York Press.

Clinton, Bill. 2005. "We Must Act Now." *Parade*. September 25:4–5.

Coleman, James S. 1961. *The Adolescent Society*. New York: Free Press.

Connors, Greg. 2002. "Action Figures." *Buffalo News*. July 14: B1.

Cooper, Allison. 2005. "Dr. Richard Rohrer, 'Strived to be the Best.'" *Brighton-Pittsford Post*. December 7: 3-B.

Corbin, C.B. 1973. "Among Spectators, 'Trait' Anxiety and Coronary Risk." *Physician and Sport Medicine*. 1 (2): 55–58.

Craig, Steve. 2002. *Sports and Games of the Ancients*. Westport, CT: Greenwood Press.

Crissey, Mike. 2004. "'Dude': It's Not Just for Surfers and Skaters." *The Post-Standard*. December 9: A-1.

Cromley, Janet. 2006. "Gyms Telling Grunters to Quiet Down." *The Los Angeles Times* (as appearing in *The Post-Standard*). December 19: E-3.

Crowe, Jerry. 2007. "Criticism of USC Football Schedule is Off by Miles." *Los Angeles Times*. July 10: D2.

Curran, Daniel and Claire Renzetti. 1994. *Theories of Crime*. Boston: Allyn and Bacon.

Curry, Timothy J. and Robert M. Jiobu. 1984. *Sports: A Social Perspective*. Englewood Cliffs, NJ: Prentice Hall.

Delaney, Tim. 1999. *Community, Sport and Leisure*. Auburn, NY: Legend Books.

———. 2002. "Sport Violence," pp. 1560–1563 in the *Encyclopedia of Crime and Punishment*, Vol.4, edited by David Levinson. Thousand Oaks, CA: Sage.

———. 2004A. *Classical Social Theory: Investigation and Application*. Upper Saddle River, NJ: Prentice Hall.

———. 2004B. "The Russian Mafia in the United States," pp. 6–17 in *Social Diseases: Mafia, Terrorism, Totalitarianism*, edited by Tim Delaney, Valerii Kuvakin, and Tim Madigan. Moscow, Russia: Russian Humanist Society.

———. 2005. *Contemporary Social Theory: Investigation and Application.* Upper Saddle River, NJ: Prentice Hall.

———. 2006A. *Seinology: The Sociology of Seinfeld.* Amherst, NY: Prometheus Books.

———. 2006B. *American Street Gangs.* Upper Saddle River, NJ: Prentice Hall.

———. 2007. "Pop Culture: An Overview." *Philosophy Now* 64 (November/ December): 6–7.

Delaney, Tim and Allene Wilcox. 2002. "Sports and the Role of the Media," pp. 199–215 in *Values, Society & Evolution,* edited by Harry Birx and Tim Delaney Auburn, NY: Legend Books.

DiCesare, Bob. 2005. "Small Hall Honors More Than Fame." *The Buffalo News.* May 31: D-1.

Douglas, Tom. 1983. *Groups.* New York: Tavistock.

Drehs, Wayne. 2008. "Inches from Tragedy, Oswego Overcomes. *ESPN.go.com.* May 16:3. Available: http://sports.espn.go.com/ncaa/news/story?id=3398247

Duderstadt, James J. 2003. *Intercollegiate Athletics and the American University: A President's Perspective.* Ann Arbor: The University of Michigan Press.

Dunning, Eric. 1986. "Social Bonding and Violence in Sport," pp. 224–244 in *Quest for Excitement: Sport And Leisure and The Civilizing Process,* edited by Norbert Elias and Eric Dunning. New York: Basil Blackwell.

———. 1999. *Sport Matters: Sociological Study of Sport, Deviance, Violence and Civilization.* New York: Routledge.

Edmonds, David and John Eidinow. 2004. *Bobby Fischer Goes to War.* New York: HarperCollins.

Edwards, Harry. 1973. *Sociology of Sport.* Homewood, IL: Dorsey.

Eitzen, D. Stanley. 1989A. "The Political-Economic Olympics," pp. 262–270 in *Sport in Contemporary Society,* 3rd edition, edited by D. Stanley Eitzen. New York: St. Martin's Press.

———. 1989B. "Black Participation in America Sport Since World War II," pp. 300–312 in *Sport in Contemporary Society: An Anthology,* 3rd edition, edited by D. Stanley Eitzen. New York: St. Martin's Press.

———. 1999. *Fair and Foul: Beyond the Myths and Paradoxes of Sport.* New York: Rowan & Littlefield.

Eitzen, D. Stanley and George H. Sage. 1989. *Sociology of North American Sport,* 4th edition. Dubuque, IA: Wm. C. Brown.

Elias, Norbert. 1978. *The Civilizing Process: The History of Manners.* Oxford: Blackwell.

———. 1986. "An Essay on Sport and Violence," pp. 150–174 in *Quest for Excitement,* edited by Norbert Elias and Eric Dunning. New York: Basil Blackwell.

ESPN. 2005. "Many Ginobili – Special Report." First aired: June 11.

ESPN.com. 2005. "The 25 Best Sports Movies." Available: http://sports.espn.go.com/espn/espn25/story?page=listranker/bestmoviesresult

Falkener, Edward. 1961. *Games, Ancient and Oriental and How to Play Them.* New York: Dover.

Feezell, Randolph. 2004. *Sport, Play & Ethical Reflection.* Urbana and Chicago, IL: University of Illinois Press.

Fendrich, Howard. 2002. "NBA Inks New Six-Year, $4.6 Billion Deals with ESPN, ABC, TNT." *The Buffalo News*. January 24:C-5.

Figler, Stephen and Gail Whitaker. 1991. *Sport and Play In American Life*, 2nd edition. Dubuque, IA: Wm. C. Brown.

———. 1995. *Sport and Play in American Life*, 3rd edition. Chicago: Brown and Benchmark.

Finney, Ben and James D. Houston. 1996. *Surfing: A History of the Ancient Hawaiian Sport*. Petaluma, CA: Pomegranate Communications.

Forbes. 2008. "Top Colleges for Getting Rich." Available: http://www.forbes.com/2008/07/30/college-salary-graduates-lead-cz_kb0730.

Foster, Janet. 1990. *Villains: Crime and Community in the Inner City*. New York: Routledge.

Freeman, William. 1997. *Physical Education and Sport in a Changing Society*. Boston: Allyn and Bacon.

Frey, James H. 1978. "The Organization of Amateur Sport: Efficiency to Entropy." *American Behavioral Scientist*. 21: 361–378.

Frey, James H. and Tim Delaney. 1996. "The Role of Leisure Participation in Prison: A Report From Consumers." *Journal of Offender Rehabilitation*, Vol. 23 (1/2):79–89.

Frey, James H. and D. Stanley Eitzen. 1991. "Sport and Society." *Annual Review of Sociology*, 17:503–522.

Geschwind, Melissa. 2001. "Orchard Park Little League Team Cries Foul." *Buffalo News*. September 1:A1.

Giles, Molly, 2005. "Family Volunteering: A Derby Dad and His Kids Help Other Kids Be Winners." *Brighton-Pittsford Post*. December 5: 4-B.

Goldman, Adam. 2008. "U.S. Eater Still Top Dog." *Daily Breeze* (Torrance, CA). July 5: A8.

Goldstein, Richard, 1996. *Ivy League Autumns: An Illustrated History of College Football's Grand Old Rivalries*. New York: St. Martin's Press.

Griffin, Pat. 1998. *Strong Women, Deep Closets: Lesbians and Homophobia in Sport*. Champaign, IL: Human Kinetics.

Guttmann, Allen. 2004. *Sports: The First Five Millennia*. Amherst and Boston: University of Massachusetts Press.

Hallman, J.C. 2003. *The Chess Artist*. New York: St. Martin's Press

Hanson, Mary Ellen. 1995. *Go! Fight! Win!: Cheerleading in American Culture*. Bowling Green, OH: Bowling Green State University Popular Press.

Harvey, Jean, Lucie Thibault, and Genevieve Rail. 1995. "Neo-Corporatism: The Political Management System in Canadian Amateur Sport and Fitness." *Journal Of Sport & Social Issue*. Vol.19, No.3: 249–265.

Hawley, Amos. 1981. *Urban City: An Ecological Approach*. New York: Ronald Press.

Higgins, Matt. 2005. "Endless Winter: A Surfing Paradise Not for the Faint of Heart." *The New York Times*. November 19: B21.

Hirschi, Travis. 1969. *Causes of Delinquency*. Berkeley: University of California Press.

Hoch, Paul. 1972. *Rip Off the Big Game: The Exploitation of Sports by the Power Elite*. Garden City, NY: Anchor.

Hoffman, Roy. 1996. "It's a Bird, It's a Plane, It's a Flying Anvil." *The Post Standard*. November 7: A-18.

Hubert, Cynthia. 2007. "Fall Down, Go Boomer." *The Sacramento Bee* (as appeared in *The Post-Standard*). January 11: E-2.

Inge, M. Thomas, editor. 2000. *Charles M. Schulz: Conversations*. Jackson, Mississippi: University Press of Mississippi.

Institute for International Sport. 2008. "National Sportsmanship Day." Available: http://www.internationalsport.com/nsd/index.cfm.

International Federation of Competitive Eating (IFOCE). 2008. "Website: About." Available: http://www.ifoce.com/about/php.

International Paralympic Committee (IPC). 2008. "About the IPC." Available: http://www.paralympic.org

Jay, Kathryn. 2004. *More Than Just a Game*. New York: Columbia University Press.

Johnson, David and Frank Johnson. 2002. *Joining Together: Group Theory and Group Skills*, 8th edition. Upper Saddle River, NJ: Prentice Hall.

Keating, James W. 2001. "Sportsmanship as a Moral Category," pp. 7–20 in *Ethics in Sport*, edited by William J. Morgan, Klaus U. Meier, Angela J. Schneider. Champaign, IL: Human Kinetics.

King, Lauren. 2001. "Afghans Revive Ancient Blood Sport That Was Banned Under Taliban Rule. *The Buffalo News*. December 29: B-3.

Lancaster, Scott. 2002. *Fair Play: Making Organized Sports a Great Experience for Your Kids*. New York: Prentice-Hall.

Leonard II, Wilbert M. 1988. *A Sociological Perspective of Sport*. New York: Macmillan.

Liptak, Adam. 2008. "1 in 100 US Adults Behind Bars, New Study Says." Available: http://www.nytimes.com/2008/02/28/ua/28cnd-prison.html.

Lumpkin, Angela. 1994. *Physical Education and Sport*, 3rd edition. St. Louis: Mosby.

Luschen, Günther. 1981. "The Interdependence of Sport and Culture," pp. 287–295 in *Sport, Culture and Society*, edited by John W. Loy, Gerald Kenyon and Barry McPherson. Philadelphia: Lea & Febiger.

Madigan, Tim. 2003. "Interview with Myles Brand." *Philosophy Now*, 41(May/June):12.

Malina, Robert. 1986. "Readiness for Competitive Youth Sport," pp. 45–50 in *Sport for Children and Youths*, edited by Maureen Weiss and Daniel Gould. Champaign, IL: Human Kinetics.

Mandell, Richard. 1984. *Sport: A Cultural History*. New York: Columbia University Press.

Marshall, John. 2008. "Games Long Gone." *The Post-Standard*. July 10: C-1, C-2.

Martens, Rainer, Robert Christina, John Harvey, Brian Sharkey. 1981. *Coaching Young Athletes*. Champaign, IL: Human Kinetics.

McHugh, Paul. 2008. "Making Mavericks: Technological Tools Help Forecast the Big-Wave Spot. *Honolulu Star-Bulletin*. January 12: A8.

McIntosh, Peter. 1993. "The Sociology of Sport in the Ancient World," pp. 19–38 in\ *The Sports Process*, edited by Eric Dunning, Joseph Maguire, and Robert Pearton. Champaign, IL: Human Kinetics.

Merron, Jeff. 2002. "Waking Up Rudy's Echoes." Available: http://espn.go.com/page2/s/merron/021202.html

Michaelis, David. 2007. *Schulz and Peanuts: A Biography*. New York: Harper.

Micheli, Lyle J. with Mark D. Jenkins. 1990. *Sportswise an Essential Guide for Young Athletes, Parents and Coaches*. Boston: Houghton Mifflin.

Michener, James A. 1976. *Sports in America*. New York: Random House.

Miller, Toby, Geoffrey Lawrence, Jim McKay and David Rowe. 2001. *Globalization and Sport*. London: Sage Publications.

Morgan, William, Klaus Meier and Angela Schneider. 2001. *Ethics in Sport*. Champaign IL: Human Kinetics.

Mowday, R. T., L.W. Porter and R.M. Stegas. 1982. *Employee-Organizational Linkage: The Psychology of Commitment, Absenteeism, and Turnover*. New York: Academic Press.

Museum of Appalachia. 2005. "July 4th Celebration and Anvil Shoot." Available: www.museumofappalachia.com.

National Amateur Dodgeball Association (NADA). 2008. "Website: About NADA." Available: http://www.dodgeballusa.com/about.html.

National Federation of State High School Associations. 2007. "High School Sports Participation Increases Again; Girls Exceeds Three Million for First Time." Available: http://www.nfhs.org/web/2007/09/high_school_sports_participation.aspx.

National Football League (NFL). 2008. "NFL Teams Implement Fan Code of Conduct." Available: http://www.nfl.com/news/story.

National Junior College Athletic Association (NJCAA). 2008. "Website: Welcome to the NJCCA." Available: http://www.njcaa.org.

National Wheelchair Basketball Association (NWBA). 2008A. "About Us." Available: http://www.nwba.org/index.

———. 2008B. "NWBA Mission Statement." Available: http://www.nwba.org/index.

NCAA Manual. 2008. Indianapolis, IN: The National Collegiate Athletic Association.

NCAA News. 2001. "2001 NCAA Drug Use Survey." October 13: 1, 17. Available: www.ncaa.org.

Nelson, Shane. 2007. "Hawaii's Legendary Surfers," pp. 51–53 in *Oahu Essence*. Honolulu: Morris Visitors Publications.

Nerz, Ryan. 2006. *Eat This Book*. New York: St. Martin's Press.

Nesmith, Jeff. 2007. "Frontier of Sports Cheating: Genomics." *The Post-Standard*. October 23: C-1, C-3.

Newton, Michael, 2004. *Savage Girls and Wild Boys: A History of Feral Children*. New York: Picador.

Nietzsche, Friedrich. 1979. *The Portable Nietzsche*. Edited and translated by Walter Kaufmann. New York: Penguin Books.

Niles Daily Star (online edition). 2008. "Irish No. 1: Intramurals Ranked Tops in Participation." Available: http://www.nilestar.com/articles/2008/07/30/ndsports4.prt

Nisbet, Robert. 1969. *The Quest for Community: A Study in the Ethics of Order and Freedom*. New York: Oxford University Press.

Nixon II, Howard L. and James H. Frey. 1996. *A Sociology of Sport*. Belmont, CA: Wadsworth.

Oklobzika, Kevin. 2008. "St. John Fisher Baseball Players Get Lesson in Life." *The Democrat and Chronicle*. May 10:A3.

Olson, Eric. 2008. "Fresno Forever: Bulldogs Celebrates World Series Title." *The Post-Standard*. June 26: C-10.

Oriard, Michael. 1993. *Reading Football: How the Popular Press Created an American Spectacle*. Chapel Hill, NC: The University of North Carolina Press.

Payne, Melanie. 2003. *Champions, Cheaters, and Childhood Dreams: Memories of the All-American Soap Box Derby*. Akron, OH: University of Akron Press.

Pennington, Bill. 2007. "Cheers & Fears." *The Post-Standard* (originally appeared in *The New York Times*). May 8: D-1.

Pfeiffer, Ronald P. and Brent C. Mangus. 2002. *Concepts of Athletic Training*, 3rd edition. Boston: Jones and Bartlett.

Phillips, John. 1993. *Sociology of Sport*. Boston: Allyn & Bacon.

Pop Warner. 2008. Home website. Available: http://www.popwarner.com/history.

Potter, Dena. 2008. "Study: Winning in Sports Really Does Bring Universities More Students." *The Post-Standard*. March 24: A-1, A-4.

Putnam, Douglas T. 1999. *Controversies of the Sports World*. Westport, CT: Greenwood Press.

Quinlan, Linda. 2006. "Soap Box Derby Dreams Come True for Six." *Brighton-Pittsford Post*. June 14: 13-A.

Rader, Benjamin. 2004. *American Sports*, 5th edition. Upper Saddle River, NJ: Prentice Hall.

Redondo Beach Chamber. 2008. "George Freeth Memorial." Available at: http://www.redondochamber.com/visitors/freeth_memorial.htm.

Ritter, Malcolm. 2008. "Pill Gives Sedentary Mice a No-Sweat Workout." *The Post-Standard*. August 1: A-3.

Roberts, Michael. 1976. *Fans! How We Go Crazy Over Sports*. Washington, D.C.: New Republic.

Robinson, Joshua. 2008. "Ball Girl? Triathlete? Amputee? All of the Above." *The New York Times*. August 29:C15.

Rushin, Steve. 2005. "Sex and the Twin Cities." *Sports Illustrated*. October 24:19.

Russian News & Information Agency. 2008. "Russia Wins 2008 Ice Hockey World Championship in Canada." Available: http://en.rian.ru/sports/20090519/107753003.

Sack, Allen L. and Ellen J. Staurowsky. 1998. *College Athletes for Hire: The Evolution And Legacy of the NCAA's Amateur Myth*. Westport, CT: Praeger.

Santibanez, Lucrecia, Gabriella Gonzalez, Peter A. Morrison, and Stephen J. Carroll. 2007. "Methods for Gauging the Target Populations that Community Colleges Serve." *Population Research & Policy Review*, 26: 51–67.

Schulz, Charles. 1999. *Peanuts: A Golden Celebration*. New York: HarperResource.

Seattle Post-Intelligencer. 2005. "Elma School Officials Ban Short Cheerleader Skirts." September 9. Available: http://seattlepi.nwsource.com.

Seddons, Peter. 2008. "Harold Abrahams: Chariot of Fire Athlete." Available: http://www.youandyesterday.co.uk/articles/Abrahams,_Harold_-_'Chariots _of_Fire'_Athlete

Sefton, Dru. 2004. "Cup Stacking: The Next Pro Sport?" *The Post-Standard.* September 19: A-16.

———. 2005. "Cheerleaders: Go, Team, Go or Go-Go Girls in Training?" *The Post-Standard.* May 15: C-4.

Seinfeld. 1997. "The Little Jerry." First air date: January 9, 1997.

Shulman, James L. and William G. Bowen. 2001. *The Game of Life.* Princeton, NJ: Princeton University Press.

Siegel, Larry L. Brandon C. Welsh and Joseph J. Senna. 2003. *Juvenile Delinquency,* 8th edition. Belmont, CA: Wadsworth.

Sieh, Maureen. 2008. "Lomong to Carry US Flag in Opening Ceremony." *The Post-Standard.* August 7: A-1, A-6.

Simon, Peter. 2000. "Student Puts Honesty Over Winning." *Buffalo News.* October 21:A1.

Simon, Robert L. 1985. *Sports and Social Values.* Englewood Cliffs, NJ: Prentice Hall.

———. 1991. *Fair Play.* Boulder, CO: Westview.

Smith, Ronald E. 1988. *Sports and Freedom: The Rise of Big-Time College Athletics.* New York: Oxford University Press.

Souhan, Jim. 2007. "Sports Provide Normalcy." *Star Tribune* (Minneapolis) (as appeared in *The Post-Standard.* August 5: C-2.

Special Olympics. 2008. "About Us." Available: http://www.specialolympics.org.

Sperber, Murray. 1990. *College Sports Inc.* New York: Holt Henry.

Sponholz, Joseph. 1997. *Winning Athletic Scholarships: Guaranteeing Your Academic Eligibility for College Sports Scholarships.* New York: Random House.

Sports Illustrated. 2008. "Video Games." July 28:19.

SportsIllustrated.com. 2005. "Going for the Jugular?" October 31. Available: http://sportsillustrated.cnn.com/2005/football/ncaa.

Stone, Gregory. 1955. "American Sports: Play and Display." *Chicago Review.* 9 (3): 83–100.

Sunkin, Ayssa. 2007. "Union Springs Students Stack to a Record." *The Citizen* (Auburn, NY). November 9: A1.

Swaddling, Judith. 1980. *The Ancient Olympic Games.* Austin: University of Texas Press.

Taylor, Nelson. 2008. "National Anvil Shooting Contest." Available: http://www.2camels.com/national-anvil-shooting-contest-php.

Teaching Tolerance. 2003. "Ho'oponopono." Fall 2003: 4.

The American Youth Soccer Organization. 2008. "Website: Homepage." Available: http://soccer.org.home.aspx.

The Citizen. 2007. "Registry Tracks Athletes With Life-Saving Device." August 21: C5.

———. 2008. "Study Says Children Exercise Less as They Age." July 16: B6.

The Moscow Times. 2005. "Russian Soccer Is Back in Europe." May 25–31:1,3.

The Post-Standard. 2005. "Scientists Find a Splash of Red is the Color of Victory." May 20: A-2.

The Simpsons. 2008. "Any Given Sundance." First air date: May 4, 2008.

Thomsen, Geoff. 2006. "Top 25 Most Popular Sports/Recreational Activities in the U.S. Available:http://www.doubledonut.com/2006/08/14/top-25mostpopular-sports recreational-activities-in-the-US.

Thompson, Jim. 1995. *Positive Coaching: Building Character and Self-Esteem Through Sports.* Portola Valley, CA: Warde Publishers, Inc.

———. 2003. *The Double-Goal Coach.* New York: Harper Collins.

Thorton, William E. and Lydia Voigt. 1992. *Delinquency and Justice*, 3rd edition. New York: McGraw-Hill.

Turner, Jonathan. 2003. *The Structure of Sociological Theory.* Belmont, CA: Wadsworth.

———. 2006. *Handbook of Sociological Theory.* New York: Springer.

Valade, Jodie. 2005. "A Life Lived Whole." *The Plain Dealer.* October 9:C3.

Van Krieken, Robert. 1999. "The Barbarism of Civilization: Cultural Genocide and the 'Stolen Generations.'" *British Journal of Sociology*, Vol. 50, No.2 (June):297–

Varner, Monica K. and J. David Knottnerus. 2002. "Civility Rituals and Exclusion: The Emergence of American Golf During the Late 19th and Early 20th Centuries." *Sociological Inquiry*, Vol. 72, No. 3 (Summer): 426–441.

Vescey, George. 2008. "An Act of Sportsmanship That Touched 'Em All." *The New York Times.* April 30: C13.

Viadero, Debra. 2008. "Exercises Seen as Priming Pump For Students' Academic Strides; Case Grows Stronger for Physical Activity's Link to Improved Brain Function." *Education Week.* Vol. 27 (23): 14–15.

Volberg, Rachel. 1994. "The Prevalence and Demographics of Pathological Gamblers: Implications for Public Health." *American Journal of Gambling Studies.* 10(4): 399–409.

Wann, Daniel L. Merrill J. Melnick, Gordon W. Russell and Dale G. Pease. 2001. *Sports Fans.* New York: Routledge.

Weir, Fred. 2008. Euro 2008: Russian Soccer Team Revives Nationalism." *The Christian Science Monitor*, June 27.

Willard, Michael Nevin. 2002. "Duke Kahanamoku's Body: Biography of Hawaii," pp. 13–38 in *Sport Matters*, edited by John Bloom and Michael Nevin Willard. New York: New York University Press.

Williams, Randy. 2006. *Sports Cinema 100 Movies.* Pompton Plain, New Jersey: Limelight Editions.

Womack, Mari. 1992. "Why Athletes Need Ritual: A Study of Magic Among Professional Athletes," pp. 191–202 in *Sport and Religion*, edited by Shirl J. Hoffman. Champaign, IL: Human Kinetics.

World Adult Kickball Association (WAKA). 2008. "Website: Your WAKA Experience." Available: http://www.kickball.com

World Sport Stacking Association (WSSA). 2008. "Website: Welcome to the WSSA." Available: http://www.worldsportstackingassociation.org.

World Sports Humanitarian Hall of Fame. 2008. "Homepage." Available: http://www.sportshumanitarian.com/about.html.

Young, Nat with Craig McGregor. 1987. *The History of Surfing*. Tucson, AZ: The Body Press.

Zimbalist, Andrew. 1999. *Unpaid Professionals*. Princeton, NJ: Princeton University Press.

Index

About the Authors

Tim Delaney earned his Masters Degree from the California State University at Dominguez Hills with a specialty in sport sociology (Master's Thesis: *A Selective Critique of Sport in American Society*) and earned his Ph.D. from the University of Nevada at Las Vegas with sport sociology as an area of specialty (Dissertation title: *Identity and Community Through Sport Boosterism*). Delaney has taught numerous sport sociology courses at both the graduate and undergraduate levels in both sociology and physical education departments. Delaney has published numerous books, chapters in books, encyclopedia articles, and book reviews. Among his published books are: *Shameful Behaviors* (2008), *Simpsonology: There's A Little Bit of Springfield in All of Us!* (2008), *Seinology: The Sociology of Seinfeld* (2006), *American Street Gangs* (2006), *Contemporary Social Theory: Investigation and Application* (2005), *Classical Social Theory: Investigation and Application* (2004), and *Community, Sport and Leisure* (1999, 2001). Delaney regularly presents papers at regional, national and international conferences. He maintains memberships in ten academic associations and has twice served as President of the New York State Sociological Association. To learn more about Tim Delaney visit his website at: www.BooksBy-TimDelaney.com

Tim Madigan is Assistant Professor of Philosophy at St. John Fisher College. He earned his B.A., M.A. and Ph.D. in philosophy at the State University of New York at Buffalo. Madigan was executive editor of *Free Inquiry* magazine from 1986 to 1998 and Editorial Director of the University of Rochester Press from 1999 to 2004. He is on the editorial board of

Philosophy Now magazine, where he writes a regular column entitled "Food for Thought." He has published dozens of articles on ethical issues, including "The Kantian Coach," which appeared in a special issue of *Philosophy Now* (guest edited by Tim Delaney) on philosophy and sport. As an instructor, Madigan specializes in applied ethics.